Alliance Diversification
and the Future *of the*
U.S.-Korean Security Relationship

Charles M. Perry

Jacquelyn K. Davis

James L. Schoff

Toshi Yoshihara

A Publication by
The Institute for Foreign Policy Analysis, Inc.
In Association with The Fletcher School of Law
and Diplomacy, Tufts University

Brassey's, Inc.

Brassey's, Inc.

(Editorial)   22841 Quicksilver Dr., Dulles, Virginia 20166 USA

(Orders)   Brassey's Book Orders, P.O. Box 960, Herndon, Virginia, 22070 USA

Brassey's books are available at special discounts for bulk purchases for sales, promotions, premiums, fundraising, or educational use.

Library of Congress Cataloging-in-Publication Data

Alliance diversification and the future of the u.s.-korean security relationship
ISBN: 1-57488-895-1; $25.00

CIP information not ready at time of publication

Designed by J. Christian Hoffman

Printed in the United States of America by Merrill/Daniels Press, Everett, Massachusetts

10 9 8 7 6 5 4 3 2 1

Contents

⹋

Illustrations

✣

Foreword

For half a century the United States' alliance with South Korea has been a cornerstone of stability in Northeast Asia and, together with the American alliance with Japan, a linchpin of the deployment of United States forces in Asia. Until recently it was generally assumed that the alliance would continue in place for the foreseeable future, although it was also recognized that there might well have to be significant adjustments in its structure to take account of changing circumstances on the Korean Peninsula and in the region.

The original aim of this book, and of the project from which it is drawn, was to set forth a road map for the two governments as they guided the alliance through these changes. However, since the initiation of the project, the situation on the peninsula and the outlook for the alliance have been clouded by deep and growing divergences between the two allies over how to respond to the threat posed by North Korea's nuclear program and, ultimately, how to deal with North Korea itself.

An asymmetry of threat and risk exists within the alliance over the issue of the North's nuclear program. The United States sees the prospect of a North Korea with nuclear weapons as an acute threat to America's national security. The combination of nuclear weapons and long-range missiles would enable Pyongyang to threaten American bases and allies throughout Northeast Asia and, perhaps in the future, American territory itself. Moreover, American policy makers looking at the world through a post-

September 11 prism fear that Pyongyang might provide nuclear materials to international terrorists who would not hesitate to use them against the United States. Thus, for some American policy makers the threat posed by a nuclear North Korea is of such magnitude that they are prepared to contemplate very serious measures, including even military action, to nullify it.

For their part, South Korean policy makers share American concerns about the prospect of a North Korea with nuclear weapons and have said that a nuclear North Korea is "unacceptable." But there is not in South Korea a strong sense of direct threat from the North Korean nuclear weapons program. In part this may be because South Korea has lived for decades with the reality of North Korea's devastating conventional weapons threat. Also, many South Koreans blithely assume that the North would never use nuclear weapons against them, their Southern cousins. Whatever the reason, there is a reluctance in South Korea to confront North Korea over the nuclear issue or even to threaten it with the loss of current benefits from South-North economic engagement to persuade Pyongyang to give up the program. Not surprisingly, South Koreans see great risk to themselves from what the United States might do to deal with the North's nuclear threat.

The Bush administration has made no secret of its skepticism that North Korea will ever give up its nuclear program through negotiations. Many influential figures in the administration and outside argue that the only way to guarantee that North Korea does not become a nuclear weapons state is through a change in the regime in Pyongyang. Thus far, however, Washington has not shaped a credible strategy to bring about regime change that does not carry a high risk of sparking a devastating military conflict. But Washington's talk of the need for regime change creates great anxiety in South Korea – perhaps more than in the North.

For the present, the United States, absorbed by the challenges of Iraq and its own electoral calendar, has encouraged China to take the diplomatic lead in dealing with North Korea. The United States has avowed a commitment to a political solution but has insisted that it will not reward North Korea's bad behavior and stipulates that Pyongyang must dismantle its nuclear program in a comprehensive, verifiable, and irreversible manner before it can expect to receive any concessions from the United States. Thus far, however, the Bush administration has not addressed the North Korean nuclear issue with any sense of urgency, and it now seems unlikely that the Chinese-led six-party process will achieve much until next year at the earliest. Whether Washington will then be prepared to engage in the give-and-take of serious negotiations or revert to the rhetoric of regime change may be influenced by the outcome of the American election, but it is impossible to predict at this point. In any event, that choice will have major implications for the United States-South Korean relationship.

Washington's decision to rely on China to lead a multilateral process to address the North Korean nuclear issue has had the effect of accelerating change in the regional context of the United States-South Korean alliance. China's growing economic power gives it greatly increased political influence within the region. On the issue of North Korea, China shares South Korea's concerns over Washington's talk of regime change. China and South Korea tend to see their respective longer-term interests with regard to North Korea as more compatible with each other than with the United States. While China has not supplanted the United States in terms of importance to South Korea, it is safe to say that Washington is no longer the only magnetic north on Seoul's geopolitical compass.

Underlying the growing dissonance in the alliance is a marked change in South Korea's view about the medium-term future of North Korea. For many years, early reunification was the consensus goal of South Korea's strategy toward the North. Recently, the South Korean vision of North Korea's future has become much more nuanced. Younger generations of South Koreans born and educated long after the end of the Korean War no longer view reunification as the country's defining goal. They fear for their own economic prosperity and social stability if they suddenly have to absorb twenty-two million impoverished North Koreans. Under former President Kim Dae-jung and now under President Roh Moo-hyun, South Korean policy toward the North has aimed at using economic engagement to reduce tensions on the peninsula and induce the sort of change within the Pyongyang regime that would bring reconciliation and, over time, some form of reunification.

South Koreans have come to learn much more about North Korea's economic condition in the six years since South-North engagement was launched, and they now see the North more as an object of charity than as a security threat. As dialogue and economic engagement have continued, albeit fitfully, South Koreans have a growing confidence that they can manage their relationship with the North on their own. While the majority of the South Korean public still appears to value the U.S. military role in the country, it is less and less tolerant of the inconvenience and implied loss of sovereignty that come with that military presence. There is a corresponding wariness about American intentions toward the North, a feeling that American reluctance to engage in direct talks with Pyongyang and Washington's talk of regime change not only fail to take account of the South's interests but are ultimately threatening to the South. Public criticism of the alliance is not a new phenomenon in South Korea, but it has clearly reached new highs in recent years.

Changes in opinion about the United States and the future of North Korea are being reinforced by a dramatic realignment of domestic politics in South Korea. In addition to a generational change of political leadership, something approximating an ideological transition is under way. After the Korean War, the South defined itself primarily as an anti-communist state, and its domestic politics reflected its national security doctrine. The spectrum of legitimate political activity in the South ranged from the right to the center. There was little legitimate political space for the left, even the center-left. Yet, what Koreans refer to as the "progressives" have a long history. They were at the forefront of opposition to Japanese rule. In the years between the end of Japanese rule and the North Korean invasion that triggered the Korean War, there were violent partisan struggles within South Korea and across the thirty-eighth parallel.

The long-delayed resurgence of progressive forces began to gather momentum with the election of Kim Dae-jung in 1998. Roh Moo-hyun's narrow victory in 2002 was a major step in the reshaping of domestic politics. But the most dramatic signal that the long dominance of the conservatives had ended was the April 2004 electoral success of the left-of-center Uri party, which gained a majority in the National Assembly. As these younger, reform-minded leaders rise to influence, recent trends toward a more independent, more assertive South Korean foreign policy are likely to grow. That is not to say that there will be a wholesale rejection of the alliance with the United States, but the pro-American elites that dominated South Korean policy toward the United States for decades are clearly in retreat, and obviously, this leftward movement of Korean domestic politics will be a severe challenge to the alliance. If and when United States policy on the North Korean nuclear issue shifts from an emphasis on multilateral diplomacy to a more confrontational approach, we may well find that South Korea will not join us. That will be an existential moment for the alliance.

For the United States in the post-September 11 world, it is not clear that the alliance with Korea plays the same sort of role in overall security planning as it did previously. An evolving military doctrine with new emphasis on technology and mobility has resulted in a decision to reposition American forces in South Korea from north of Seoul to south of the city. U.S. military planners also want to have the flexibility to use forces currently based in South Korea elsewhere should certain contingencies occur. If the already restive South Korean public begins to perceive that American forces are in Korea primarily for the convenience and interests of the United States and not just for the deterrence of North Korean aggression, their tolerance for the disruptive presence of foreign troops will diminish and the alliance will begin to unravel.

For some South Koreans the alternative to the alliance with the United States is greater accommodation with North Korea, consciously deciding to seek security by making North Korea dependent on economic aid from the South. Such a strategy would carry considerable risk and would be fiercely opposed by conservative forces in the South, which remain formidable. But in the evolving political environment of South Korea and the atmosphere of increasing strain with the United States, the possibility of such a scenario cannot be dismissed.

Stephen W. Bosworth,
former U.S. Ambassador to the Republic of Korea,
and Dean of The Fletcher School, Tufts University

Preface

///

When this research project was first conceived in 2000, the prospects for change on the Korean Peninsula seemed quite promising. The leaders of the Republic of Korea (ROK, also South Korea) and the Democratic People's Republic of Korea (DPRK, North Korea) held an historic summit meeting in June of that year. Just two months later, about two hundred Koreans were reunited briefly with family members for the first time since the Korean War. Past attempts at reconciliation between the two countries paled in comparison, and the president of the United States began seriously considering a North Korean offer to visit its capital, Pyongyang, and meet with its "Dear Leader," Kim Jong-il.[1] Meanwhile, American military planners began to wonder if events might overtake them, and that they could be left with a U.S.-ROK alliance singularly designed to counter a threat that no longer existed, much like the North Atlantic Treaty Organization (NATO) after the collapse of the Berlin Wall and then, later, of the Soviet Union.

Although U.S. officials, policy analysts, and scholars had for years seriously studied the potential impact that Korean unification might have on the U.S.-ROK alliance, the policy research remained conceptual in 2000. Washington had hardly begun the process of building a consensus with officials in Seoul as to what kind of security relationship a united Korea might want to have with the United States. Should U.S. forces continue to be based on the peninsula, and if so, in what configuration? What would be their function, and how would they interact with Korean forces? This research project began as an attempt to move beyond earlier studies and answer these questions in more detail. The goal was to prepare a plan for American policy makers to achieve a constructive, post-unification security relationship with Korea, as it seemed that Washington might be running out of time.

During the course of this project, however, the strategic landscape of the region and the political environment on the peninsula changed significantly. Today, the prospects for imminent reconciliation or reunification seem dimmer than before. At the same time, the foundation of the U.S.-ROK alliance is being undercut by societal change in South Korea and a widening gap in the allies' threat perceptions and security priorities. As it turned out, the question of alliance legitimacy and durability did indeed become as pressing as we predicted, though not necessarily for the same reasons we expected.

It has become increasingly clear that the U.S.-ROK alliance is fast approaching (and in some ways has already arrived at) a major turning point in its history. Some American and Korean alliance managers have recognized this fact and are trying to address the situation in bilateral talks, but the current dialogue is insufficient to remake the alliance. A concerted effort by the leadership in both countries (involving the general public) to refashion the alliance is almost certainly needed in the near term if the alliance is to survive in the future. Left untended, the fissures that have emerged in the alliance will grow wider, and the strength of the bilateral security relationship will diminish over time. There are those who argue that such deterioration in the alliance is not altogether unexpected or unhealthy, given South Korea's economic accomplishments and growing ability to look after its own security. It would be unusual, some might say, for an alliance forged fifty years ago not to undergo such significant change.

America's other major alliances (NATO and Japan) have in fact been transformed throughout their history, more recently through formal reviews and legal processes. This is not to say that the U.S.-ROK alliance has gone unchanged since its inception, but the adjustments to date have not opened up the alliance to new roles and missions (as was the case with NATO and Japan) or allowed it to shift from its central focus on deterring and defeating possible aggression from the North.

Although South Korean forces have served alongside Americans in places like Vietnam and now Iraq, these deployments were more of a response to extraordinary events than they were a systematic retooling of alliance responsibilities. Indeed, it was only well after initial ROK dispatches to Iraq that the United States and South Korea finally revised their mutual logistics support agreement (MLSA) to include airlift services, underscoring how focused their security relationship has been on the peninsula.[2] In many ways, the missions were undertaken as *a result* of the countries' alliance, not as *a part* of the alliance agreement.

In contrast, U.S. Marines stationed in Okinawa, Japan, have recently been sent to serve in Iraq and the Philippines, demonstrating Japanese understanding that its alliance with the United States includes the hosting of U.S. forces that can serve in missions around the region and around the world. Japanese ships also provide logistical support for U.S. operations in Afghanistan, which shows an increasingly deep integration of Japanese forces with Americans serving abroad in joint missions under the rubric of the U.S.-Japan alliance. NATO troops today conduct stabilization and counter-terrorist missions outside of Europe, far beyond its original area of responsibility. These kinds of modifications have not been attempted to the same degree within the U.S.-ROK alliance for various reasons, not the least of which is ROK hesitancy to make similar commitments while the peninsula remains divided.

It may be the case that, for a variety of political, security, demographic, and cultural reasons, the U.S.-ROK alliance will ultimately weaken over time, particularly in the aftermath of Korean unification. However, this possibility (some might even say, likelihood) does not mean that the alliance should be permitted to wither away, as both Washington and Seoul have much to gain from a revitalized partnership. This monograph demonstrates that both countries should actively strengthen the alliance by diversifying their security relationship and adjusting to current political and strategic realities. Yet, while the U.S.-ROK alliance has the potential to pay long-term dividends, both for the allies and for the region, it will require a significant investment of time, money, and political capital.

For the United States, even if the end result is an alliance without a permanent U.S. troop presence in Korea, the process of engaging South Korea in a dialogue on diversification will be worth the effort, primarily in the form of a methodical and coordinated transition to a new, mutual security arrangement, the probability of a versatile access agreement, and a stronger overall bilateral relationship. Failure even to try to diversify the alliance risks a precipitous and acrimonious decline in U.S.-ROK ties at some point in the future, potentially during a period of reconciliation on the peninsula, which is precisely when the United States will want to secure a constructive role for itself in a vital and transforming region. The task is all the more urgent because alliance failure could produce consequences in Northeast Asia that harm broader U.S. security interests. As a result, there is a need to anticipate and respond to any threats to alliance cohesion.

One way to think about alliance diversification is the concept of preventive diplomacy or preventive defense. This notion of a preventive posture centers on the idea that proactive and early actions can be taken to 1) preclude foreseeable disputes between actors from arising in the first place; 2) keep existing disputes from escalating or deteriorating into crisis or conflicts (including political, diplomatic, economic, and military ones); and 3) limit the spread of damage should crises or conflicts emerge. In the context of the U.S.-ROK alliance, both sides should engage in active planning and exercise preventive alliance management to avert foreseeable probable problems and to prepare for unexpected shocks. The recommended action, in this case, is to diversify what the alliance stands for and what it does.[3]

The present conditions offer Washington and Seoul an opportunity to take a seedling from their alliance "tree" and replant it in more fertile soil nearby, recognizing that this well-rooted and sturdy relationship is aging and is being subjected to new stresses and strains. It may soon reach a point when this tree, which has weathered many storms in the past, might not be able to sustain the next heavy shock to its system. The prudent action is to plant several new cuttings from that tree while it remains healthy, and then nurture those seedlings that show the most promise. One cannot wait until the tree shows visible signs of collapse before trying to start anew.

This approach is reinforced by the growing maturity and increased complexity of the overall U.S.-ROK relationship, which has expanded beyond the security focus that characterized bilateral ties for so much of the Cold War. U.S.-South Korean ties offer many additional benefits, in terms of valuable trade and investment, shared democratic values, and consequently a growing socio-cultural connection that provide fertile ground for a new legacy of prosperity, cooperation, and mutual support. This book explains why we think such diversification of the alliance should be pursued, and it examines ways that American policy makers can prepare themselves for this task.

With the generous support of the Smith Richardson Foundation, the Institute for Foreign Policy Analysis (IFPA) carried out field research, convened workshops, and conducted interviews with dozens of U.S. and ROK officials to consider the alliance's future in both the short term (to address the continued threat from North Korea and its nuclear weapons program) and the long term (to prepare for a North-South reconciliation process that would presumably remove a central rationale for the alliance and risk casting it adrift). The authors are grateful to the Smith Richardson Foundation for its support of this research project and for providing the opportunity to explore these issues in detail. In particular, we would like to thank Allan Song, who provided valuable guidance throughout this process.

The authors would also like to thank all of the government officials and policy experts who participated in workshops, interviews, and in other ways, and who contributed so much to the project and this book. With respect to the academic and broader policy community in the United States, this includes, among others, Stephen Bosworth, Victor Cha, Ralph Cossa, Robert Einhorn, Thomas Fargo, Michael Finnegan, Michael Green, "Chip" Gregson, Mark Groombridge, Andrew Hoehn, Thomas Hubbard, Charles Jones, Charles Kartman, James Kelly, Christopher LaFleur, Leon LaPorte, Richard Lawless, Michael McDevitt, Eric McVadon, Barry Pavel, Jonathan Pollack, Jack Pritchard, Evans Revere, David Straub, and "Chip" Utterback. From the academic and policy communities of the Republic of Korea (ROK), this includes Ban Ki-moon, Cha Young-koo, Cho Tae-yong, Choi Kang, Choi Young-jin, Huh Chul, Kim Hee Sang, Kim Jae Chang, Lee Chung Min, Lim Sung-nam, Moon Chung-in, Park Jin, and Sheen Seongho. Others who provided helpful insights on Japanese and Chinese perspectives, in particular, include, from Japan, Jimbo Ken, Kanehara Nobukatsu, Kawakami Takashi, Saiki Akitaka, Sugiyama Shinsuke, Takamizawa Nobushige, Tokuchi Hideshi, and Yamaguchi Noburo, and, from China, Chen Qimao, Wu Baiyi, Xia Liping, Yang Mingjie, Yao Yunzhu, Zhang Chenggang, Zhu Chenghu, and Zhuang Jianzhong. At IFPA, we received invaluable research assistance from Derek Boc and Guillermo Pinczuk, editorial assistance from Adelaide Ketchum, and graphic art and publication design support from Christian Hoffman. The views expressed in this book, of course, are the authors' alone.

In this book, Korean and Japanese names are written with the family name first and the given name second, as is the custom in those countries. Interestingly, the American news media tends to write Korean names (and Chinese names) in this manner (that is, family name first), but it often writes Japanese names in the Western style, with the family name given last. This inconsistency underscores a prevailing view that Japan is somehow more "Westernized" than Korea, which often influences, however subtly, the way that U.S. government officials deal with their Korean counterparts and suggests that some fundamental cultural gaps remain to be bridged.

Charles M. Perry
Jacquelyn K. Davis
James L. Schoff
Toshi Yoshihara
April 2004

Notes for the Preface

1   The presidential trip never took place, of course, as President Clinton deemed progress in talks to control North Korea's missile program insufficient to warrant such a high-level visit. It was not clear that the DPRK ever fully agreed to the U.S. terms for disman-

tlement and verification. With a change in administrations pending, the Clinton administration ran out of time to try and smooth out the final details.

2 The revised MLSA was signed by the two countries in February 2004, in time for a larger deployment of ROK troops to Iraq.

3 The preventive defense concept was well presented in Ashton B. Carter and William J. Perry, *Preventive Defense: A New Security Strategy for America* (Washington, D.C.: Brookings Institution, 1999). See also Victor D. Cha, "Values after Victory: The Future of U.S.-Japan-Korea Relations," *Comparative Connections, E-Journal on East Asian Bilateral Relations,* Pacific Forum CSIS, special annual issue, July 2002, http://www.csis.org/pacfor/annual/2002annual.html. Cha applied this concept to U.S.-Japan-Korea security cooperation in the context of helping these alliances develop a new identity beyond the Cold War.

THE EAST ASIA REGION

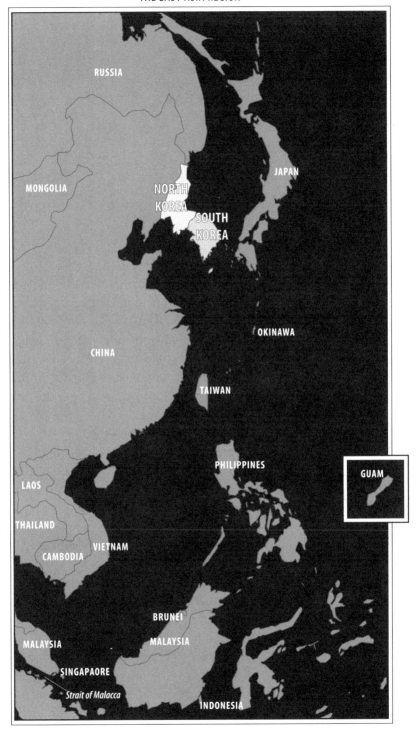

THE KOREAN PENINSULA

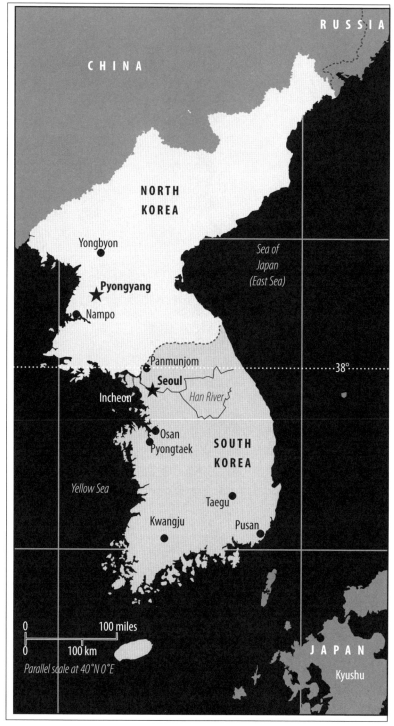

CHAPTER ONE

The Shifting Landscape *in a* New Century

History may eventually judge that the dawn of the twenty-first century marked the beginning of the end for a divided Korean Peninsula. Future generations may see this as a time when a confluence of global developments and domestic changes within Northeast Asia and the United States finally coalesced to form a sharp point, on top of which precariously rested the future of Korea, with peaceful reconciliation on one side and open hostility on the other. Since 2000, the prospects for relations between the southern Republic of Korea (ROK) and the northern Democratic People's Republic of Korea (DPRK) have teetered back and forth in a manner suggesting that the existing stalemate on the peninsula, so common in the past, may no longer be sustainable.

To be sure, the history of North-South relations has long been marked by periods of conflict, interspersed by attempts at entente, but there are reasons to believe that transformational changes are astir. In the last four years in particular, the direction of North-South interaction has at times tilted convincingly toward economic engagement, with the possible establishment of a peace regime that could eventually lead to gradual reconciliation, if not reunification. At other times, however, it has leaned in the direction of greater isolation and the seemingly inevitable collapse of the North, possibly leading to military conflict and necessitating a more grueling, painful process of reconstruction and integration. The political and strategic environment, on the peninsula and around the region, has changed significantly since

2000, and it may finally force this see-saw of inter-Korean relations to land on one side or the other. The various personalities and policy choices in this historical drama will be a fascinating and instructive tale for posterity, but we cannot know yet if the story will be one of triumph or of tragedy.

A number of recent events and developments seem for various reasons to be pushing the Korean Peninsula toward the start of some form of unification or reconciliation process in the next decade. Various national policies and mitigating factors could either accelerate or postpone the final outcome, and there is no guarantee that the process will be peaceful, but the roots of that outcome seem to have firmly taken hold in only the last four years. A few of the most important developments include:

- The failure of the Clinton administration's negotiations with North Korea regarding its missile program in the administration's waning days and the transition to the George W. Bush administration
- Changes in U.S. defense and security strategy (particularly military transformation), especially in the aftermath of the September 11 terrorist attacks and the priority placed on preventing the proliferation of weapons of mass destruction (WMD) to terrorist organizations, and President Bush's inclusion of North Korea as a part of a so-called axis of evil in his 2002 State of the Union speech
- The historic inter-Korean summit between Kim Dae-jung and Kim Jong-il at Pyongyang in June 2000 and its strong repercussions, both positive and negative (such as reunions of family members, increased commercial interaction, and the awarding of the Nobel Peace Prize to Kim Dae-jung, versus the subsequent failure to maintain momentum for a return visit or other initiatives in the face of raised expectations, complicated by a political scandal that the summit was facilitated by the South's transfer of nearly $200 million to the North)
- The political empowerment of South Korea's younger, digitally connected generation (nearly half of the voting-age population are in their twenties and thirties),

embodied in the election of President Roh Moo-hyun in 2002 (who was only seven years old when the North-South cease-fire was signed in 1953)

- Japanese Prime Minster Koizumi Junichiro's visit to Pyongyang in 2002, the signing of the Japan-DPRK Pyongyang Declaration, and the resulting stalemate in Japan-DPRK negotiations caused by North Korea's admission that it had abducted Japanese nationals over the course of several years and its eventual refusal to allow the families of abducted Japanese (left behind in the DPRK) to return to Japan (the way the abducted individuals themselves returned)

- The People's Republic of China's (PRC) accession to the World Trade Organization (WTO) in 2001, its leadership changes in 2003, and its emergence as a more mainstream member of the international community and stronger diplomatic force in the region, a key interlocutor on North Korean nuclear issues, and a major trading partner with South Korea, on top of a near doubling of its trade with the United States since 1999, contributing the most to America's record trade deficits

- The closer security relationship between Russia and the West as demonstrated, in part, by the relatively uneventful U.S. withdrawal from the Treaty on the Limitation of Anti-ballistic Missile Systems in 2001 and the creation of the NATO-Russia Council in 2002, further limiting the DPRK's ability to drive a wedge between the regional powers

During this time the North Korean economy has remained stagnant, despite halting experiments with economic reform, and Pyongyang has forced the region to address the North's predicament by overtly pursuing a nuclear deterrent and eventually withdrawing from the Nuclear Non-proliferation Treaty (NPT) in 2003. The implications of these events (and evolving associated dynamics) are multi-faceted, but overall they point to changing perceptions of the status quo and an ever shrinking amount of political and strategic space in which to accommodate the positions of the major players in the region.

All of these developments have had their own particular impact on the current situation and have contributed to the crystallization of the North Korean WMD challenge as it stands today. But, it is fair to identify four of these factors that are the most influential and provide the strongest argument why the United States needs to be proactive on alliance diversification: 1) the global war on terror (GWOT); 2) the rising political clout of South Korea's younger generation; 3) China's growing regional and international prominence; and 4) the military transformation underway in the United States. These are the primary reasons why some of the recommendations regarding U.S.-ROK alliance enhancement made up to ten years ago can no longer be avoided.

Against this backdrop, North and South Korea seem destined for a significantly different relationship in the near future. If the DPRK ultimately trades away its nuclear program for diplomatic recognition and some degree of economic engagement, then the die is cast for a new North-South relationship (indeed, a new relationship between North Korea and the world). If Pyongyang refuses to give up its nuclear deterrent, then there seems to be little chance that it can avoid collapse or conflict with the West. Either course puts the North and South on a path toward reunification, even if it might be an arduous process and take several years to be fully realized. It also means that the United States is running out of time to decide how aggressively it wants to pursue alliance diversification with the ROK, because the issue will probably be overwhelmed in Seoul by an obsession with national reconciliation at that time.

The Challenge for American Policy Makers

The operative question for this study is, what do these developments mean for U.S. policy makers as they contemplate the future of America's security relationship with the ROK and, by extension, with a Korean Peninsula undergoing some form of political and military reconciliation (or perhaps confrontation) in the future? In 2003, the fiftieth anniversary of the U.S.-ROK alliance was celebrated with a modicum of fanfare and a great deal of discussion. While much was written and talked about regarding the alliance's future, relatively little was decided. In many ways, the dialogue about how Washington and Seoul could ideally manage the current and impending transitions on the peninsula had only just begun.

Work proceeds – both within the ROK and the United States, and in various bilateral dialogues – on clarifying options for re-balancing and restructuring the U.S.-ROK alliance to make it more relevant and sustainable over the longer haul, but the effort has not been sufficiently focused. The discussions so far have dwelled more on the ROK's role in a global realignment of U.S. military force structure than on the prospective U.S.-ROK security relationship in a post-Korean reconciliation/reunification scenario. Consequently, the allies have dealt mostly with near-term, concrete issues, such as adjustments to the composition, location, and investment in the U.S. Forces Korea (USFK) and the ROK military, as well as some reassignments of certain roles and missions and the possible revision of the existing command structure. The Future of the Alliance Policy Initiative (FOTA) – launched late in 2002 by the countries' defense chiefs at the Korea-U.S. Security Consultative Meeting to "[adapt] the alliance to changes in the global security environment" – is the primary example of this dialogue.[1]

Despite its title, the FOTA has to date focused less on the abstract future of the alliance and more on hammering out a mutually acceptable plan and timetable to reassign certain missions and physically relocate the USFK and its command facility within South Korea. This has left little time to discuss broader, long-range strategic issues regarding the alliance, though U.S. officials are pressing this aspect of the agenda in 2004. The fast pace of the talks is being driven by a desire in Washington to keep the USFK in line with a global transformation of how U.S. forces are deployed overseas. U.S. military planners are trying to make near-term headway in what may admittedly be a rather long-term adjustment. The process, however, risks alienating the ROK public by creating an impression that the United States could be imposing a hardship on the ROK (in the form of adventurous off-peninsula missions or larger than expected increases in ROK defense spending on top of one-time base relocation costs), thereby giving alliance opponents fuel for argument and possibly undermining the main goal of strengthening the security relationship for the future.[2]

There are a variety of practical reasons why the FOTA is pressing forward with USFK realignment now, and the initiative can have a positive effect on the alliance if it is managed adeptly. The FOTA, however (at least as it was conducted in 2003), is not a substitute for a structured, broader discussion about designing a mutually beneficial alliance for the future that is worthy of strong public support in both countries. One wonders if there is enough time in 2004 for the FOTA to fully transition from negotiating a short-term base realignment plan to redefining the long-term future of the alliance. The problem is that the FOTA cannot be both a part of America's global strategic transformation process and a Korea-specific dialogue on the future of the alliance at the same time, if for no other reason than that the latter would take much longer than the former.

Moreover, the FOTA is not designed to deal with the particular changes going on in South Korea, to solicit public input, or to bend too far to public demands in that country, because it is part of a world-wide effort driven, first and foremost, by America's needs and national interest. The FOTA is a valuable forum, but this study contends that the United States is still in need of a more comprehensive, long-range plan for managing the military transition on the Korean Peninsula that is better attuned both to changing ROK domestic political dynamics and to emerging strategic priorities, and it is to assist in this effort that the energies of this research project were directed.

The key point is that the U.S.-ROK alliance faces significant challenges created by transitions in both countries and within the broader region, and it will take more than eight or ten months in 2004 to build a broad, common understanding and a shared vision for the future. These changes, particularly in South Korea, are substantive and are likely to have long-term implications. Given South Korea's burgeoning democracy and young population, the public will need to be more involved in this process of alliance redefinition. The fiftieth anniversary of the U.S.-ROK alliance might have coincided with the beginning of the end of a divided Korea, but it may have also marked the beginning of a new era of U.S.-ROK relations built around a more diversified security partnership to complement the nations' economic ties. The next few years could have a dramatic impact on America's strategic future in Northeast Asia. Crafting and implementing policies that effectively serve U.S. long-term interests will not be easy for American policy makers, diplomats, and military planners, but the stakes are too high to shrink from these challenges.

Summary of Conclusions

This study looks methodically and comprehensively at the issues surrounding the potential for diversifying the U.S.-ROK alliance, beginning with an examination of the relevant changes taking place in both countries that are forcing policy makers to consider a new approach. The book then reviews a decade of research on these topics (and on the geostrategic prospects for the region) to take advantage of this extensive body of work and to provide the context for the contributions of this particular project. The literature review is followed by a description of an ideal future U.S.-ROK alliance from an American perspective, which involves building a loose, but coherent, coalition of willing security partners in the region and integrating South Korea (and eventually a unified Korea) into that coalition, preferably as a core member. The next three chapters explore all of the obstacles to achieving this ideal scenario (in the ROK, the United States, and around the region), followed by another chapter that details the scenarios and options for a U.S. military transition on the peninsula in the face of these obstacles. The final chapter explains conclusions and recommendations based on the results of this research project and lays out a plan for American policy makers to begin pursuing alliance diversification with South Korea. A brief summary of these recommendations follows below.

To begin with, the United States and South Korea must acknowledge their different threat perceptions and conflicting security priorities, and then take steps to bridge these gaps as much as possible. As a part of this process, the United States needs to better define and articulate its goals for the alliance and make a greater effort to convince the ROK and its citizens of America's continued, strong commitment to South Korea's security, as well as to explain the potential benefits to the ROK of alliance diversification. In order to achieve this, the United States should encourage Seoul to define and articulate its own goals more clearly, especially now that South Korean foreign policy appears to be in a period of transition.

For example, a "main strategic goal" for the Roh administration is to "improve U.S.-Korea relations and independent national defense simultaneously." This is potentially a sign that South Korea is looking for some detachment in the alliance, or it could be a convenient opening to diversify the alliance in a way that fits with ROK aspirations. South Koreans themselves are probably not yet sure which way to lean, and herein lies the opportunity for American foreign policy. U.S. officials will have to listen carefully to Seoul's positions and demonstrate that they understand South Korea's perspective, trying to accommodate its priorities as best they can, without compromising America's primary security objectives.

Achieving alliance diversification and reinvigorating the U.S.-ROK security relationship will require a comprehensive bilateral dialogue specifically designed for this purpose. Although the FOTA talks have been productive, they were not able to stimulate a thorough enough debate, either in government circles or among the public, about how the future of the alliance could be shaped, let alone provide a forum for exploring, detailing, and deciding upon alternative visions. This new dialogue could quite easily pick up from where the FOTA leaves off (call it FOTA 2), but it will ultimately be a different process, one that is more ambitious and open ended, as well as one that more directly enjoys presidential imprimaturs in both countries.[3]

FOTA 2 might still be led by the Office of the Secretary of Defense (OSD) in the United States and the ROK's Ministry of National Defense (MND), but both presidents will need to invest more political capital in the process, and the White House and the Blue House will need to play a larger role in energizing and driving the dialog. There is almost as much work to be done creating a consensus on the alliance's future within each government as there is between the two countries, so a careful balance between the domestic and bilateral discussions will need to be managed in the early stages of the talks.

The initial goal should be an agreement on a broad set of alliance diversification principles, which could then be turned into something akin to the U.S.-Japan Joint Declaration on Security, signed by President Bill Clinton and Prime Minister Hashimoto Ryutaro in 1996. That document set the stage for a review and revision of the Guidelines for Japan-U.S. Defense Cooperation (Defense Guidelines), which ultimately allowed for such unforeseen developments as the provision of Japanese logistical support for operation Enduring Freedom (Afghanistan) and the application of the allies' acquisition and cross-servicing agreement to U.S. and Japanese troops serving in Iraq.

The first round of U.S.-ROK FOTA talks was launched at the ministerial level, but a more comprehensive set of discussions that would truly remake the alliance would have to be inaugurated in some form by the presidents of the two countries. A U.S.-ROK joint declaration should *initiate* a process of alliance diversification rather than seek to *conclude* the discussion before the public and elected officials have a chance to participate.

It might be possible, indeed even advisable, to break down FOTA 2 into two different discussion tracks, one focused on long-term issues related to alliance diversification and the future of the security relationship, and the other dedicated to short-term, crisis management contingencies that could arise in the next few years while the two governments are working on the longer-range details.[4] The two-track process recognizes that the alliance faces two distinct challenges, one in the form of North Korea's nuclear weapons program and the potential for a clash over its proliferation activities, and the second being the nations' diverging strategic priorities complicated by, among other factors, societal change in South Korea. It is clear that progress on the longer-term issues depends in large part on how effectively the allies manage the North Korean problem in the short term.

The first step, therefore, is to initiate an interagency discussion in the U.S. government to consider different USFK-ROK armed forces transition alternatives that support its defense transformation goals and that can also appeal to the ROK. Three possible alternatives are outlined in chapter 8, and the research suggests that the third option, a "regional/hemispheric posture" that involves a more mobile USFK working jointly with ROK forces, deserves particular attention. The regional/hemispheric posture assumes a gradual and methodical reunification process that integrates North Korea with the South. This process is not without its challenges and hardships, of course, but it is promising enough that a more healthy form of Korean nationalism emerges. Consequently, the combination of a greater sense of security and a more confident national psyche enables Seoul to embrace many of the regional security obligations commensurate with its emerging middle power status.

While this internal debate is taking place, the United States should engage ROK officials and listen to their thoughts regarding the long-term future of the alliance, incorporating their feedback into the discussions in Washington. The goal is to propose various diversification concepts at the first few meetings, ideally settling on a rough framework that administration officials in both countries can build upon to prepare the alliance for a united Korea. This process began in 2004 to some extent, but it has not been as substantive a dialogue as it needs to be in order to reorient the alliance. Some initial fundamentals of diversification are as follows:

- In the intervening period prior to Korean reconciliation and unification, diversification is supplemental to (and does not detract from) defense of the ROK against DPRK aggression.
- For the United States, a diversified alliance provides versatility to U.S. forces for carrying out counter-terrorist and stabilization missions off-peninsula that are supported by a more capable and complementary ally.
- For the ROK, a diversified alliance facilitates a non-threatening (to neighbors) and cost-effective power projection capability to ensure its basic national security goals, including self-defense and the protection of its economic and energy security interests, in addition to enhanced independence in a more stable region.
- Diversification lays the groundwork for a post-unification, U.S.-Korea security relationship, should one be desired by the two countries at that time.

- Diversification involves bridging multiple gaps between the separate tracks of the alliance relationship (that is, military, diplomatic, economic, and civil society).
- Diversification is part of a regional effort that aims to dampen military competition and enhance security cooperation in the Asia Pacific as a whole.

The second step is to move beyond a discussion about broad concepts and begin detailed negotiations on a road map for diversifying the alliance that both presidents can endorse. The 1996 Japan-U.S. Joint Declaration on Security was a sweeping document, expressing the president's and the prime minister's concurring beliefs regarding a number of issues, including the bilateral alliance, the mutual security treaty, and bilateral, regional, and global cooperation under their security relationship. Within the declaration were both broad statements and specific proposals. The declaration provided a strategic direction and a political foundation for the subsequent Defense Guidelines revision process, and it put presidential credibility on the negotiating table. Such a development is needed for the U.S.-ROK security relationship to thrive.

Once the basic road map for alliance diversification has been agreed to by the two presidents, the third step is for both sides to flesh out the details regarding logistics, implications, and limitations. The alternatives detailed in chapter 8 include a discussion of the potential impact on the roles and missions for the U.S. and ROK militaries, force structure, command structure, and weapons system procurement. These are all important issues for negotiators to discuss in order to determine the proper balance going forward. From an institutional and legal perspective, there will also likely be a need to revise parts of the U.S.-ROK mutual defense treaty, as well as possibly enter into new agreements that could further facilitate the provision of logistical support, cross servicing, and supply procurement.

Even though alliance diversification is intended to function in the context of a unified Korea, the United States and South Korea should not wait until unification to discuss and implement a diversification plan. The alliance adjustments recommended in this study are pertinent to today's security environment, and it is important that these new patterns of alliance behavior be well established and generally accepted before a tumultuous re-unification process begins. Alliance diversification can also be supportive of such a process in several ways. If ROK forces are stretched thin as they deploy to the North to provide security and participate in humanitarian missions, then the USFK can be a source of stability and reassurance in the South. The USFK could take advantage of increased mobility to assist ROK forces with specific missions in the North, such as securing and dismantling WMD sites, monitoring the terms of a reunification process, managing a refugee problem, and providing food, medical, and energy supplies to people in need.

In the regional/hemispheric posture, during and following the consolidation of Korea as a reunited entity, Seoul assumes primary responsibility for its defense and security. However, unlike some other scenarios explored in chapter 8, a more confident Korea seeks to further complement and enhance U.S. military capabilities in the region and beyond. While the U.S. military is no longer involved directly with the defense of Korea, the United States incorporates Korea's defense posture into its own planning for extra-regional and hemispheric activities. In many ways, the burden-sharing arrangements between Washington and Seoul increasingly resemble the outcomes flowing from the U.S.-Japan alliance revitalization process in the 1990s, during which planners on both sides shifted away from the defense of Japan to contingencies beyond the home islands. Borrowing from the legacy of the pre-unification era, the level of bilateral cooperation and joint operational planning continues to deepen.

Similar to some of the other alternatives, under the regional/hemispheric posture, Korea downsizes its armed forces across the board. The heavy ground forces that have long characterized the ROK military would be replaced by rapid deployment capabilities with elite units intended to fulfill extra-regional tasks. In the meantime, air-naval expeditionary forces become the centerpiece of Korea's force structure. The U.S. military, for its part, withdraws most of its ground forces (except for highly mobile units) and expands its air and naval presence to complement and reinforce Korea's security posture. A part of the rationale for the apparent redundancy is to fill in Korea's capabilities deficit during the transition on the peninsula. The U.S.-ROK forces

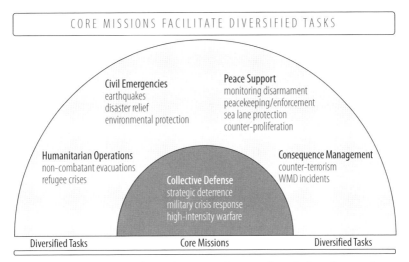

would engage in regular joint exercises and training focused on interoperability in certain capabilities, such as interdiction of illicit weapons or drug trading, counter-terrorism operations, and off-peninsula stabilization, peacekeeping, and humanitarian relief missions. As illustrated above, the alliance becomes increasingly focused, over time, on carrying out these diversified tasks in concert with other allies and security partners in the region.

As further integration between the two forces proceeds, the alliance may adopt operational concepts similar to NATO's combined joint task force (CJTF). The CJTF concept is explained in more detail in chapter 8, but in short it is intended to facilitate an alliance's ability to cope with non-collective defense contingencies (and, when required, to operate alongside other non-allied states). In the U.S.-ROK alliance context, both sides would develop doctrines and force structures for a flexible and readily deployable task force designed for operations other than mutual defense. Each would then be able to tailor its forces based on the operational requirements, size, and location of the crisis, and the unique capabilities that each can bring to bear on fairly short notice. In operational terms, the United States and Korea would boast the capacity to detach "organic assets" – parts that are essential to a larger military unit – from their respective military organizations and capabilities for a combined and joint operation. These are examples of the types of issues that could be discussed in this third step of the dialogue.

As alluded to earlier, one of America's main objectives should be to build a regional coalition in East Asia that is prepared to fight terrorism and promote regional stability. The rationale for this coalition and how it relates to the U.S.-ROK alliance is discussed in chapter 4, but briefly stated it would center around America's treaty and major non-NATO allies in Asia: Japan, the ROK, Australia, Thailand, and the Philippines (and involve other security partners such as Singapore). The coalition should also involve other regional powers, namely Russia and the PRC, as much as possible. China is particularly important in this effort, both in terms of what it can contribute to the region and because of the destabilizing effect an isolated China (real or imagined) could have in Asia. U.S.-ROK alliance diversification should be a part of a broader effort to enhance regional security cooperation, and the bilateral negotiations will need to be mindful of this goal. The allies do not necessarily have to consult with Chinese officials during the talks, but some method of reassuring Beijing will pay dividends over the long term.

As for the ROK, it can decide how aggressively it wants to participate in this coalition, but every effort should be made to facilitate its involvement. A benefit of focusing regional security cooperation on fighting terrorism and promoting regional stability is that it can be convened without the appearance of trying to contain China. In fact, as noted above, this coalition would seek to include the PRC as much as possible.

The final major recommendation of this study is for the United States to adopt policies aimed at strengthening the non-military aspects of the bilateral relationship, much in the same way that it does with Japan and other European allies. While it is true that a military alliance can be founded (and even endure, to some extent) solely based on mutual strategic interest, such a relationship tends to be vulnerable to obsolescence when strategic interests begin to diverge. By the same token, a military alliance that is embedded within a strong and multi-faceted bilateral partnership can still lose its relevance under similar circumstances, even if the other aspects of the relationship continue to flourish. The threshold for alliance deterioration, however, is much higher in the latter scenario, which is to say that a wider gap in common interests can be accommodated in a broad-based alliance and still retain its military component. The U.S.-ROK alliance is certainly not a one-dimensional, military-only relationship (as this study demonstrates), but neither does it have the same depth as the U.S.-European or U.S.-Japanese relationships, and there are steps that U.S. policy makers can take to address this deficiency.

Though there is no easy way to strengthen bilateral ties at the grassroots level, educational and professional exchange programs are effective over the long term, such as those supported by the Japan-United States Friendship Commission, the German Marshall Fund of the United States, or other organizations. A similar, U.S.-based foundation to promote U.S.-Korean ties does not currently exist, but it could be a productive investment in an important alliance relationship. Another valuable program supported by government money is the Mike Mansfield Fellowship Program, which enables U.S. federal government employees to learn Japanese and experience long-term placements in Japanese government offices. This could be a model for a new, Korea-specific program.

Expanding involvement in Korea by organizations such as the U.S. National Endowment for Democracy is yet another opportunity to strengthen the relationship, as is fostering interaction between U.S. and Korean non-governmental organizations (NGOs) in humanitarian and relief activities. This would take advantage of a flourishing of NGOs in the ROK. These kinds of efforts only supplement official military and governmental exchanges and do not include the vast amount of private sector interaction that is arguably the most important channel, but they do underscore a commitment to common values of democracy and human liberty that has the potential over time to be the strongest bond between our two nations. Despite this potential, the current relationship is marred by bilateral ignorance, mutual misunderstanding, and miscommunication. This is a situation that needs to be addressed. All of these efforts, tied together, can be part of a proactive American strategy to redesign and reinvigorate the U.S.-ROK alliance amid a period of dramatic change in both countries.

In order for such a forward leaning alliance strategy to succeed, several important analytical steps need to be taken to understand more clearly the challenges ahead and to formulate a workable set of policies. This study begins to take these steps and endeavors to make the journey for U.S. policy makers that much shorter.

First, the contemporary developments on the Korean Peninsula and the conditions of U.S.-ROK relations are the central contexts within which the current policy debates are taking place. The starting point for analysis, therefore, is necessarily a review of key geostrategic, political, socio-economic, and military trends surrounding the partnership. Second, a sound conceptual framework is required to provide overall guidance and analytical grounding to this study. In particular, past scholarly works on regional security issues related to the U.S.-ROK alliance and innovative policy prescriptions offer important insights on the possibilities of and limits to proactive alliance management. Third, an ideal roadmap for the future of the alliance and the possible complications to navigating the alliance management process bring sharper focus to the realistic policy alternatives. The rest of this book seeks to highlight each of these policy drivers and parameters to arrive at policy recommendations that anticipate and adequately cope with the emerging challenges to the alliance and that set the stage for revitalizing the security partnership for a more stable and productive future.

Notes for Chapter One

1 The Future of the Alliance Policy Initiative was established by U.S. Defense Secretary Donald Rumsfeld and ROK Minister for National Defense (MND) Lee Jun at the December 2002 Korea-U.S. Security Consultative Meeting to "[adapt] the alliance to changes in the global security environment" and "develop options for modernizing and strengthening the alliance." It is sometimes also considered to be phase 2 of a joint study of the U.S.-South Korean alliance. The two-year initiative, led by U.S. Deputy Assistant Secretary of Defense for Asia-Pacific Affairs Richard Lawless and ROK MND Deputy Minister for Policy Lieutenant General Cha Young Koo, met five times in 2003 before presenting a variety of interim implementation plans to the November 2003 Security Consultative Meeting in Seoul.

2   This is despite the fact that ROK defense planners in the mid to late 1990s were already calling for slowly increasing South Korea's defense budget and developing a more independent defense capability, so U.S. pressure is clearly not the only force behind these changes.

3   FOTA 2 might not require the launching of a new, formal set of talks. It could be managed within the Policy Review Subcommittee (PRS) of the Security Consultative Meeting, provided the PRS meets often enough and adopts a method of interacting with elected officials and/or the general public. See chapter 9 for more detail.

4   In this case, "crisis management contingencies" refers less to purely military situations, such as incursions from the North, for which U.S. and ROK forces regularly prepare, and more to incidents with a significant political dimension, including an attempt to interdict DPRK drugs or weapons shipments, or how to respond to a North Korean nuclear weapon or long-range missile test.

CHAPTER TWO

U.S.-ROK Relations
in an Era *of*
Transition *&* Transformation

Over the past few years, it has become increasingly apparent that the transformation taking place in U.S.-South Korean relations is accelerating. This transformation is in part a result of the changing political culture in the ROK, including a generational shift that reflects a different world view from that of the previous generation and lacks the personal memory of the Korean War and the sacrifices made by South Koreans and Americans in reversing the invasion by North Korea. Related to this generational shift is an emergent Korean national confidence that demands new respect for the ROK's post-war achievements, particularly its higher global economic standing. On the diplomatic front, the younger generation tends to consider engagement with North Korea, even if it possesses nuclear weapons, as preferable to isolating its neighbor or the possibility that the United States might provoke a confrontation with Pyongyang.

These trends are triggered in part by the ROK's new-found economic power, but they are also fueled by pride felt in its success in co-hosting the 2002 World Cup Soccer tournament, as well as by indignation at such incidents as the acquittal of U.S. soldiers in the accidental death of two Korean schoolgirls in 2002, and even in minor incidents like the disqualification of an ROK speed skater at the 2002 Olympic Games in Salt Lake City that allowed an American to win the gold medal.[1] Together, the rise of the so-called 2030 generation (voters in their twenties and thirties who helped elect President Roh in 2002) and the resurgence of Korean nationalism, replacing anti-communism as a uniting force, are symptomatic of a changing political culture in Seoul that challenges the current rationale for a fifty-year U.S.-ROK alliance and expects to see changes in the U.S.-ROK military relationship to reflect more clearly South Korea's emergence as a mature partner.

These changes within South Korea are accompanied by dramatic and fast-paced adjustments to America's national security strategy in the face of new global and regional strategic landscapes. U.S. foreign policy is currently undergoing more significant change than it did immediately following the end of the Cold War. Even well after the collapse of the Soviet Union, the United States viewed the North-South standoff on the Korean Peninsula largely as a holdover from the Cold War, and the allies' strategic approach to the problem changed relatively little over the years. In the past, there have been adjustments and disagreements, of course, particularly in the early 1970s when the United States withdrew the 7th Infantry Division from South Korea and established relations with the PRC, or when President Carter sought to bring home the 2nd Infantry Division later in that decade. Still, the overall force posture and nature of the alliance commitment was fundamentally consistent over the last fifty years.

Since the declaration of a U.S.-led GWOT following the September 11, 2001, terrorist attacks in the United States, however, policy makers in Washington have begun to look differently at regional alliances and at the arrangement of American military assets in East Asia. Previously firm policies regarding U.S. troop levels in the region, or a U.S. "tripwire" strategy along the thirty-eighth parallel in Korea, are being replaced with new approaches. These circumstances create both stress and opportunity for alliance relations, and it will require careful thought and effective communication at various levels (including the public level) to minimize the strains and to capitalize on the opportunity. The U.S.-ROK alliance can and should evolve, but successfully navigating this transformation first requires a thorough understanding of the forces at work in each country and around the region.

Political Transitions within South Korea

As alluded to above, there are internal and external factors contributing to the changes taking place in South Korea. Internally, the December 2002 presidential election demonstrated that the roots of democracy are deepening throughout the country, and it marked the end of the "three Kims" era (namely, that of Kim Young-sam, Kim Dae-jung, and Kim Jong-pil, who competed and dominated ROK politics on and off for over thirty years). The election results, however, also revealed a nation divided politically, regionally, and demographically. The two candidates, Roh Moo-hyun of the center-left Millennium Democratic Party (MDP) and Lee Hoi-chang of the more conservative Grand National Party (GNP), ran on markedly different platforms and essentially split the vote tally (49 percent to 47 percent).

At the same time, the election reaffirmed a geographical division between the southeast and southwest, albeit less pronounced than in previous elections, and revealed a growing generational gap (twice as many "2030" voters chose Roh, and those over age fifty overwhelmingly supported Lee). Although Roh won the presidency and selected the cabinet (State Council), he has had to reckon with the strong legislative power of the GNP and members of his former party, which held a majority of seats in the National Assembly until April 2004. During the election campaign, domestic attitudes toward the alliance with the United States and USFK were polarized, with a demonstration against the USFK often followed shortly thereafter by a pro-U.S. alliance rally. South Korea's relations with the United States and the status of the USFK have become critical issues for the Roh administration, and they remained a subject of intense debate going into an important National Assembly election in April 2004 that altered the legislative balance of power.

Ever since Roh's election, ROK national politics have continued down a fractured and chaotic path, leading ultimately to an unprecedented vote to impeach the president just weeks before the April 2004 poll for election law violations. This followed the breakup of the MDP, infighting at the GNP, and the appointment of an independent counsel to investigate alleged corruption involving illegal campaign funding for both parties' presidential candidates.

As of this writing, Roh's future as president rests with the nine-member Constitutional Court, which must rule on the matter within 180 days. For his part, Roh responded by announcing that he would view the April election as a referendum on his presidency. Throughout this time, South Korean relations with the United States have been a divisive issue in the Roh administration, resulting in a major shakeup in his foreign policy team in early 2004.[2]

Roh's own standing in the polls dropped significantly since his inauguration, from an approval rating peak of about 92 percent down to about 38 percent a year later.[3] He even lost support among his core political base of voters, those in their twenties, thirties, and forties, because of a combination of a perceived lack of leadership and experience in dealing with issues of labor strife, corruption, a weak economy, and managing relations with North Korea and the United States. This disappointment contrasted sharply with the high expectations for the reform-minded politician at the beginning of 2003, and it contributed to the steep drop of public confidence in the president. The absence of a popular alternative to Roh, however, means that he can still wield political influence, and it appears that the impeachment vote ironically boosted his support, as many voters were annoyed by the politics behind the action.

Both of the leading political parties fought amongst themselves in 2003, and it led to an unexpected result in the April 2004 elections. Legislative supporters of Roh split from the MDP in September 2003 and formed their own group (the Uri Party), further weakening the MDP in relation to the GNP. The new Uri Party then rode a wave of anti-impeachment sentiment to victory in April, capturing 152 of the 299 seats in the National Assembly.

The GNP did not benefit from the malaise surrounding Roh and his former party, in part because the GNP was also caught up in the illegal funding scandal and seemed unresponsive to public calls for greater transparency in political financing and decision making. Its members also bickered among themselves, contributing to a surge of party lawmakers and candidates deciding not to seek re-election in April. The GNP also suffered from the fact that the majority of South Koreans still support the basic tenets of the sunshine policy and engagement with the North, an approach that conservative elements in the GNP often deride, which limited the election gains for the party.

The April elections were, to some extent, an important turning point for political parties in South Korea. Political parties in South Korea are trying to transcend their regional origins and offer the public a choice between policy approaches to such issues as dealing with North Korea, reforming the economy, and managing relations with the United States and other nations. The new two-ballot voting system, for example, helped the issue-oriented Democratic Labor Party eclipse the MDP to become the third largest voting block. If the parties are successful, over time the citizens of South Korea will indirectly exercise greater influence over policy making than they have in the past.

Signs of this trend are already evident, as shown by the growth of politically active non-profit organizations and their use of the Internet as a tool for promoting this activism. South Korea has one of the largest Internet populations in the world (number six with about twenty-eight million users) and a high penetration rate (over 58 percent).[4] Some interesting examples of political mobilization via the Internet include opposition to the ROK's purchase of American F-15 fighter jets in spring 2002 and the push behind an anti-American movement during the presidential election campaign later that year. The April elections represented one small step toward a more ideologically oriented, less regionally organized political party structure.

While this development may complicate alliance management in the short term, it can ultimately strengthen the alliance if a concerted effort is made to involve the public and to listen and respond to its concerns. The United States took deliberate steps in this direction by launching a public diplomacy campaign when anti-American sentiment was running high in 2002. This policy of active communication and openness (through public events, speeches, exchanges, and so on) should continue and become a more permanent component of American foreign policy, rather than a reactive, damage control device. USFK commander General Leon LaPorte broke new ground in this regard when he conducted a live debate with young South Koreans via the Internet in February 2004. Such an approach would represent the manifestation of a U.S. policy of welcoming, encouraging, and engaging a more vibrant democratic process in South Korea.

For their part, ROK political leaders must actively join (and preferably lead) a campaign that explains to the public how the alliance contributes to Korea's national interests and how that alliance can be enhanced. U.S. officials cannot effectively make this argument by themselves. One problem to overcome is that some South Korean politicians have a tendency to pander to anti-American voter sentiment in public, while privately trying to reassure their American friends of their commitment to the alliance. Moreover, in their weakened state, it is questionable how effective the parties can be in the short term while domestic politics remains in flux and intensely competitive.

Demographic Transitions within South Korea

Characterizing a generation is fraught with difficulties and can often lead to unhelpful – even misleading – generalizations and over-simplifications. There has been a good deal of hyperbole surrounding discussions of the 2030 generation, and some skepticism is warranted regarding blanket claims that it cares little for an alliance with the United States. It might also become necessary to differentiate between those in their twenties and their slightly more radical, thirty-something seniors. There seems to be no doubt, however, that important changes are underway in South Korea, that these changes are tied to a demographic shift, and that all this could have a profound impact on the country as a whole and its relations with other nations.

Demographically, South Koreans in their twenties and thirties account for 45 percent of the voting age population (about 34 percent overall), which means that they will be a politically influential group for many years to come.[5] A variety of surveys have been conducted of younger ROK citizens since the September 2001 terrorist attacks on the United States, and the results suggest declining support for the status quo of the U.S.-ROK alliance (even adjusting for especially negative reactions immediately following certain events such as President Bush's labeling North Korea as part of an "axis of evil" or accidents involving the USFK). Overall, the surveys indicate 1) a trend of declining pro-

American sentiment due to perceived American "unilateralism" and "arrogance," America being dismissive of the ROK, or its interference in ROK affairs; 2) a view of North Korea that sees it less as a threat than as a burden or object of charity, and consequently a view that is more concerned with the potential threat of a "provocation" by the United States than it is with an "unprovoked" attack from the North; 3) a view that the ROK's ties with the PRC will become more important over time than those with the United States; and 4) a general wariness about getting too deeply enmeshed in the American-led war on terrorism.[6]

Perhaps more disturbing, a poll conducted after the U.S.-led war in Iraq began in the late spring of 2003 showed that more than twice as many South Koreans were "disappointed" rather than "happy" with the lack of Iraqi resistance to the United States during the war (a number slightly more sympathetic than Pakistan but less supportive of the United States than Brazil, Russia, and even France).[7] When pressed to elaborate on the reasons behind their various pro- and anti-American feelings, it seems clear that the more positive responses tend to be rooted in the past (for example, fighting together in the Korean War and planting the seeds of democracy), while many of the negative reasons are relatively recent in origin. This suggests that an overall goal for the United States should be to build upon the legacy of strong relations and create a modern alliance that makes a visible, positive contribution to addressing today's security challenges and that demonstrates clear, mutual benefits to both publics. The emphasis on *mutual benefit* is important, since more than half of young South Koreans think that the United States benefits more from the alliance than does the ROK.[8]

It is also important to remember that changes in South Korea are taking place within a regional and global context. The shock waves of the September 11 attacks in the United States and the intensified GWOT continue to reverberate in the ROK, primarily in the form of U.S. policy initiatives – for example, the greater emphasis placed on combating the proliferation of WMD from North Korea, the U.S.-led war and occupation in Iraq, changes in military strategy including proposals for realigning U.S. forces in South Korea and in the region (consequentially requiring greater ROK defense spending), and even such seemingly innocuous issues as U.S. opposition to the newly established International Criminal Court (ICC), which includes a judge from South Korea. In some cases, these policies alienate a majority of South Koreans, but in others they have brought the two countries closer together (examples include cooperation in the GWOT and stepped-up consultation on policies regarding North Korea and USFK realignment). It is worthwhile underscoring that these developments can affect the alliance in both positive and negative ways.

There is a direct correlation between demographic and political change in the ROK. As one South Korean scholar noted, the younger generations, "who made up an absolute majority in [the] electorate, did not share their parent and grandparent generations' *jaksarang* or 'unrequited love' for America originating from before 1953…[in 2003] the young acquiesced in following U.S. leadership not because of its idealization of U.S. intentions, but because of Korea's harsh international political reality." While the Cold War was an era in which "people gave U.S. policy makers diffuse trust and loyalty," the end of that era "ushered in a new two-level political game where Korean foreign-policy makers had to take into account domestic political pressures to a degree unknown before."[9] In other words, South Korean foreign policy has become an increasingly important domestic political issue, and younger South Koreans have become a powerful domestic political force. If the "harsh reality" of the DPRK threat were to fade, then South Korean acquiescence to U.S. leadership could quickly disappear.

Transformation of American Foreign and Security Policy

The trend of change in U.S. foreign policy under the Bush administration's leadership and in response to the 2001 terrorist attacks is a dramatic departure from that which emerged during the Cold War or in the decade following its conclusion. It is not so much that America's basic foreign policy objectives are different, but that its perception of what threatens those objectives most and how the United States can best counter those threats has fundamentally transformed in the early twenty-first century. Following World War II, America's strategic organizing principle centered on the containment and defeat of expansionary communism. This was true in Asia as much as anywhere else in the world. The United States "reversed course" in its occupation policy in Japan, redirected foreign aid, struck new basing arrangements in the region (at times with undemocratic governments), and fought in Korea, Vietnam, and in smaller skirmishes to achieve its policy goals vis-à-vis the threat of communism.

Today, the GWOT and preventing failed states from becoming havens for terrorists and criminal groups have become the new organizing principle for defense planners. Some political commentators have gone so far as to describe this development as the advent of World War III, or a conflict between the "world of order and the world of disorder."[10] Comments by General Richard B. Myers, the chairman of the Joint Chiefs of Staff, are illustrative of what this means for the U.S. strategic response. Following recent war games, he said, "Most of the Joint Chiefs weren't happy with a couple [of the assumptions on worldwide commitments]." Because of the critical nature of deployments in Afghanistan and Iraq, what needs to change is "our posture in the rest of the world."[11]

The transformation in defense policy actually began before the September 11 attacks, as articulated in the 2001 Quadrennial Defense Review, which recognized the terrorist threat and abandoned the "two-major-theater war" or specific "threat-based" construct for planning in favor of a capabilities-based approach.[12] The concepts continue to be debated and refined, but by 2003 the U.S. Department of Defense (DoD) was already taking steps to expand the number of U.S. installations around the world while at the same time striving to reduce their footprint in each host country. Douglas Feith, the U.S. under secretary of defense for policy, explained, "One of the key assumptions in the past was that our forces were likely going to be fighting where they are based. We no longer think we know that."[13]

Underscoring the U.S. trend of seeing its enemies more as amorphous terrorist groups than nation states, Deputy Assistant Secretary of Defense for Strategy Andrew Hoehn remarked, "If you had to wait a month in order to respond to intelligence about the enemy...he probably won't be there."[14] At a different venue, he later added, "In this era, it's our view that we need to think about the assignment of forces globally, and the movement of forces to where and when they are needed [and not just in the context of their regional commands]."[15]

It is worthwhile noting that the term "transformation" has been perhaps confusingly applied to a variety of technological and policy changes proposed by the Pentagon in recent years. Some see transformation as limited almost exclusively to "revolutionary" developments in military technologies. An introduction to one study dealing with transformation suggests that "[t]he growth and diffusion of stealth, precision, and information technology will drastically alter the character and conduct of future wars, yielding a revolution in military affairs (RMA)."[16] This same study attributes some of the original thinking about RMA and military transformation to Soviet strategists in the 1970s, though the vision became clearer to all when the U.S. coalition demonstrated the power of its modern weaponry during the 1991 Gulf War.[17]

More recently, however, the Bush administration's military planners have broadened the concept of transformation beyond technology and tactics to include the way in which U.S. forces are positioned around the world, how the United States works with its allies and partners, and even what types of missions (including "stability operations") its soldiers are trained to conduct. Some of these changes were pondered by the Bush administration before the September 11 terrorist attacks, but the GWOT has certainly influenced the urgency and character of this effort. As Under Secretary Feith explained, "A key facet of transformation is realigning our global defense posture [including] updating the types, locations, numbers, and capabilities of our military forces, and the nature of our alliances."[18]

It is against this backdrop that the United States is pursuing talks with South Korea regarding the FOTA and relocating (and probably reducing, eventually) U.S. forces on the peninsula. The impetus behind the FOTA, therefore, is directly linked to this evolving concept of defense transformation, and this limits the flexibility for U.S. negotiators when faced with competing demands from their ROK counterparts. Adding to the issue's complexity, the allies' perceptions of threats and priorities are growing farther apart, which, given the current alliance structure, places a severe strain on the ability of both countries to satisfy their policy objectives and constituents in a complementary and mutually reinforcing manner.

During the Cold War, the ROK was a steadfast partner of the United States, and it shared America's anti-communist fervor well beyond its own borders. In early 1954 ROK President Syngman Rhee offered, without solicitation, to send a Korean Army element to Vietnam to assist in the war against the communists. Though that offer was turned down, eventually the ROK deployed over fifty thousand military personnel to Vietnam from 1964 to 1969, a number greater than all other non-American contributors (Australia, Thailand, Philippines, and three other nations) combined.[19]

Over the years, South Korea took on more responsibility for providing for its own defense, including larger defense budgets and increasing production and procurement of modern weapon systems, as well as combining operational command with the United States. At the start of the twenty-first century, the ROK contributes about 35 percent of the costs of stationing American soldiers in the country.[20] The ROK's overall defense budget will reach close to $16 billion in 2004, which supports nearly seven hundred thousand active troops, a large reserve force, and a procurement program that includes F-15K fighter aircraft and short-range, surface-to-surface missiles.

But while South Korea continues to base much of its defense policy on the threat from the North, the standoff is no longer seen in an anti-communist context and instead is focused on the autocratic regime of Kim Jong-il. In 1992, the ROK normalized relations with one of its enemies from the Korean War, communist China, and today China is arguably South Korea's largest trading partner and destination for direct investment, despite still being governed by a communist regime. Nationalism is a far stronger unifying force in South Korea today than anti-communism (or anti-terrorism, for that matter). Moreover, since the mid to late 1990s, ROK military planners have explicitly focused on slowly shifting away from a preoccupation with the North to meeting post-unification requirements and developing a "reasonable defense sufficiency" (and what is today often called an "independent defense capability" by the Roh administration).

Although South Korea is generally supportive of U.S. global efforts in the GWOT (as seen, for example, in its contributions to operation Enduring Freedom in Afghanistan and operation

Iraqi Freedom), this support is nowhere near the scale seen in the fight against communism, and the gap in perceived national interest threatens to grow wider as the United States seeks greater flexibility in the composition and deployment of its forces in South Korea. Developing a new arrangement that satisfies both countries now and into the future is a daunting challenge for U.S. policy makers. The United States will not only need to consider its military needs in the context of transformation, but it will also have to adjust to the changes going on in South Korea and prepare for the prospect of a reconciled Korean nation that seeks an independent defense posture and specialized power projection capabilities.

Change in U.S. foreign policy, however, is not without its mitigating factors. Although the September 11 attacks did cause a shift in the administration's thinking on national security priorities, the long-standing structural features of the Asia-Pacific region (a divided Korea, rising China, the uncertain status of Taiwan, sensitivity to Japanese militarization, the importance of stability and open trade routes for regional economic prosperity, and so on) will exert pressures of continuity on America's (and the ROK's) strategy for the region and temper the pace of change. Continuity will be helpful, since the United States needs to be careful not to get too far ahead of opinions in the South Korean policy community and the public on alliance transformation issues, lest it allow itself to be surprised by a lack of logistical support (for example, refusal to allow the USFK to launch an off-peninsula operation), as happened with Turkey at the outset of the war with Iraq.

Other External Influences

There are also other, broad external factors affecting the U.S.-ROK relationship, such as the shifting regional strategic landscape in the aftermath of September 11, which is characterized by closer collaboration between the United States and both the PRC and Russia, in addition to the more active Japanese military cooperation with the United States. America's relationships with the PRC and Japan in particular can influence politicians and young voters in South Korea, though at this point it is difficult to predict what kinds of ripple effects improved (or strained) U.S. relations with the regional powers would have on ROK public attitudes toward the alliance.

Improved U.S.-China ties could mean greater harmony in developing U.S.-ROK ties in a multilateral context, but with how strong a "special" U.S.-ROK component is unclear. Poor U.S.-China ties could create a more precarious situation that could force South Korea to choose sides and favor one country over another. If the ROK feels threatened or intimidated by China, it could strengthen U.S.-ROK cooperation, but if ROK-China ties (especially in trade and investment) continue to grow, then South Korea might feel a need to distance itself from the United States to placate China. Good U.S.-Japan relations are generally a positive force in the region, unless they get too far ahead of U.S.-ROK ties or cause China to feel targeted or isolated. Both the United States and South Korea have some important thinking to do regarding their strategic interests, and how they can reconcile their goals with each other, as well as with the major players in the region.

Of course, the most prominent external factor is South Korea's neighbor to the north. The DPRK's policies and actions contribute to divisiveness in the South, at times courting the ROK while it demonizes the United States and Japan, and at other times alienating South Koreans with unreasonable demands, illegal fishing and drug trade activities, or by threatening death and destruction in Seoul at the slightest perceived provocation. The ROK's policy of engagement with the North ("sunshine" under Kim Dae-jung and "peace and prosperity" under Roh) is one of the clearest policy delineators between the MDP (and now the Uri Party) and the GNP, and this will continue to be a major topic of debate in future elections. How South Korea deals with the North, in turn, affects domestic budgets and public investments, relations with the United States and other countries, the inward foreign investment climate, and the overall economy.

The Push and Pull of the U.S.-ROK Relationship

The confluence of internal and external transitions is pushing the two countries together and pulling them apart at the same time.

The challenge for alliance managers is to navigate these conflicting currents toward a mutually agreeable destination while keeping the alliance afloat. Among the "push" factors, the strengthening of democracy in South Korea solidifies common political values with the United States. The same is true on the economic side as the ROK economy increases transparency (albeit slowly), grows more economically diverse, and further opens to foreign investment. South Korea sends the third largest number of young people to study at American colleges and universities, not far behind India and China, which have populations twenty times larger.[21] Moreover, there is a religious affiliation unlike any other U.S. relationship in Asia, since more than 35 percent of South Koreans who subscribe to a specific religion are Protestant Christians, with Roman Catholics adding another 7 percent.[22] Although there are sizable Christian populations in other Asian countries, only South Korea has a Protestant majority like the United States.

The "common interests, common values" mantra repeated so often in a U.S.-Japan context can increasingly be applied to the U.S.-ROK relationship. South Korea's international activism in peacekeeping operations meshes well with U.S. goals, as shown by the ROK deployment of thirty-two hundred troops (in eight rotations over four years) to assist the Australians and the United Nations (UN) in East Timor in 1999, and in the dispatch of ROK military personnel to Afghanistan and Iraq to support reconstruction in 2003 and beyond. The planned dispatch of some three thousand ROK troops to Iraq is particularly significant, as it represents the second largest non-U.S. contingent in the country, behind Great Britain. Strong economic ties between the United States and the ROK, including increased bilateral trade in services and greater U.S. foreign direct investment in South Korea, is another push factor for the allies.[23] As will be discussed in more detail in chapter 4, even though Chinese trade with the ROK has increased dramatically in the last ten years, the United States is still by far the largest investor in South Korea and continues to buy the biggest share of the ROK's most valuable export items.

There are other factors, however, pulling the allies apart. The two countries' top security priorities are currently in conflict. For the United States, few (if any) policies are more important than preventing the proliferation of WMD to terrorist organizations, but North Korea has threatened to do just that in order to attract aid and security guarantees. Aggressively pursuing a policy of "not tolerating" a nuclear North Korea, however, could precipitate a war on the Korean Peninsula, the prevention of which is the ROK's primary foreign policy goal. South Korea simply believes that it has less at stake in the GWOT compared to the United States. Also, a more cynical reading of the dispatch of ROK troops to Iraq is that South Korea merely wants to stay on America's "good side" during the North Korea nuclear standoff and maximize access to lucrative post-war rebuilding contracts for South Korean construction and engineering firms. There are also some voices in ROK government circles that seek a quid pro quo with the United States for greater support in Iraq, namely U.S. acquiescence to the ROK's policy approach with regard to the DPRK nuclear weapons program, angering some U.S. officials who believe that the two issues should not be linked.

Moreover, from a political and ideological standpoint the realpolitik, conservative Bush administration and the pro-dialogue, liberal Roh administration are not a good fit, as exemplified by the cordial but overall unexceptional May 2003 presidential summit meeting in Washington. The two governments recognize the high stakes involved and to their credit are trying hard to bridge the gap. The FOTA is an example of this effort, and the fact that the United States and South Korea are talking and consulting on these "pull" factors is encouraging. But the discussion will need to become broader, deeper, and more sustained if it has any chance of reshaping the alliance for the future. As alluded to earlier, it is possible that these discussions might transition to something similar to those between the United States and Japan in the 1990s that focused on revitalizing and redefining their security relationship for the post-Cold War era (and that resulted in the U.S.-Japan Joint Security Declaration in 1996 and revision of the Japan-U.S. Defense Guidelines).

Although it is tempting to apply the U.S.-Japan model to the U.S.-ROK security relationship, there are also reasons why the two alliances will likely evolve differently. Foremost among these is the fact that there is a greater structural imbalance between the United States and South Korea (in terms of the economy, population, defense budget, defense posture, and military command structure) than there is in the U.S.-Japan case. Japan has a clearer strategic incentive to ally with the United States, given that its constitution limits the country to an exclusively defense-oriented military posture. South Korea has no such restriction. Moreover, so much of the U.S.-ROK security alliance has been centered on the North Korean threat that it will be even more difficult than in the Japanese case (which long had a regional application) to broaden the applicability and enhance the versatility of the alliance. Can the United States and South Korea acknowledge and accept this challenge?

Ironically it was the DPRK threat that helped the United States and Japan to adjust slowly and transform their security alliance in the post-Cold War environment (including revision of the Defense Guidelines so that Japan could provide more robust logistical support in certain "situations in the area surrounding Japan"). Yet it is precisely this threat from the North that keeps the U.S.-ROK alliance narrowly focused and, particularly in the minds of the South Korean public, so seemingly one dimensional. North Korea is therefore both the central pillar and consequentially the potential bane of the U.S.-South Korean security relationship. When North Korea ceases to exist, will it take with it the U.S.-ROK (Korean) alliance?

This question remains worryingly unanswered, and the uncertainties surrounding it are all the more vexing because there is nothing inherently predetermined about the alliance's relevance in a post-DPRK era. Indeed, the singular focus on the North, while understandable and inevitable, leaves the alliance unprepared to cope with the many sets of future outcomes in Northeast Asia. As early as the mid 1990s, however, analysts began to examine the consequences of, and possible responses to, reconciliation and reunification for the U.S.-ROK partnership. These important works provide projections of regional dynamics that range from the pessimistic to the sanguine, and they accordingly offer modest to radical policy prescriptions for the alliance. The next chapter provides an overview of past writings on alternative futures in order to identify more clearly the value that this study can add in the context of a larger body of work on the U.S.-ROK alliance.

Notes for Chapter Two

1   Even a seemingly minor incident like this can leave strong impressions on the South Korean public. Nearly two years after the speed skating incident, the American involved decided against participating in a World Cup event in the ROK after receiving death threats via e-mail, despite an offer of special security protection from the Korean Skating Federation. *Boston Globe,* "Miscellany: Threats keep Ohno out of South Korea," November 22, 2003.

2   Foreign Affairs-Trade Minister Yoon Young-kwan was pushed to resign in January 2004 to take responsibility for remarks made by his subordinates against Roh and Roh's policy toward the United States. Two officials in the ministry's North American Bureau were reassigned shortly thereafter. President Roh also fired his defense and national security advisers that same month.

3   Park Song-wu, "Roh's Approval Rating Slumps to 38 percent," *Korea Times,* February 24, 2004.

4   Nielsen/Netratings Global Q1 2002 survey. For comparison, the United States has a total internet population of about 166 million and a penetration rate of about 60 percent; Japan is at 51.3 million and 40 percent, Germany at 32.2 million and 39 percent, the United Kingdom at 29 million and 48 percent, and China at 56.6 million and about 5 percent.

5   U.S. Census Bureau, *International Data Base,* July 2003 version, http://www.census.gov/cgi-bin/ipc/idbsum?cty=KS, (January 15, 2004). The voting age in South Korea is twenty.

6   Some of the surveys are cited in other footnotes and include Korea Gallup polls, surveys by various Korean newspapers, and a Pew Research poll. One of the most interesting, though less statistically conclusive because of its small sample size, was an opinion survey of the "Next Generation Leaders in the ROK" carried out by Potomac Associates at the very end of 2001 with the support of the Institute for National Strategic Studies at America's National Defense University. This project interviewed a relatively small number of carefully selected young leaders in the fields of politics, business, media, military, academics, and nonprofit organizations.

7   Pew Research Center for the People and the Press, "Views of a Changing World 2003," June 3, 2003.

8   William Watts, "Next Generation Leaders in the ROK: Opinion Survey Report and Analysis," Potomac Associates, April 2002. These findings are corroborated by other polls taken in 2002 and 2003.

9   Kim Byung-Kook, "To Have a Cake and Eat It Too: The Crisis of Pax Americana in Korea" (paper presented at the International Conference on East Asia, Latin America, and the "New" Pax Americana, sponsored by the Weatherhead Center for International Affairs, Harvard University, February 13-15, 2003).

10   Thomas L. Friedman, "Peking Duct Tape," *New York Times*, February 16, 2003.

11   Tom Philpott, "JCS Chairman Sees 'Global War' Forcing Mission Shift," *Newport News Daily Press*, September 5, 2003.

12   The 2001 QDR was developed before the September 11 attacks, though its official release came a few weeks later. For a discussion of the implications of America's global strategy for the Asia-Pacific region, see Charles M. Perry and Toshi Yoshihara, *The U.S.-Japan Alliance: Preparing for Korean Reconciliation and Beyond* (Herndon, Virginia: Brassey's, 2003), 18-33.

13   Mark Mazzetti, "Pax Americana: Dispatched to Distant Outposts, U.S. Forces Confront the Perils of an Unruly World," *U.S. News and World Report*, October 6, 2003.

14   Ibid.

15   Remarks by Andrew Hoehn at the thirty-fourth IFPA-Fletcher Conference on National Security Strategy and Policy: Security Planning and Military Transformation after Iraqi Freedom, December 2, 2003.

16   Thomas G. Mahnken and James R. FitzSimonds, "The Limits of Transformation: Officer Attitudes toward the Revolution in Military Affairs," Newport Paper no. 17 (Naval War College, Newport, Rhode Island, 2003), 1.

17   Ibid.

18   Douglas J. Feith, U.S. Under Secretary of Defense for Policy, "Transforming the U.S. Global Defense Posture" (speech before the Center for Strategic and International Studies, Washington, D.C., December 3, 2003).

19   Department of the Army, *Allied Participation in Vietnam*, by Lieutenant General Stanley Robert Larsen and Brigadier General James Lawton Collins, Jr. (Washington, D.C., 1985), 23, 120, 131.

20   *The Embassy of Korea in the U.S.A.*, http://www.koreaembassyusa.org/bilateral/military/eng_military5.cfm.

21   Institute of International Education, *Open Doors Online*, http://www.opendoors.iienetwork.org/. There were over fifty-one thousand South Korean students in the United States in 2003 compared with about seventy-four thousand from India and almost sixty-five thousand from the PRC. Japan was fourth at about forty-six thousand.

22   Hahm Chaibong, "Anti-Americanism, Korean Style," in *Anti-Americanism in Korea: Closing Perception Gaps*, Issues and Insights, vol. 3, no. 5 (Honolulu: Pacific Forum CSIS, July 2003).

23   Marcus Noland and Taeho Bark, *The Strategic Importance of U.S.-Korea Economic Relations*, NBR Special Report, no. 4 (Seattle: National Bureau of Asian Research, 2003).

CHAPTER THREE

A Decade of Analysis

Since the mid 1990s, analysts have spent considerable intellectual capital speculating on the future contours of security dynamics in Northeast Asia, as well as about the prospects for significant adjustments in the U.S.-ROK alliance. Overarching structural changes brought about by the end of the Cold War along with major politico-military developments (both anticipated and unexpected) on the Korean Peninsula have prompted much of the animated discourse. The analysis and findings of these studies provide a rich source of data points regarding assumptions about the region's future and the basis for policy implementation. Even a cursory glance at this body of work quickly reveals that a wide range of (sometimes conflicting) views have co-existed alongside each other. To date, however, few have tried to make sense of this cacophony of analysis and to assess how each study stands in relation to the rest. There is thus a need to organize these articles and reports into a conceptually coherent spectrum of perspectives. Such a canvass introduces a useful starting point for identifying the locus and the direction of the current policy debates.

As a way to present this spectrum, the following is a brief literature review that outlines the "state of the field" regarding the future of the Korean Peninsula and associated long-term U.S. strategy. Far from being academic, this exercise represents a practical step toward better understanding realistic policy options for Washington to consider. The overview is not exhaustive, but it does offer a selective sampling of the literature intended to 1) trace the evolution of expert analysis and discussions; 2) identify inadequacies or gaps in the arguments; 3) evaluate the varying schools of thought; and 4) address and expand upon the most policy-relevant aspects of the debate.

To set the stage for this review, it is worth noting that the most dominant analytical framework used to assess the future of the Northeast Asia region is the balance-of-power theory. As a consequence, many studies often contain straw-man-like qualities, which lead to outcomes consistent with this framework. Most analysts have predicated their discussions on traditional zero-sum terms that tend to underscore the competitive drivers in Asia.[1] A typical view holds that "Asia's future will resemble Europe's past; that it will be marked, in other words, by competitive great power politics, shifting alliances, costly arms races, periodic crises, and occasional wars."[2] Even those emphasizing the trends toward regional integration have conceded that realpolitik ultimately forms the backdrop to cooperative patterns of interstate behavior.[3] Balance of power theory, however, has often failed to produce distinct policy recommendations for the United States. The debate between Thomas Christensen and Robert Ross on the future of Asia perhaps best exemplified this phenomenon. Each side proposed a distinct theoretical lens with which to understand the region (in this case, the theories of the security dilemma and great-power balancing, respectively).[4] Yet, despite diametrically opposed visions for the region, both prescribed very similar U.S. policy objectives, particularly in terms of troop levels, centered more or less on the status quo.

Clinton-Era Analysis

Overall, Korea watchers detected early on that the United States needed to anticipate and respond proactively to strategic change on the peninsula. As early as 1995, a joint U.S.-South Korean task force assessed the potential for profound changes, including unification, on the Korean Peninsula and the likely impact such shifts would have on the U.S.-ROK partnership.[5] Based upon a careful examination of mutual interests, emerging challenges, and alternatives for the alliance, the study concluded that both countries would stand to gain substantially from preparations for a new alliance-based posture. The study then outlined four security alternatives (from a robust status quo to a weak political alignment) that the alliance could pursue during the transition phases toward unification. The authors determined that Washington and Seoul would have to prepare now to develop a regionally-oriented structure for the unification process.

In a forward looking analysis, Michael O'Hanlon laid out the case for maintaining restructured U.S. forward deployed forces after Korean unification.[6] He argued that the compelling rationales for keeping U.S. military presence on the peninsula are twofold: 1) deterring threats (emanating from Korean-Japanese hostility and the rise of China); and 2) fostering regional security cooperation. O'Hanlon's prescriptions for a future U.S. force structure ranged from an enhanced version of the status quo to a posture based on air and naval power. He concluded that a more balanced approach that focuses on broader regional security missions, such as counter-terrorism and peacekeeping, would adequately meet the necessary deterrence and reassurance requirements for the alliance.

In a book published before the inter-Korean summit, Michishita Narushige approached the future of the U.S.-ROK alliance premised on the eventual demise of North Korea.[7] The alliance, he contended, would survive the North's dissolution and continue to play an important reassuring role among regional powers still mired in memories of historical rivalries. Furthermore, a rejuvenated alliance could bolster regional and global security, enhance burden sharing between Japan and South Korea, provide a hedge against a rising China, and promote shared democratic values. Without providing any specific data on future force structures, he concluded that while U.S. force levels would likely be reduced in the post-confrontation era on the peninsula, the American military would still take the primary responsibility for maintaining regional security. In the meantime, Japan and South Korea would assume the main burden for their own defenses.

These studies, while useful, contain a few shortcomings. Most importantly, the works have limited policy utility and currency today because they are necessarily circumscribed by assumptions and projections made at the time of writing. In this instance, the studies of the late 1990s were conceived in the context of the Agreed Framework and the apparently imminent economic collapse of the North. Given that the DPRK was reined in temporarily in terms of its nuclear ambitions and appeared to be nearing implosion, discussions of a prospective unification, a term used liberally in all the works noted above, were not unfounded. This study, too, is premised on the expectation that some type of reconciliation process (either planned or spontaneous) will at least begin in the near future, but the diplomatic and strategic environment is significantly different than it was a decade ago.

The previously obscure threat posed by "global terrorism" has become the most important factor in American defense planning, and thus the imperative and the opportunity for diversifying the alliance are manifest. At the same time, it is clear that alliance activity in the GWOT involves more than defensive military action and includes countering WMD proliferation, humanitarian assistance and development aid, democracy promotion, and other missions. This coincides with dramatic domestic changes in South Korea and a desire in that country to develop a more independent foreign policy and defense capability, as well as greater apparent stability in the DPRK, at least compared to the mid 1990s. Rather than preparing the alliance for a unified Korea that follows a sudden collapse of the North, it is quite possible that reunification will be a protracted process (even if that process is initiated in some form in the next decade).

The rationale for, and method of, restructuring the alliance, therefore, must be applicable to both the current strategic environment *and* a post-DPRK world. What is encouraging is that some South Koreans are open to the idea of diversifying the alliance, as long as it is not perceived as being solely focused on supporting the United States in the GWOT and includes a broader range of missions that can serve both countries' interests.

Adjusting to the Post-Post-Cold War Era

From the regional perspective, Ralph Cossa analyzed the Bush administration's alliance-based approach toward Asia, which pledged to focus on traditional bilateral security relationships such as those with Japan, South Korea, and Australia.[8] He noted that this emphasis on long-standing allies dovetailed with past policies and demonstrated more continuity than change. Most notably, Washington remained on track to revitalize its security relationship with Japan while a "comprehensive approach" to the Korean Peninsula was still primarily premised on existing diplomatic mechanisms, including the South's sunshine policy, the Agreed Framework, and the U.S.-Japan-ROK Trilateral Coordination and Oversight Group (TCOG) process. Further, Sino-U.S. relations had reverted to constructive cooperation, a far cry from earlier efforts at labeling Beijing as a "strategic competitor." Cossa appeared to endorse the return to business as usual in East Asia.

Nicholas Eberstadt examined the evolution of American bilateral ties in Northeast Asia following the outbreak of the war on terrorism.[9] The enhanced security cooperation between the United States and Japan demonstrated an alignment in strategic interests that was closer than at any time since the postwar period. Similarly, the maturation of Sino-U.S. relations enabled China to endure major geostrategic shifts (including unprecedented American military presence in Central Asia) that would have been unthinkable a few years ago. In contrast, he observed that the new U.S. strategic outlook and security posture following the terrorist attacks could threaten to undermine alliance cohesion with South Korea. As Washington viewed the DPRK through the lens of terrorism and non-proliferation, its policies became increasingly at odds with Seoul's, which were still wedded to the process of reconciliation.[10] He warned that the vitality of the military alliance could come under increasing stress unless both sides clarified the common interests and goals that sustained the partnership and provided specific policy options.

Recent analyses of the Korean Peninsula have also emphasized the status quo and short-term policies based primarily on linear projections. While Nicholas Eberstadt acknowledged the emergence of new challenges to the strategic order on the peninsula, he maintained that geopolitics remained the defining element in shaping the rationale for U.S. policy toward the two Koreas.[11] For the short to medium terms, he observed, "Even with the presumption of genuine rapprochement between North and South and some measure of stability on the Korean Peninsula, a U.S. withdrawal from Korea at this juncture would create a 'security vacuum' in the area, and invite a latter-day version of that 'Great Game' of realpolitik the Pacific Powers played so roughly in the region a century ago." As such, the requirement for a continuing U.S. military presence persisted. Over the longer term, he added, "If and when the day arrives that the North-South struggle is no more, however, a compelling rationale for a continuing ROK-U.S. alliance can still be made: a rationale based upon deterring instability in an economically important, militarily powerful, and not-yet-solidly-liberal international expanse." Similar to those balance of power theorists, the author advocated a version of the status quo centered on U.S. military power on the peninsula.

James Miles argued that the international community should adopt policies intended to wait out the North Korean regime until it collapses.[12] He noted that elements of severe political and economic instability have forced Pyongyang into "a period of terminal systemic crisis." Far from pushing the regime toward collapse, he argued that the Bush administration's efforts at isolation and coercion were more likely to produce a backlash (perhaps a violent one) from Pyongyang. Instead, Miles proposed a set of near-term engagement measures (including economic ties and aid) tailored to stave off confrontation and to set the stage for the demise of the DPRK.[13] According to a later study by Marcus Noland, however, a policy of "cooperative engagement" would likely reduce the chances of regime change in North Korea to less than 1 percent, largely because of the unique political and economic nature of the DPRK, whose society needs relatively little to survive.[14]

Lee Sang-hyun assessed the growing divergence in perceptions concerning the utility of the U.S.-ROK alliance between Washington and Seoul. He stressed in particular the domestic political developments in the South as the main catalyst for the schism between the two sides. The author argued that democratic evolution and the emergence of a new generation of South Koreans have contributed to a new set of expectations for South Korea's place in the region, its security role vis-à-vis the United States, and its posture toward the North.[15] These new perspectives have increasingly driven ROK policies that conflict with U.S. interests.

To forestall the negative consequences of such a trend, Lee recommended a set of policies aimed primarily at damage control. He offered vague prescriptions for shoring up public diplomacy on both sides and for dampening anti-American sentiments in the South, and he urged the two allies to postpone discussions surrounding U.S. force reductions on the peninsula and the transfer of operational command to the South.

Even some of the more provocative analyses urging more radical shifts in U.S. policy have been confined to short-term solutions. For instance, analysts at the Heritage Foundation urged a series of escalatory steps intended to stave off and deter North Korean belligerency. In addition to enhancing jointness and active defenses for American and ROK forces, the report called for increases in U.S. troop levels and hinted at the reintroduction of nuclear weapons on the Korean Peninsula.[16] At the other end of the spectrum, the CATO Institute advocated a withdrawal of U.S. forces in the face of an imminent threat. The premises of the argument have centered on improvements in the South's own deterrent capabilities and the need to end the phenomenon of "free riding" by transferring the security responsibility to the powers in the region, where it belongs. Such extreme policy prescriptions, however, based almost entirely on the cost and benefit analysis of the current threats posed by the North, tend to lose sight of America's long-range foreign policy goals in Asia.

Adjusting to the New Century

Some scholars, however, have gradually recognized that systemic forces of regional change are afoot. These newer studies argue that broader structural changes in the region and new dynamics on the peninsula have begun to challenge the assumptions that have underwritten U.S. policy since the postwar era. Indeed, the most recent literature points in significantly different directions for Asia in general and the Korean Peninsula in particular. Flowing from a new set of parameters for understanding the region, these works have produced imaginative projections of Asia's future and forward-looking prescriptions for U.S. policy (though there is by no means a consensus on the issues).

David Kang provides a theoretical innovation that overturns dominant conventional wisdom in the field.[18] He argues that international relations theory based upon the European experience is being inappropriately applied to Asia and that empirical evidence undermines predictions of competition and balancing in the region. In particular, historical patterns demonstrate that Asian states have tended to accommodate Chinese dominance. Indeed, stability in the past derived largely from strategic alignments of deference centered on a strong China. The absence of balancing today, he contends, bears out this historical continuity. Moreover, as the power of China and other Asian countries continues to climb, the role of the United States will be challenged, and Washington will be forced to reckon with an Asian reality far removed from long-standing expectations. From this cogent analysis, Kang identifies a profound implication for future U.S. policy: "Whether some type of U.S. withdrawal would be deleterious for the region is far more questionable." In other words, the emergence of a new Asian regional order might render American forward presence increasingly obsolete (at least, at the current U.S. force level and configuration).

A separate article asserts that emerging dynamics in Northeast Asia, facilitated in part by deliberate and inadvertent U.S. policy, will begin to fundamentally redefine America's regional role.[19] Most controversial is the authors' contention that the "hub and spoke" regional structure based upon traditional U.S.-led bilateral relationships is giving way to an unprecedented Sino-U.S. entente. Tensions within the U.S.-ROK alliance, Japan's declining influence, and China's increasing assertiveness have all contributed to this China-centric trend. More broadly, the authors observe that "[t]he diffusion of power brought about by economic success in Asia and American preoccupation with the war on terrorism will diminish the American focus on regional security, much as the end of the Cold War led to decreased interest in European security." The article hints implicitly at future regional alignments that could lead to another round of U.S. strategic readjustments (if not disengagement) as countries begin to seek more independent courses and new relations with each other. In other words, without a proactive posture, Washington may find itself overtaken by events and become a bystander to rapidly changing realities.

In an article aptly titled "The End of Alliances," Rajan Menon forecasts what he considers an inevitable outcome of the post-Cold War era: the obsolescence of U.S.-led alliances in the absence of a clear organizing principle from which nations forge security partnerships. He argues that alliances have always been premised on particular contexts and that, as circumstances change over time, so too does the objective value of military relationships.[20] While inertia and nostalgia might serve to prolong the lifespan of alliances, erosion of their structure invariably occurs as the lack of coherent, mutual interests becomes more evident. In the context of the Korean Peninsula, the consolidation of the South's democracy and an increasingly multi-dimensional strategic outlook will enable the South to pursue policies that are less and less in line with U.S. interests. He predicts that "[w]hat is certain is that the emergence of a reunified Korea will cause the case for permanent U.S. bases to crumble. American troops may have to remain on the peninsula for a relatively brief transitional phase, but that will be all."

In terms of an alternative U.S. security posture, Menon concludes, "America will revert to a pattern it has followed for most of its history, operating in a world without fixed, long-term alliances and pursuing its interests and safeguarding its security in cooperation with a range of partners…the United States will be best served by agile and creative statecraft that looks beyond – but does not exclude – traditional friends and solutions, and that musters alignments and coalitions that vary according to context." Such a dramatic shift would require maximum flexibility as the guiding principle for action, which the author presents as the historical norm for U.S. behavior.

Premised on predictions of major structural changes in Asia, William Tow provides a different vision for the future of U.S. alliances in the region.[21] He observes that the concept of exclusive bilateralism, which has underwritten the hub-and-spoke security arrangements between the United States and its traditional allies, is increasingly out of step with regional realities. The growth of multilateral institutions and the tightening web of interdependence have substantially enhanced mutuality of interests among

Asian states. South Korea is particularly notable for its activism in promoting economic and security dialogue with its neighbors. In response to such trends, and against the backdrop of the Bush administration's determination to focus on interests rather than threats as the organizing principle for alliance management, Tow urges a new approach based on what he terms "extended bilateralism." In essence, while the core U.S. strategy would still be based on its bilateral alliances, these ties would be extended to each other and build upon or complement multilateral institutions as a bridge to accommodate the convergence of interests among the various regional players. Without providing specific policy prescriptions, he envisions the existing system giving way to "a more fluid set of dyadic alliances in which what occurs in each alliance has a clear impact upon the others."

In a variation of the same theme (and predating Tow's paper), Dennis Blair, the former combatant commander of U.S. Pacific Command, calls for a fundamental shift away from the competitive balance-of-power mentality, which has dominated interstate relations in the region, through the promotion of shared interests.[22] Similar to Tow, he believes that the road to future stability runs through America's bilateral alliances with Japan and South Korea in the form of "enriched bilateralism." According to Blair, this new structure "principally involves greater consultation and policy coordination with the nations of the region regarding the full range of U.S. policies that affect their security interests, going beyond those that affect only bilateral arrangements." Such an arrangement would then become the forum in which other regional powers are involved as active participants. He envisions the inclusive process as serving as a stepping stone toward genuine multilateral mechanisms. He points to such precedents as the TCOG process and the four-party talks (of the mid to late 1990s) in coordinating regional responses to North Korea as successful experiments in enriched bilateralism. The more recent six-party talks on the DPRK (in 2003 and 2004) appear to bear out his assessment.

While promoting a different kind of inter-bilateral collaboration, Victor Cha puts his assessment of U.S.-led Asian alliances in far more pessimistic terms.[23] Cha predicts, "[The future geostrategic] landscape is unfavorable to U.S. interests. For reasons of geography, history, culture, power, economics, and demography, trends in Asia may emerge such that domestic politics of Korean unification push the U.S. military off the peninsula." Yet, in contrast to the determinism that characterizes the discussions of balance of power theorists, Cha advocates a far more proactive stance. Borrowing from the concept of preventive defense, he argues that "[t]he imperative for the United States is to forestall these unfavorable geostrategic currents in Asia that would follow unification. At its core, this long-term necessity compels Washington to promote stronger relations between its two main Asian allies and to consolidate the trilateral U.S-Japanese-Korean relationship." In contrast to the bilateral approaches noted above, the author argues for an even more ambitious project that accelerates the traditional alliance-based arrangement in Northeast Asia toward trilateralism. In another contrast, under this new construct, Washington, Seoul, and Tokyo together would serve as a unified platform to address threats (such as hostile force projection and counter-terrorism) rather than to promote multilateralism.

A key characteristic of Cha's article that distinguishes it from the studies examined above is the high level of policy specificity. Cha concludes his analysis with a careful and concrete examination of the future requirements for such a new trilateral security posture, including force structure, command structure, basing, and public diplomacy (both domestic and international). A few other works similarly discuss a range of concrete policy recommendations designed to cope with the potential structural shifts on the Korean Peninsula. Derek Mitchell posits several "pillars for post-unification strategy" centered on anchoring future U.S. military presence in Asia and on the peninsula.[24] Notable policy options include 1) a shift away from heavy forces to a flexible posture that emphasizes mobility, agility, and power projection; 2) a command overhaul that abandons the Combined Forces Command (CFC) and adopts two parallel command structures between U.S. and ROK forces; 3) the full integration of U.S. forces on the peninsula with other forces in the region; and 4) the establishment of new access and basing arrangements to facilitate training and exercises and the pre-positioning of military assets.

Premised on an anticipated unification process on the peninsula, another study focuses on organizational changes to the command structure and shifts in the roles and missions of the U.S. armed services.[25] The author proposes a successor organization to the existing command arrangements. He envisions a Northeast Asia command (a sub-component operating under the Pacific Command) that would unify and replace U.S. Forces Korea and Japan.[26] Given the long working relationships developed over the years and the potential political sensitivities to the introduction of a new service (in this case, the navy), the army and the air force should, he argues, continue to dominate the force presence on the peninsula. The article also recommends adjustments in the force structure among the services. The army should draw down most of its heavy forces and replace them with lighter and expeditionary brigades, the air force should vacate one of the two major airbases and rely on long-range, precision strike capabilities, the marines should devise access agreements with a unified Korea, and the navy should maintain its power projection capacity.

Toward an Integrated Analysis

The emerging literature has clearly demonstrated higher levels of sophistication and specificity compared to earlier studies, at the same time that short-term uncertainties on the peninsula have become more pronounced. Yet, even these more recent works contain some shortcomings that deserve attention.

First, regional projections that predict momentous structural changes, particularly the shift away from the hub-and-spoke dynamic in Asia, often come up short in terms of policy recommendations. Sweeping statements about a more flexible and non-aligned posture are not accompanied by useful guidance for policy makers. In particular, both Kang and Menon fail to provide adequate prescriptions on exactly how the United States should prepare for the eventualities and systemic shocks that they foresee.

Second, while the analytical efforts to advocate policy options surrounding the Korean Peninsula are commendable, they similarly fail to identify concrete mechanisms by which to translate ideas into action. Indeed, some studies tend to offer a wish list of policies without couching them in terms of feasibility and prioritization. Among the most egregious, one study fires off twenty-two recommendations under the rubric of a "strategic plan" in the span of two pages.[27] In Cha's study, there is an apparent disconnect between the compelling rationales for a trilateral U.S.-Japan-Korea mechanism and the means to achieve such an objective. It is not clear how his policy proposals focused almost exclusively on the U.S.-ROK alliance can serve to bridge the chasm that divides Japan and South Korea.

Third, based on these above observations, an analytical gap has emerged between those discussing broad structural changes and those focused on Korea-specific issues. For the former, tectonic geopolitical shifts are increasingly obviating the strategic centrality of traditional U.S.-led alliances in the region. Indeed, the very relevance of alliances and U.S. forward presence is being questioned. The latter analyses require that preparations for reconfigurations in the region and on the Korean Peninsula be centered on those same alliances. Rather than disengagement, they advocate a deepening and broadening of the security partnerships centered on variations of bilateralism. This bifurcation in analysis remains to be reconciled.

Nevertheless, important shifts in the policy community have emerged in the literature reviewed here. While consensus remains far from clear, analysts have certainly begun to grapple with the systemic changes that are likely to challenge U.S. interests and posture in Asia. More importantly, the collection of studies provides a broad road map from which this monograph can draw to chart a practicable and long-term course for the U.S.-ROK alliance.

This study seeks to reconcile the apparent rift between the regional perspectives that envision an end to the post-World War II order in Asia and the Korea specialists who advocate a more proactive posture to rescue the U.S.-ROK alliance from inevitabilities posited by the former. Indeed, there is no contradiction between the two. It is precisely the negative geopolitical trends emerging over the horizon that require policy makers on both sides of the Pacific to actively reshape the alliance for the future. In this context, discussions surrounding enriched bilateralism, extended bilateralism, and even U.S.-ROK-Japan trilateralism are helpful concepts to develop further. Building upon these initial analytical forays, this study examines how strengthening the bilateral dimension with an eye toward broader regional cooperation can be achieved, while also dealing with the more pressing challenges, such as the ongoing DPRK nuclear crisis, surrounding the alliance today.

Notes for Chapter Three

1   For a pessimistic assessment, see Paul Dibb, David D. Hale, and Peter Prince, "Asia's Insecurity," *Survival* 41, no. 3 (autumn 1999): 5-20.
2   Aaron L. Friedberg, "Introduction," in Richard J. Ellings and Aaron L. Friedberg, eds., *Strategic Asia: Power and Purpose 2001-02* (Seattle: National Bureau of Asian Research, 2001), 7.
3   See Amitav Acharya, "A Concert of Asia?" *Survival* 41, no. 3 (autumn 1999): 84-101; and Joshua Kurlantzik, "Is East Asia Integrating?" *Washington Quarterly* 24, no. 4 (autumn 2001): 19-28.
4   See Thomas J. Christensen, "China, the U.S.-Japan Alliance and the Security Dilemma in East Asia," *International Security* 23, no. 4 (spring 1999): 49-80; and Robert S. Ross, "The Geography of Peace: East Asia in the Twenty-First Century," *International Security* 23, no. 4 (spring 1999): 81-118.
5   Jonathan D. Pollack and Young Koo Cha, *A New Alliance for the Next Century: The Future of U.S.-Korean Security Cooperation* (Santa Monica, Calif.: RAND, 1995). In 1999, RAND produced another useful study that forecasted the potential unification scenarios on the Korean Peninsula. The alternative outcomes included peaceful integration, collapse of the North and absorption by the South, war, and "disequilibrium" (a persistent state of near collapse). In assessing the probable outcomes, the authors concluded that, "On balance, it seems highly unlikely that Korean unification will unfold in a predictable or conflict-free manner. The stakes, risks, and potential for 'messy' outcomes seem very high." The monograph then briefly projected the challenges that a unified Korea could pose to the major players in the region and outlined the implications that each of the unification scenarios could have for U.S. Army planning for contingencies on the peninsula. See Jonathan D. Pollack and Lee Chung Min, *Preparing for Korean Unification: Scenarios and Implications* (Washington, D.C.: RAND, 1999).
6   Michael O'Hanlon, "Keep U.S. Forces in Korea after Reunification," *Korean Journal of Defense Analysis* 10, no. 1 (summer 1998): 5-19.

7 Michishita Narushige, "Security Arrangements after Peace in Korea," in Nishihara Masashi, *The Japan-U.S. Alliance: New Challenges for the 21st Century* (Tokyo: Japan Center for International Exchange, 2000); and Michishita Narushige, "Alliances after Peace in Korea," *Survival* 41, no. 3 (autumn 1999): 68-83.

8 Ralph A. Cossa, "The Bush Administration's 'Alliance-based' East Asia Policy," *Asia-Pacific Review* 8, no. 2 (2001): 66-80.

9 Nicholas Eberstadt, "American Security Relations with Northeast Asia after 9-11," *Korea and World Affairs* 26, no. 3 (fall 2002): 335-56.

10 See also Robert E. Hunter, "After 9/11: U.S. Policy in Northeast Asia," *Asia-Pacific Review* 10, no. 1 (2003): 1-19. In sharp contrast to Eberstadt, Hunter argued instead that September 11 and the wars against Afghanistan and Iraq did little to alter Washington's options toward North Korea, and he urged a return to the diplomatic status quo and a freeze on deliberations surrounding changes to the U.S. force posture in Asia.

11 Nicholas Eberstadt, "Korea," in Ellings and Friedberg, eds., *Strategic Asia,* 159.

12 James Miles, "Waiting Out North Korea," *Survival* 44, no. 2 (summer 2002): 37-49.

13 See also James J. Przystup, "Anticipating Strategic Surprise," *Strategic Forum*, no. 190 (Institute for National Strategic Studies, National Defense University, Washington, D.C., March 2002). The author argued that the United States should actively seek to engage the North (premised on the principles of transparency, reciprocity, and verification) in an effort to prod Pyongyang toward economic and political opening. In contrast to Miles's premise, the objective in this case is to avoid a backlash *from the South* during an emotionally charged election year in the ROK.

14 Marcus Noland, *Korea after Kim Jong-il*, Policy Analyses in International Economics, no. 71(Washington, D.C.: Institute for International Economics, 2004).

15 Lee Sang-hyun, "Past, Present, and Future of the Korea-U.S. Alliance," *East Asian Review* 15, no.2 (summer 2003): 71-86. For a similar argument, also see Don Oberdorfer, "Korea and the United States: Partnership under Stress," *The Korea Society Quarterly Perspectives* 3, no. 2 (summer/fall 2002).

16 Balbina Y. Hwang, Larry M. Wortzel, and Baker Spring, "North Korea and the End of the Agreed Framework," Heritage Foundation Backgrounder, no. 1605 (October 18, 2002).

17 Doug Bandow, "Cutting the Tripwire: It's Time to Get Out of Korea," *Reason*, July 1, 2003; and Ted Galen Carpenter, "Options for Dealing with North Korea," CATO Institute Foreign Policy Briefing, no. 73 (January 9, 2003).

18 David C. Kang, "Getting Asia Wrong: The Need for New Analytical Frameworks," *International Security* 27, no. 4 (spring 2003): 57-85.

19 Morton Abramowitz and Stephen Bosworth, "Adjusting to the New Asia," *Foreign Affairs* 82, no. 4 (July/August 2003).

20 Rajan Menon, "The End of Alliances," *World Policy Journal* 20, no. 2 (summer 2003): 1-20.

21 William T. Tow, "Assessing Bilateralism as a Security Phenomenon: Problems of Under-Assessment and Application" (working paper for the Hawaii International Conference on Social Sciences, June 12, 2003 [with permission from the author]).

22 Dennis C. Blair and John T. Hanley Jr., "From Wheels to Webs: Reconstructing Asia-Pacific Security Arrangements," *Washington Quarterly* 24, no. 1 (winter 2001): 7-17.

23 Victor D. Cha, "Focus on the Future, Not the North," *Washington Quarterly* 26, no. 1 (winter 2002-03): 91-107. See also Victor D. Cha, "Korea's Place in the Axis," *Foreign Affairs* 81, no. 3 (May/June 2002): 79-92. Cha proposes the concept of "hawk engagement" to open the way for closer trilateral cooperation for the long term.

24 Derek J. Mitchell, "A Blueprint for U.S. Policy toward a Unified Korea," *Washington Quarterly* 26, no. 1 (winter 2002-03): 123-37.

25 Carl E. Haselden, Jr., "The Effects of Korean Unification on the US Military Presence in Northeast Asia," *Parameters* 32, no. 4 (winter 2002-03): 120-32.

26 For another proposed command structure, see General John H. Tilelli and Major Susan Bryant, *Northeast Asian Regional Security: Keeping the Calm* (Arlington, Virginia: Association of the United States Army, 2002), 41. The authors argue that PACOM should relinquish its authority over Northeast Asia. Instead, they recommend a separate Northeast Asian unified combatant command, which would oversee an area of responsibility encompassing China, Japan, Taiwan, and the two Koreas. They argue, "Northeast Asia is simply too important to the security of the United States to be lumped together under such a large and diverse regional command that includes the Asian Subcontinent, Southeast Asia and the South Pacific." This new arrangement, they contend, would foster narrower focus and deeper expertise on Northeast Asia on the part of the combatant command and thus create an environment more conducive to sound long-term policies.

27 Kim Dong Shin, "The ROK-U.S. Alliance: Where Is It Headed?" *Strategic Forum*, no. 197 (Institute for National Strategic Studies, National Defense University, Washington, D.C., April 2003): 3-4.

America's Ideal
U.S.-ROK Alliance

Taking into account the global and regional developments discussed in the previous chapters, as well as its own national security strategies, the United States must clarify what it believes is the ideal future alliance relationship with the ROK (and, eventually, a unified Korea), before it can seriously engage Seoul in formal discussions on the topic. The issue of USFK realignment, being discussed in the FOTA, is currently enmeshed within America's plans for global military transformation and evolving strategies for fighting the GWOT. This situation, combined with the Pentagon's preoccupation with stabilizing Iraq and Afghanistan (not to mention expanding force levels, maintaining readiness, and looking to realign bases at home), means that U.S. policy makers have not been able to focus sufficient attention on building a consensus specific to the integration of Korea in their regional and global initiatives. This chapter will examine how America's national security strategies are changing, and it will outline an ideal scenario for enhancing regional stability by building a loose but coherent coalition of willing nations, rooted in bilateral agreements, to combat specific threats, promote stability, and establish new patterns of security cooperation in East Asia. The effort to incorporate the ROK into this coalition essentially becomes the process of alliance diversification, and it is a means to bridge the gap between U.S. military transformation goals and South Korean foreign and security policy aspirations.

Global Considerations, Regionally Tailored

The United States is transforming its military posture around the world to respond to the demands of the GWOT and to take advantage of newer military technologies. Closely related to this development are the issues of how U.S. forces interact with those of its allies and to what degree America's allies should adjust their own forces and military doctrines to solidify their security relationships with Washington. Although to some degree "military transformation" means different things to different people, there is a broad consensus emerging among U.S. officials regarding the ideal for certain alliance relationships. In the U.S.-ROK case, some basic observations can be made as to what Washington is looking for in a diversified alliance.

Alliance Stability

First and foremost, the United States desires a stable alliance committed to the principles of the Mutual Defense Treaty, signed by the two nations in 1953. However, the mere existence of the one-page treaty is not sufficient to ensure a stable alliance, since it is primarily a means by which the allies can establish arrangements and activities in pursuit of agreed-upon goals. True stability requires either a shared vision for what the alliance seeks to achieve or, in the absence of a shared vision, a sufficiently compatible and mutually acceptable tradeoff whereby each country believes it is receiving certain vital benefits from the alliance that it could not obtain by some form of lesser agreement of cooperation. Furthermore, whatever foundation is laid for the future of the alliance must be clear and compelling enough to endure changes in administrations and governing political parties. For roughly forty years, until the collapse of the Soviet Union, the United States and South Korea more or less maintained a shared vision for the alliance, but they have since been shifting to a more complementary arrangement in which each side increasingly must be able to fulfill particular security needs of the other.

During the Cold War, the two countries' largely overlapping vision for the alliance provided the ROK with a needed patron power to defend the nation against aggression and intimidation from the North, and allowed it to rely on America's protective cover to rebuild and develop its own economic and political systems. The United States, for its part, was eager to forge security ties with different partners to form a staunchly anti-communist bulwark and thwart further communist expansion in Asia. As the alliance matured over the decades, the rationale for security ties remained premised, at its most basic level, on the defense of a democratic and capitalist South Korea (notwithstanding the slow pace of democratic development in the ROK). The alliance consensus, however, has been slowly unraveling for at least the last decade, and, for various reasons noted in previous chapters, this trend has begun to accelerate.

It is not that the United States commitment to ROK defense is weakening, but rather that U.S. military planners and political leaders are looking to broaden the role of the alliance to extend beyond the peninsula, or at least to integrate the USFK more fully into the U.S. global military posture. At the same time, diverging threat perceptions, fears of becoming entangled in the GWOT, and growing national confidence are causing South Koreans to think differently about their security relationship with the United States. Although the heretofore simple, shared purpose or vision for the alliance may be losing its currency, the two countries still have several interests in common, and some form of a new "grand bargain" between the United States and the ROK serving both their interests is not yet out of reach. Developing such a bargain is vital to the alliance's long-term stability and viability.

Flexible Force Structure, Aligned with Global Priorities
Beyond restoring stability to the alliance, the United States government has certain global and regional goals in mind as it engages its ROK counterpart in discussions about the future of the bilateral alliance. In June 2003, Peter Rodman, assistant secretary of defense for international security affairs, explained before a House International Relations Subcommittee, "U.S. regional defense postures need to be based on global considerations, not just regional." This means that the regional approach to military readiness should conform to global priorities of mobility, increased capability of U.S. forward forces, combined and joint operations, forward infrastructure to support long-range attack capabilities, and promotion of greater allied contributions.[1]

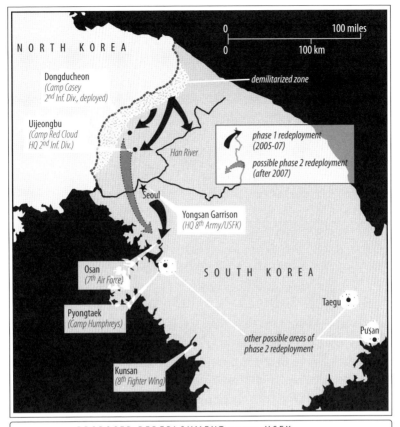

NORTH KOREA

0   100 miles
0   100 km

Dongducheon
(Camp Casey
2nd Inf. Div., deployed)

demilitarized zone

Uijeongbu
(Camp Red Cloud
HQ 2nd Inf. Div.)

phase 1 redeployment
(2005-07)

possible phase 2 redeployment
(after 2007)

Han River

Seoul

Yongsan Garrison
(HQ 8th Army/USFK)

Osan
(7th Air Force)

SOUTH KOREA

Taegu

Pyongtaek
(Camp Humphreys)

Pusan

other possible areas of
phase 2 redeployment

Kunsan
(8th Fighter Wing)

PROPOSED REDEPLOYMENT OF THE USFK

By nearly all of these measures, the current USFK posture is a poor fit with these emerging priorities, and this explains DoD's effort to reconfigure and invest in those forces. This situation is similar in some other countries as well, particularly Germany.

Most of the current U.S. force structure in Korea is composed of heavy artillery and army personnel concentrated in a handful of bases near or north of the Han River, with the primary purpose of deterring and, if necessary, repelling a surprise North Korean attack on the South. Approximately 80 percent of all U.S. Army personnel in Korea are stationed in seven bases around the country, and five of these bases, representing about half of the USFK total troop presence, are located within thirty-five miles of the demilitarized zone (DMZ) that divides the peninsula. Prominent bases in this group of five include Camp Casey and Camp Red Cloud. Tentative realignment plans envision consolidating the most-forward deployed U.S. forces to locations near these two facilities in the next few years, before reassigning them another thirty-five miles or so south to new bases yet to be constructed, possibly near Osan. Much of the equipment at these five bases consists of relatively difficult-to-transport heavy armor, such as M1 *Abrams* tanks, M2 *Bradley* fighting vehicles, and self-propelled howitzers. The United States does plan to replace some of this hardware with more modern and mobile weapons systems, such as *Stryker* combat vehicles.

Relatively speaking, current U.S. forces south of Seoul possess greater mobility than their counterparts farther north. Camp Humphreys, about thirty-five miles south of Seoul, houses a number of AH-64D attack helicopters and Ch-47 *Chinooks*. Nearly all U.S. Air Force personnel are located at either Kunsan Air Base (109 miles south of the DMZ on the southwest coast) or Osan Air Base (48 miles south). The latter, situated north of Camp Humphreys, houses the 51st Fighter Wing, along with approximately twenty A-10s (designed for close air support) and twenty-four F-16 multi-role fighter aircraft. Underscoring the short-range nature of its mission, the USFK does not maintain their own mid-air refueling capability.

How does America's force posture in the ROK fit within the broader U.S. defense planning construct? America's security strategy centers on policies intended to *assure* friends and allies; *dissuade* future military competition; *deter* threats and coercion against U.S. interests; and *defeat* any adversary should deterrence fail.[2] To ensure that the United States can fulfill these four objectives, the Defense Department envisions "regionally tailored forces forward stationed and deployed in Europe, Northeast Asia, the East Asian littoral, and the Middle East/Southwest Asia."[3]

Beyond these critical planning parameters, which largely predate the September 11 terrorist attacks, new priorities have emerged to complement America's current security strategy and to cope with the emerging threats in the context of the GWOT. According to the most recent National Security Strategy, "America is now threatened less by conquering states than we are by failing ones. We are menaced less by fleets and armies than by catastrophic technologies in the hands of the embittered few."[4] These types of threats are, by their nature, less threatening to U.S. allies than they are to the United States, and they are less susceptible to American dissuasion and deterrence than any threat posed by a potentially hostile national army. Almost by default, therefore, America's military strategy is already shifting from "assure, dissuade, deter, and defeat" to something along the lines of *support* friends and allies in their battle against domestic or neighboring terrorist elements, *stabilize* weak or failing states, *preempt* threats in unstable regions, and *defeat* any adversary that emerges in a combatable form. This is true not only in Asia; NATO is also moving to take on more stabilization and preemptive missions in troubled nearby regions.

Share the Burden for Efficiency and Effectiveness

In addition to enhancing alliance stability and adjusting the USFK to be more in tune with global and regional strategic priorities, the United States is looking to develop a network or loose coalition of allies in East Asia that would be ready and willing to conduct certain counter-terrorism, counter-proliferation, and stabilization missions in support of regional security, and the ROK can be an important partner in this effort. Alliance diversification, as contemplated in this study, is primarily targeted at involving the ROK (and a future unified Korea) in this coalition to the greatest extent possible.

The precedent and experience of NATO are instructive. Immediately following the end of the Cold War, few would have predicted that NATO could be reconfigured and motivated to carry out the kinds of peacekeeping, peace enforcement, and commercial shipping protection operations that it is performing today. NATO took the lead in a peace-enforcement/peacekeeping mission in Kosovo in 1999, and it still maintains a force there of close to eighteen thousand, as of the end of 2003. In August 2003, NATO took over command and coordination of the International Security Assistance Force in Afghanistan, following the ouster of the Taliban government in that country, its first-ever deployment outside Europe. Though the commitment of roughly fifty-five hundred troops is relatively small, NATO defense ministers decided in December 2003 to expand the peacekeeping mission progressively beyond Kabul in the ensuing months, after the UN Security Council authorized such an expansion in October.

Equally groundbreaking is NATO's naval operation in the Mediterranean Sea following the September 11 terrorist attacks, when Alliance assets were deployed in support of Article 5 operations for the first time in its history.[5] NATO has contributed airborne warning and control system aircraft (AWACS) to the United States, as well as ships from its standing naval forces to the Eastern Mediterranean, to deter terrorist attacks and weapons proliferators by monitoring ship traffic around the strategically important Strait of Gibraltar. In February 2003, NATO extended the so-called operation Active Endeavor to include escorting non-military ships traveling through the strait to maintain security in the area. As of the end of October 2003, about 350 ships had been escorted and over 36,000 merchant vessels had been monitored by the NATO force. In April 2003, the operation Active Endeavour task force began to conduct selective ship-boarding operations in order to "enhance the effectiveness of the current naval operations against suspected terrorist activities in the Mediterranean."[6] These kinds of operations are illustrative of what the United States could look for in a coalition of willing allies and partners in Asia.

It took NATO decades to develop the institutions and processes that facilitated its evolution into a more multi-faceted alliance after the Cold War, and the transformation has been neither easy nor complete. Though it is unrealistic to expect several Asian nations to come together quickly and begin imitating NATO, there is some hope for building narrow and specific patterns of non-threatening cooperation among a small group of countries to carry out certain NATO-like missions. The political and logistical challenges are immense, but there are at least a few peacekeeping, commercial ship protection, and counter-terrorism missions in which participation by several regional players can be viewed as serving mutual national interests and maintaining the peace in Asia.

Building such coalitions might facilitate the creation in the long term of a more stable environment that is conducive to developing bold security architectures hitherto unseen in Asia's history. What the end-state of such a regional order might look like is not clear. However, the ongoing U.S. efforts to maximize the security partnership with NATO suggest that regional collaboration in East Asia is possible and desirable, and it could lead to tighter and deeper institutional security cooperation both among the East Asian nations themselves and in conjunction with the United States. There already exists a web of formal and informal arrangements based upon multilateral and bilateral mechanisms intended to promote regional stability. Iterative and regular interactions within and among these relationships are likely to foster new expectations concerning peace and war.

Such a phenomenon could gradually evolve into widely accepted norms of behavior that in turn serve as the basis for creating permanent institutions of regional cooperation. Both China and South Korea have made official statements supportive of exploring how the six-party talks on North Korea's WMD programs could be expanded into a forum for Northeast Asian security.[7] In this long-range context, diversifying the U.S.-ROK alliance to accommodate regional missions might be one important step toward such a worthwhile ambition. In the meantime, a more agile partnership could also help the United States achieve its defense transformation goals and be a convenient way for South Korea to get more involved in off-peninsula missions, as well as to position the alliance to survive eventual Korean reconciliation and unification.

Building a Coalition of Allies and Partners for Regional Security

The effort to achieve America's defense policy goals will benefit significantly from the assembly of a stable, regional coalition of willing nations, each contributing specific assets and capabilities as part of an integrated whole, with the common mission to promote stability, facilitate humanitarian relief operations, and combat some of the root causes and manifestations of terrorism in Asia. How aggressively the United States should pursue the creation of such a coalition, what it should be prepared to sacrifice to ensure its realization, and how formal an arrangement is possible (or desirable) are all open questions that could occupy a separate study. The central question for this study, however, is what role the U.S.-ROK alliance could play in such a coalition, since the United States and other countries appear committed to exploring at least the possibility of building some kind of security network in the region and around the world. To begin to answer this question, it is useful to think about what a regional security coalition might look like in the future.

The foundation of this coalition would likely be America's treaty and major non-NATO allies (MNNAs) in the area: Japan, the ROK, Australia, Thailand, and the Philippines.[8] Singapore has also been supportive of U.S. security policies in Asia, and at times it is not inconceivable that countries like Russia, China, India, and Vietnam could be involved in specific regional initiatives. Russia, for example, will join NATO naval and air force exercises in 2004, despite the fact that it is not a formal member of that alliance. China-U.S. military ties have warmed considerably since a U.S. spy plane and Chinese fighter collided in April 2001. Relations with Vietnam have progressed as well: a U.S. defense secretary and Vietnam's defense minister met in November 2003 for only the second time since the Vietnam War to discuss security cooperation. This meeting was followed shortly thereafter by the first-ever U.S. Navy port-of-call visit to Ho Chi Minh City.

Independent cooperation between some of these nations is also increasing. China and India held their first-ever joint military exercises at the end of 2003, a series of naval maneuvers partially focused on counter-terrorism. In addition, the United States is engaging Muslim states like Indonesia and Malaysia in talks regarding anti-terror cooperation, counter-proliferation measures, and development assistance. Washington is also contributing in small ways to a recently established anti-terrorism center in Kuala Lumpur for members of the Association of Southeast Asian Nations (ASEAN) and other countries in the region. A coalition arrangement of this sort suggests that the extent and nature of military cooperation would vary widely from country to country. Some members might allow for a substantial U.S. land, air, and naval presence, primary command and control assets, and pre-positioned supplies and equipment. Other countries, however, would likely want tighter limits on U.S. force presence or restrict cooperation to access agreements in certain contingencies with varying degrees of intensity in joint training.

It is important to note that the international component of America's national security strategy involves several non-military activities that should ideally exist symbiotically with each other in an alliance relationship. These include diplomacy (including democracy promotion, human rights issues, and conflict prevention), intelligence sharing, development aid, and the promotion of economic growth and free trade. It is becoming increasingly difficult to separate such activities from the military aspects of an alliance, given the amorphous nature of the enemy and its reliance on political and economic despair as a source of recruits and platforms of support. If the United States and its partners identify a local community providing refuge for a terrorist group, for example, should they shower that community with aid or with bullets? Perhaps it will be some precarious balance of the two? Answering these questions and managing such a multi-faceted network of alliances is obviously going to be difficult, but at least one benefit will be that each bilateral relationship need not encompass all of these components to be a constructive contributor to regional stability. Indeed, such an arrangement would provide the opportunity for less capable parties to specialize in their respective strengths, thus ensuring an inclusive framework for participation without overtaxing certain member states.

The core or "founding members" of this coalition would probably agree to a comprehensive relationship that includes a significant military function, but other (lesser) partners might be able to pick and choose those support activities that best suit their national interests and local political conditions.[9] Not all of the activities (in fact, relatively few of them) would be militarily oriented. Singapore, for example, could cooperate on a number of fronts including intelligence sharing, combating terrorist financing, naval exercises (for anti-piracy, distressed ship rescue, and possibly interdiction of illegal cargoes), and other diplomatic and economic efforts. It has already taken steps in this direction in January 2004 by joining the Proliferation Security Initiative (PSI), which is a multinational program aimed at stopping the illegal trade of WMD by coordinating law enforcement efforts and intercepting illicit WMD cargoes.[10] Chinese and Russian involvement might be less robust, but these two countries could still be vital partners in counter-proliferation initiatives and military confidence building measures (CBMs), and their diplomatic support on certain issues (such as North Korean nuclear development) would be critical. Coalition management will be a daunting and delicate task, but it is by no means insurmountable as long as the basic arrangement respects prevailing geostrategic realities.

It does not require too much imagination to think of a plausible scenario or two that could easily wreak havoc on a fragile anti-terror coalition as outlined above. If Taiwan were to declare independence, for example, and precipitate an armed conflict with China across the Taiwan Strait, not only might the United States and China find themselves in a serious confrontation, but it is also possible that a Chinese missile threat could deter countries like Japan or South Korea from actively supporting U.S. military action. It is equally plausible that a cross-strait crisis might lead to a split among the founding members, with Japan choosing to support the United States while the ROK either opts to stay neutral or side with the PRC. Either outcome would deal a devastating blow to any coalition. Similar problems would arise with conflicts involving other disputed islands in the region, ethnic or separatist rebellions within certain countries, and other real or perceived infringements on national sovereignty.

It is clear, however, that the United States cannot effectively pursue its new security strategy by simply relying on its regional security relationships as they are currently structured, so some form of adjustment is necessary. Thus, rather than focus on the limitations of an anti-terror coalition in East Asia, it is more productive to consider what can be gained by even an imperfect arrangement among willing partners, to design acceptable roles and missions, and to facilitate consultation that will contribute to regional and U.S. national security. The geopolitical security dilemmas that exist today in East Asia will endure regardless of whatever policies the United States pursues in the short term, and so knitting together a coalition to protect trade and combat the sources and lethal potential of terrorism in the region can only be a net positive for those who choose to participate.

While it is tempting to suggest that the United States and its allies ought to pursue some kind of treaty alliance organization (along the lines of NATO) or a looser organization for cooperation (such as a security companion to Asia-Pacific Economic Cooperation, APEC), the track record in the region is not encouraging when it comes to establishing well-structured, efficient, and decisive multilateral institutions. APEC and ASEAN have made valuable contributions to regional prosperity and stability, but their consensus-oriented decision-making process and aversion to political controversy serve as a poor model for sensitive security issues. Even the ASEAN Regional Forum (ARF), designed to promote open dialogue on political and security cooperation in the region, has achieved only modest success at implementing basic CBMs and promoting preventive diplomacy. These organizations will remain important as forums for discussion and policy coordination, but not for action.

Coalition Management

Something akin to APEC, perhaps an Asia-Pacific Security Cooperation forum, might indeed some day become a useful tool for maintaining regional stability, or perhaps the six-party talks will prove to be the seed for a Northeast Asian security organization. But a more productive, near-term approach for the United States is to build upon its bilateral relationships and lead a loose coalition on an issue-by-issue consensus basis. The approach is not far removed from the "enriched bilateralism" described by the former U.S. ambassador to the ROK, Stephen Bosworth, William Tow's "extended bilateralism," or the "wheels to webs" construct articulated by retired Admiral Blair and John Hanley. At the time those concepts were developed, however, there was little focus for this thickening web of security relationships, beyond vague objectives of regional stability, transparency, and greater confidence. What is different today from the pre-September 11 situation is that there exists now a potentially powerful unifying theme of counter-terrorism that can sharpen the attention of political leaders and military planners in Asia (even though the coalition could focus on more than just the GWOT). Perhaps equally important, this kind of coalition centered on the United States, the ROK, Japan, and Australia can understandably be convened without appearing as an alliance aimed at containing the PRC, which would likely (and unconstructively) add to regional tension. In fact, the coalition would seek the involvement of the PRC, and Russia, whenever possible.

The key to managing a broad, counter-terrorist coalition is solidarity among its founding members. The core members of this group must agree upon a base-level, common set of goals, missions, and operating parameters. The United States can then design into bilateral agreements with these countries the necessary basing and access arrangements to carry out the appropriate missions. An important component of these agreements would be language to promote complementary force capabilities and enhance interoperability through procurement, standardized operating procedures, and coordinated joint exercises.

This is not to suggest that counter-terrorist functions will become the primary rationale for all of the U.S. alliance relationships in the region. In the case of the ROK, for example, counter-terrorist functions will likely remain only supplementary to the defense of South Korea and the central tenets of the Mutual Defense Treaty. The same is true for Japan and the U.S.-Japan Security Treaty. Moreover, these countries understandably do not view the GWOT with the same primacy as does the United States, and they have their own priorities that can be incorporated. Indeed, one country's counter-terrorism mission can be another country's relief or development mission (as in Iraq), and in some cases these efforts are combined so as to be inseparable. Some U.S. counter-terrorism support missions in the Philippines, for example, combine military operations with the provision of medical and dental clinics for local populations. The commitment to fighting terrorism, however, should be sufficiently strong that America's partners will make the required investments in equipment, training, and political capital, explaining to their citizens the need for the coalition and the tangible benefits and potential sacrifices of participation.

Legal, financial, and operational frameworks for the coalition would be rooted in bilateral agreements, but the agreements could be renegotiated aggressively to accommodate and support the new missions in a coordinated fashion. Bilateral training would continue, but multilateral exercises would increasingly become important and more ambitious. Coalition members without bilateral agreements with the United States would be welcome to participate in those missions that they believe support their nations' interests. In one of the bolder recent proposals along these lines, U.S. Chief of Naval Operations Admiral Vern Clark suggested that navies around the world should join forces to combat terrorism and form a nautical equivalent of the North American Air Defense Command (NORAD). He proposed that the navies could share intelligence about terrorist threats and coordinate resources on a global basis.[11] While it is not clear that such an initiative will be launched any time soon, the proposal does demonstrate how far the frontiers have been pushed for thinking about multilateral security cooperation.

Coalition Functions

Counter-terrorism would be the primary organizing principle behind the coalition, but even in this narrow context it could actually refer to a rather wide range of activities. As noted above, some of these activities would involve non-military efforts in the areas of diplomacy, law enforcement, developmental aid and investment, trade, and financial regulation. More specific military-related functions would likely focus on prevention and policing, through intelligence sharing, early warning measures, addressing potential vulnerabilities (such as at ports or along critical sea lanes), and counter-proliferation initiatives, as well as military training, counter-insurgency, crisis response, peacekeeping, and consequence management exercises. Consistent with the concept of capabilities-based planning, counter-terrorist functions coexist with, but do not replace, other important and traditional missions of forward deployed U.S. forces, such as defeating the military forces of other nation states. Theater missile defense cooperation might also become an aspect of coalition activity, but because this issue overlaps with geopolitical rivalries, system development and command and control issues will probably remain in the bilateral arena.

In the last few years, the United States Pacific Command (PACOM) and other regional commands have already begun reorganizing themselves to be better prepared to combat decentralized non-state terrorist groups. After a period of experimentation following the September 11 attacks, the regional commands, with the approval of DoD and the National Security Council (NSC), throughout 2002 and 2003 worked to establish the Joint Inter-agency Coordination Group for Counterterrorism (JIACG/CT) to strengthen multi-agency planning for complex (essentially offensive) missions. As PACOM Commander Admiral Thomas B. Fargo explained to the Senate Armed Services Committee in March 2003, "We have established [JIACG/CT] to coordinate DoD and other government agency activities [e.g., Department of State, Treasury, and Justice, and the Central Intelligence Agency] in PACOM's area of responsibility, [in order to] develop targets for future military or [U.S. government] operations, plan PACOM regional and country counter-terrorism campaigns, and enhance U.S. and partner nation counter-terrorist capabilities in support of national objectives in the GWOT."[12] Within PACOM, the JIACG/CT reports to the director for operations (J-3), but PACOM places an emphasis on key nations in the region and its relationships with ambassadors and country teams. A counter-terrorism liaison program allows for certain personnel to be placed within American embassies to provide communication between JIACG/CT and the field, though they often serve under the command representatives in-country so as to remain unobtrusive.[13]

Officials involved with JIACG/CT describe it as "developing a framework to reach beyond the military into diplomatic, law enforcement, and fiscal matters...The improvement in counter-terrorism capabilities includes the theater security cooperation plan, security assistance, foreign military sales, exercises, and international military education and training. Other agencies also have their own means."[14] To date, JIACG/CT has largely focused on intelligence and law enforcement matters and primarily in a bilateral manner with certain Southeast Asian countries, such as Singapore, Malaysia, Indonesia, and the Philippines. U.S. forces based in Northeast Asia, however, also play an important role in these efforts.

Joint exercises in the Philippines, for example, rely heavily on U.S. Marines based in Okinawa, Japan. In November 2003, U.S. Marines and Navy personnel along with their Filipino counter-parts took part in a fifteen-day exercise, Talon Vision 2004, in Luzon, Philippines. The exercise sought to improve and maintain interoperability, combat readiness, and professional relationships between the two countries' armed forces, but it also included humanitarian and civic assistance projects, such as joint medical and dental missions to certain areas.[15] Increasing this kind of flexibility and diversifying deployments throughout the region is an important goal of U.S. defense planners. At the same time, another objective is to support allies' efforts to provide for their own deterrence and defense while improving interoperability and interagency cooperation to respond to the changing security environment. Over time, it is conceivable that the counter-terrorism mission (or asymmetric defense) will replace allied defense as the primary function for U.S. forces in countries like the ROK and Japan.

The U.S.-ROK Role in a Coalition

The United States would clearly benefit from the ROK becoming a willing and enthusiastic founding member of this regional coalition. Because U.S. troops will remain in South Korea regardless to help defend the nation and deter any potential DPRK aggression, reconfiguring force structure and alignment to allow for simultaneous off-peninsula, counter-terrorist activities is an efficient, economical, and prudent adjustment in the GWOT. The commitment to ROK defense will still be the primary mission for the USFK as long as Korea remains divided, but South Korea also has a vital stake in promoting regional stability, and these adjustments should be seen as an important, mutual investment in support of that goal. These efforts can be supportive of the ROK's stated objective of establishing a Northeast Asian multilateral security system.

The United States would also benefit from partnering with a stronger ROK military that keeps pace with evolving American military technology and operating procedures. This partnership could also provide the United States with more options than Japan-based facilities alone when considering the use of forward deployed assets in regional operations. Turkey's denial of access to its territory for use as a coalition launching pad for operation Iraqi Freedom was an important lesson for U.S. planners regarding the value of base and access diversification. Moreover, if North and South Korea are eventually successful in crafting a plan for a peace regime on the peninsula that can lead to reunification, then moving the USFK off the DMZ and establishing a rationale for the alliance other than countering the DPRK will dilute criticisms that the USFK is physically and metaphorically an obstacle to Korean reconciliation. It will also lay the groundwork for a long-term U.S.-Korean relationship containing a strong security component that could serve as a valuable hedge against potential risks for both countries. A strong partnership would be able to cushion any unforeseen shocks to the alliance, reassure the Korean public during the transition on the peninsula, and stabilize the regional balance of power during what would likely be a lengthy and potentially volatile unification process.

From the South Korean perspective, broadening the scope of the U.S.-ROK alliance has several attractive aspects. First, as alluded to above, regional stability is an important national interest to which the ROK has continually proven willing to commit military resources (as seen, for example, in its contribution of a peacekeeping force in East Timor), and for which an East Asian security coalition would be designed. Second, Southeast Asia is a crucial trade lifeline for South Korea, and Seoul currently has no independent means of responding to disruptions to this trade by terrorist threats, hegemonic pinching, or regime failure in countries like Indonesia or the Philippines. Indonesia, for example, is the ROK's fourth largest trading partner and a valuable source of natural gas, crude oil, and wood pulp. The bulk of South Korea's energy resources pass through the Straits of Malacca, dividing Sumatra and Malaysia. The Philippines is the ROK's sixth largest trading partner, supplying copper and electrical capacitors, and purchasing South Korean televisions, cameras, and autos. ROK direct investment in the Philippines was over $1 billion in 2002.

In addition, although the proposed reconfiguration of the USFK would require South Korea to increase its defense spending and independent capabilities, the increase is arguably less dramatic than would be the case if U.S. forces were to pull out altogether. Indeed, as early as 1997, ROK military planners were forecasting annual defense budgets of close to $30 billion by 2002 in their Mid-Term Defense Plan (in 2004 this budget is just over $16 billion), primarily because of weapons procurement plans required to support a more independent defense and power-projection capability. Facilitating American military transformation on the peninsula, therefore, can be seen as a way for the ROK to gradually and affordably invest in a truly self-sufficient defense capability that is commensurate with its growing confidence and long-term aspirations.

Looking to the future, as long as the size and composition of the USFK remains modest, the presence of U.S. forces in Korea could indicate to neighboring nations a low likelihood for military conflict on the peninsula, by restraining an ROK arms buildup while limiting the ability of a regional heavyweight to intimidate a temporarily fragile country obsessed with the task of unifying the nation. Russia, China, and Japan could thereby reduce the amount that they would need to spend on border or coastal defense. A long-term U.S. military presence on the Korean Peninsula, therefore, can be viewed as a means to help limit regional military expenditures, allowing for greater investments in productive infrastructure and brightening the prospects for peace and prosperity. Even if the competitive dynamics of regional relations lead to a more intense arms race in Northeast Asia, the American forward posture would still play a constructive balancing and reassurance role among Korea and its neighbors.

By sticking relatively close to the United States, the ROK can also assure its continued access to U.S. military technology and operating techniques. Moreover, being an insider of this East Asian coalition would allow South Korea to secure for itself greater influence on related initiatives and policy choices in the region than would otherwise be the case. Similarly, the ROK would also retain a certain degree of leverage with the United States in discussions regarding policy coordination vis-à-vis North Korea and other domestic priorities. As one former U.S. diplomat argued, South Korea could follow the example of British Prime Minister Tony Blair in the Iraq war, which is to "embed yourself into Washington's policy" (borrowing the image of journalists embedded with coalition troops during the war). The point was that by siding so clearly with President Bush, Blair was then able to gain more access to and influence on U.S. decision making (including, most prominently, the White House's concession to seek a second UN Security Council resolution before embarking on operation Iraqi Freedom) than had he stood ambiguously apart.[16]

In the long run, it is in South Korea's interest to diversify the U.S.-ROK alliance rationale beyond its near singular focus on the DPRK threat, primarily because it is so difficult today to determine the ROK's future strategic imperatives. At this time, Seoul cannot know what the regional strategic landscape will look like during and immediately following a reunification scenario, whenever that might take place. It should thus be looking to maximize alliance flexibility and prepare a set of practical, supplemental reasons for continuing close security cooperation with the United States, if such an arrangement is later deemed advantageous.

The alternative for South Korea is to rebalance the burden-sharing arrangement within the bounds of the status quo without undermining the alliance's ability to deter and defeat the DPRK's Korean People's Army (KPA). Seoul could seek a gradual draw-down of forward deployed U.S. forces along with a corresponding increase in ROK military expenditures that would be sufficient to free up additional American troops and equipment to redeploy for other global duties. The danger in this approach, however, is twofold. First, the enhancement of the ROK's armed forces and the reduction of the U.S. military presence could inspire unwarranted confidence in Seoul and raise fundamental questions about South Korea's need to rely on the United States. Many observers in Washington and Seoul have long contended that the ROK is already capable of coping with the DPRK threat alone. In light of this, even a methodical shift in defense responsibilities toward the South might provide political ammunition to those arguing for an early and complete U.S. military disengagement from the Korean Peninsula.

Second, it is unclear exactly what minimum number of forward deployed U.S. troops on the peninsula is deemed credible among South Koreans. It is entirely possible that a slow and deliberate rebalancing process, with negligible impact on the prevailing military balance, could still nonetheless cross a psychological threshold at which Seoul lowers its assessment of the U.S. security commitment and loses confidence in America's political will to defend it. These two closely interrelated points together suggest that notions of commitment and credibility are ultimately in the eyes of the beholder and are more fragile than one might think.

Beyond these shorter-term, transitional considerations, South Korea will also need to address issues and dilemmas that could emerge in the post-unification era. Seoul could lose popular support for the alliance as the North Korean threat dissolves, even though the ROK government might want to retain a comprehensive security relationship to protect itself against unforeseen geopolitical tensions. For instance, will Seoul want to maintain its partnership with the United States and a limited USFK presence as a hedge against changes in Russian or Chinese leadership or foreign policy direction? Will a unified Korea someday become more dependent on energy pipelines that are effectively controlled by those countries? Would a security alliance with America be an effective way to stifle the potential for an expensive military rivalry with Japan? In the absence of alliance diversification, how will Korean leaders argue politically that the USFK should remain beyond reconciliation, especially if the alliance requires some Korean investment in base relocation at a time when the public will be focused on the costs of reunification? The ROK will always be able to move away from a close alliance with the United States if, at some point, it believes it must. It could be far more difficult, however, to re-engage its U.S. ally or make significant adjustments (and investments) in the alliance during or after reunification, precisely at the moment that nationalism would likely reach a zenith. In terms of the timing of alliance diversification, sooner is better than later, since it maximizes flexibility and the time available to implement changes.

The Korean Peninsula's geopolitical environment and the region's security dynamics further complicate Seoul's calculus and future options. The difficulty of Korea's position is abundantly clear when compared to Germany's at the time of its unification. For Germany, the continued hosting of U.S. bases was a less contentious issue than it would likely be in Korea. After all, U.S. troops stationed in West Germany were not really there to defend against East Germany; they were there to counter the broader global threat posed by the Soviet Union. Even after the Soviet Union collapsed, there was sufficient wariness in Eastern Europe toward Russia to warrant a security bias to the West.

Moreover, the united Germany was quickly absorbed into an existing and stable collective security structure in the form of NATO, and thus a continued U.S. military presence was less of a national issue than it was a collective alliance decision. None of these factors that supported the continued U.S. forward basing in Germany will likely be present for a unified Korea.

Despite the various arguments in favor of a new, diversified rationale for the U.S.-ROK alliance, however, there are several complicating factors within the United States, South Korea, and around the region that could ultimately thwart the ambitions of U.S. military planners and force them to look elsewhere for the support they need to foster greater security cooperation in East Asian and carry out the war against terrorism. These dynamics are discussed in detail in the next three chapters. At this time, it is not clear whether U.S. and South Korean officials will be able to overcome the myriad of obstacles to greater security cooperation. Failure to craft a more diverse and enduring partnership will not in and of itself lead to a fracture of the alliance, but the importance of this opportunity and the potential costs of inaction should not be underestimated. The fifty-year-old alliance is more than just a proud legacy, it is a valuable pillar of strength that, when combined with other U.S. relationships in Asia, can become the foundation for regional peace and prosperity.

Notes for Chapter Four

1   Assistant Secretary of Defense for International Security Affairs Peter Rodman, "U.S. Security Strategy in the Asia-Pacific Region," prepared statement for the hearing before the Subcommittee on Asia and the Pacific, House International Relations Committee, June 26, 2003.

2   Department of Defense, *Quadrennial Defense Review Report* (Washington, D.C., September 30, 2001), 11.

3   Ibid., 20.

4   The White House, *The National Security Strategy of the United States of America* (Washington, D.C., September 2002), 1.

5   Article 5 of the North Atlantic Treaty states, "The Parties agree that an armed attack against one or more of them in Europe or North America shall be considered an attack against them all and consequently they agree that, if such an armed attack occurs, each of them, in exercise of the right of individual or collective self-defence

recognised by Article 51 of the Charter of the United Nations, will assist the Party or Parties so attacked by taking forthwith, individually and in concert with the other Parties, such action as it deems necessary, including the use of armed force, to restore and maintain the security of the North Atlantic area."

6   For NATO's explanation regarding operation Active Endeavor, see "Operation Active Endeavour," *Regional Headquarters Allied Forces Southern Europe*, http://www.afsouth.nato.int/operations/ Endeavour/Endeavour.htm (March 9, 2004).

7   The six-party talks include the United States, the ROK, the DPRK, China, Japan, and Russia.

8   The benefits of major non-NATO ally status are largely symbolic, implying a close working relationship with a country's defense forces. MNNAs do not enjoy the same mutual defense and security guarantees afforded to members of the North Atlantic Treaty Organization. The granting of MNNA status, however, does carry some advantages in the foreign-assistance process. Major non-NATO allies are eligible for priority delivery of excess defense articles, stockpiling of U.S. defense articles, purchase of depleted uranium anti-tank rounds, participation in cooperative research and development programs, and participation in certain military equipment purchase financing schemes. The Philippines was designated an MNNA in October 2003, and Thailand joined the group in December 2003.

9   Other scholars have proposed similar arrangements, labeling some "level one" coalitions and others "level two." See, for example, Dana Robert Dillon, "The Shape of Anti-Terrorist Coalitions in Southeast Asia," Heritage Lecture, no. 773 (Washington, D.C., Heritage Foundation, January 17, 2003).

10   The original PSI participants are Australia, France, Germany, Italy, Japan, the Netherlands, Poland, Portugal, Spain, the United Kingdom, and the United States. Five other countries later joined the effort: Canada, Denmark, Norway, Singapore, and Turkey.

11   Robert A. Hamilton, "Navy's Top Officer Calls for a Global Naval Force," *New London* (Conn.) *Day*, October 28, 2003.

12   Admiral Thomas B. Fargo, U.S. Navy, Commander, U.S. Pacific Command, statement before the Senate Armed Services Committee on U.S. Pacific Command Posture, March 13, 2003.

13   Colonel Charles N. Cardinal, Commander Timber P. Pangonas, and Ambassador Edward Marks, "The Global War on Terrorism: A Regional Approach to Coordination," *Joint Force Quarterly*, no. 32 (autumn 2002): 50-51.

14   Ibid., 52.

15   *Philippine Star*, "U.S. Troops Arrive for Talon Vision 2004," October 31, 2003.

16   Based on comments made by a former U.S. diplomat at a U.S.-ROK-Japan trilateral dialogue workshop convened by IFPA to discuss

WMD challenges on the Korean Peninsula. See James L. Schoff, "WMD Challenges on the Korean Peninsula and New Approaches: A Trilateral Dialogue Report" (IFPA, Cambridge, Mass., July 2003).

CHAPTER FIVE

Competing Priorities & Complicating Factors *in the* United States

///

Despite the zeal with which OSD is pushing military transformation, the policy does have its detractors. Moreover, even among those who support the overall pursuit of transformation, there are disagreements over the details, such as what would constitute the ideal combination of forces, weapons, bases, access agreements, command structure, and alliance relationships. An additional question is how far the United States should go in compromising its priorities in order to appease critics and improve the political climate vis-à-vis U.S. forces in each host country. Should alliances only be viewed in terms of their military utility, or are there other valid and broader political and economic benefits of an alliance worthy of consideration?

As America heads into a presidential election year, there is also likely to be considerable domestic debate about the future direction of U.S. foreign policy in general, and the cost of pursuing those policies more specifically. There is no guarantee that the same leadership will be in place at the State Department, the Pentagon, or even the White House in 2005. Is 2004 a "wait and see" year for America's allies, or can U.S. officials follow through on their priorities regardless? Finally, U.S. policy toward North Korea could also be a complicating factor for a smooth transition to a more diversified alliance with the ROK. This chapter examines the potential implications of these issues.

Ambiguities of Transformation and Force Realignment

In the United States, the same issue that most complicates negotiating a diversified alliance with South Korea (or any ally) is also a major driving force behind the need for change, military transformation, or more specifically, the uncertainty surrounding the end-state of transformation. Although alliance managers in the United States do not have to worry as much as their ROK counterparts about how these security talks might impact domestic politics, they do face one challenge that the South Koreans do not have, which is how to balance the give and take in multiple discussions with various countries on security matters. During this era of technological change and geostrategic upheaval, the challenge can be daunting.

Too Many Dependent Variables

The massive scale of the military transformation and force realignment effort, involving simultaneous discussions with literally dozens of countries, produces a complex process whereby the negotiations with any one country are inevitably affected to some degree by progress (or lack thereof) on a separate bilateral track with Seoul. Given the ambitious goals for transformation, it is perhaps unavoidable that multiple discussions with several countries regarding base and access agreements proceed at the same time, but it nonetheless complicates the job for American negotiators, who are, after all, engaged as much in a delicate political and diplomatic process as they are carrying out a military planning exercise.

Some analysts have been critical of what they see as the Bush administration's apparent disregard for the potential adverse affects of such a vast and speedy undertaking. A former Clinton administration defense official wrote, "The shifts would have a compelling military logic. But they would also carry significant human, financial, and diplomatic costs, [and] to ensure that the costs of changing to the new posture do not overwhelm the benefits, the Bush administration needs to carefully think the plans through, in all their dimensions. But so far, the military planning has advanced far beyond the supporting political and diplomatic process."[1]

Because DoD and State Department officials involved in these talks come from similar regional departments, many of the same people who participate in the FOTA with South Korea, for example, are also part of separate talks with Japan, dubbed the Defense Policy Review Initiative (DPRI).[2] There is also some, though not complete, overlap among those charged with crafting new agreements with Australia, Thailand, the Philippines, and Singapore. Effective cooperation between the regional bureaus of the State Department and DoD helps ameliorate some of the problems associated with coordinating multiple negotiations, but it does not change the fact that U.S. officials are unable to articulate exactly how the U.S.-ROK alliance and the USFK will factor into a regional defense or counter-terrorist strategy, for the simple fact that the degree of necessity or redundancy of USFK and ROK assets depends on the ultimate (and currently unknown) contributions by other nations. How can Washington place a value on the support it receives from the ROK when it does not yet understand how ROK-based capabilities will complement other U.S. and allied capabilities in the region?

When NATO began converting from a threat-based planning approach to a capabilities-based approach in the late 1990s, its members faced similar policy coordination challenges as those experienced by America's friends in Asia today. In the NATO case, however, there was a well-established mechanism for discussing and coordinating such security policy issues, a structure that does not exist in Asia. Even within the NATO organization, development of a new integrated set of complementary capabilities has taken several years and continues today.

The example of the U.S.-Japan Defense Guidelines revision launched in the mid 1990s is also instructive. Those negotiations were strictly bilateral and proceeded virtually in isolation from other U.S. alliance considerations in the region, yet that process too required several years before the two countries were able to coordinate logistical support activities, such as those conducted in operation Enduring Freedom. It seems clear from recent experience that adjustments to alliance functions stemming from transformation require a significant amount of time to negotiate, to implement, and to take hold.

Time, however, is not necessarily on the ROK's side, since South Korean intransigence could result in the United States planning not to use ROK-based assets for off-peninsula contingencies, relying instead on U.S. forces in Japan or elsewhere. Washington has been particularly aggressive in pursuing broader contingency-based planning with Japan and Australia, in addition to looking at options for expanding its own capabilities in the region. Options being reviewed include basing a second aircraft carrier in the Pacific theater (although cost considerations have caused the Pentagon to distance itself from this idea since it was first proposed in 2003), shifting long-range bombers and fighter jets to Guam, and increasing the amount and location of pre-positioned hardware.

Moreover, there is an ongoing debate in Washington about where to draw the line between preserving an alliance simply because it strengthens a comprehensive bilateral relationship, versus letting it fade away if it falls short of directly supporting America's strategic priorities. Some officials argue that the United States should consider more than just military or tactical factors when evaluating the relative merits of an alliance, and that important economic or political ties could become a casualty of narrowly focused negotiations. Others, however, suggest that such thinking is a geopolitical anachronism of the Cold War and carries less weight in today's geostrategic environment. They would argue that preserving an alliance simply because its absence might weaken a political relationship in the abstract is not sound security policy.

The prospect for significant redundancy between the USFK and the U.S. Forces Japan (USFJ) is probably most apparent in this regard. Japan hosts the largest and most versatile U.S. military force in the Asia-Pacific region, including America's only Pacific-based aircraft carrier group. The USFJ consists of roughly eighteen thousand marines, thirteen thousand navy military personnel, a contingent of special operations forces, and a balanced array of fighter, airlift, early warning, and mid-air refueling aircraft. Assuming a scenario in which Korea is completing a peaceful process of reunification and maintains positive relations with its neighbors, one could argue that there are relatively few off-peninsula, stabilization, or counter-terrorist missions in and around Northeast Asia that could not be adequately managed by a robust USFJ in collaboration with the Japanese and ROK militaries. Regardless of developments in the U.S.-ROK alliance, Washington appears committed to strengthening its security relationship with Japan. In June 2003, Lieutenant General Chip Gregson, then commander of the U.S. Marine Corps Bases, Japan, told a news organization shortly before assuming command of U.S. Marine Forces, Pacific, "I think [realignment] will enhance the importance of Okinawa, and it will enhance the importance of our bases in Japan overall."[3]

The strengthening of the U.S.-Japan security relationship extends beyond pure military operations and includes intelligence gathering. A day after Gregson's comment, Japanese and U.S. officials revealed that they were exploring the possibility of relocating the headquarters of its Hawaii-based Pacific Fleet patrol and reconnaissance force to the U.S. base in Misawa, Japan. A Japanese defense official said, "The United States is positioning Japan as an intelligence-gathering strongpoint because Japan's geographical and strategic advantage is high."[4] This revelation came on the heels of an announcement that the U.S. Navy was set to relocate one of its Pacific Fleet's reconnaissance aircraft divisions from Yokohama to Misawa. Consequently, at the request of U.S. forces, the Japanese government began work to extend the runway at Misawa to three thousand meters in order to coordinate these types of missions.[5] The strengthening of the allies' intelligence capabilities at Misawa is one of many examples of how the United States and Japan are quietly, but steadily, enhancing their security relationship.

If U.S. power in Northeast Asia can be adequately projected from bases in Japan (with support from Guam and other locations), what then is the added value of the USFK in a scenario where Korea no longer faces an imminent threat? Is it simply to give U.S. military planners more launching options when planning regional operations? For example, Washington will need alternatives if Japan finds itself in a politically difficult position (perhaps due to diplomatic pressure from its neighbors) to allow a particular mission to originate from its territory. Or, does South Korea (or a particular USFK configuration) offer some specific advantages? Seoul, for instance, may be more amenable than Tokyo to permitting base access for a broader range of U.S. missions given the latter's constitutional and other political constraints. However, if these questions are not assessed in a way that convinces Washington of Seoul's strategic utility, then it is possible that the U.S.-ROK alliance might lose its relevance by a simple act of omission or negligence.

Moreover, if the ongoing talks on USFK realignments in South Korea run into delays and difficulties, or if opponents of alliance redundancy eventually win the day in Washington, then the security ties could become increasingly ill equipped to cope with future security challenges and defense requirements. The resulting inadequacies could in turn produce several unintended consequences.

Most prominent among them is the impact on the U.S.-Japan alliance of a sudden U.S.-ROK alliance failure or a precipitous decline in alliance cohesion. The shock of a breakdown in U.S.-ROK defense relations and a rapid American military withdrawal from the peninsula could bring about the much feared "singularization" phenomenon, whereby Japan would find itself uncomfortably hosting a substantial U.S. forward presence essentially alone in Asia.

In such a scenario, Tokyo might come under increasing internal pressure to follow Korea's lead and develop its own independent defense capability. Conversely, if Japan were to accept greater regional security responsibilities (in concert with the United States) at a time of deterioration in U.S.-ROK ties, then alliance diversification with Seoul could seem less relevant and more difficult to achieve for Washington. Such an outcome would essentially present Seoul and Washington with a fait accompli that could have been avoided with preventive measures.

Obviously, neither scenario would serve mutual allied interests or regional stability. The prospect of a precipitous U.S. disengagement from Asia or the exclusion of a united Korea from an American-centered regional architecture would be unfortunate, if not dangerous, for the region's future, at least in the short term, since each regional power would seek to maximize its relative strength and influence, simultaneously casting a suspicious eye on its neighbors' efforts to do the same.

In contrast, a well-negotiated and deliberate process to diversify the U.S.-ROK alliance would avoid or lessen the blows of the worst outcomes noted above. Clearly, a more agile alliance would enable the United States to maximize its basing options and ensure that Korea remains tied into a security framework and that Japan continues to serve as a stabilizing force in the region. Even if the U.S.-ROK alliance were ultimately to weaken, the political energies dedicated to preventing foreseeable threats from damaging the relationship would ease the harm that might spill over to the U.S.-Japan alliance. In particular, if Washington and Seoul were to succeed in engineering a gradual, soft landing for the alliance, then there might be adequate time for Tokyo to adjust to changing strategic realities without resorting to drastic policy options that could fray its ties with Washington in the process.

Strategy and Technology

Transformation and force realignment are also inextricably linked to strategic doctrine, developments in military technology, and weapon system procurement plans, though the direction of causality between these two sets of factors is unclear. Does technology drive transformation? Is technology an enabler that allows the United States to determine its own capabilities first and foremost, such as the ability to strike opponents from fewer, more distant "hub" bases located only in U.S. territories and on the soil of its staunchest allies, a category in which the ROK might, or might not, fall? Or do strategic planning and the demands of transformation drive research and military technological development? Should military research, development, and procurement seek to complement the broadest possible arrangement of regional alliances, basing agreements, and division of roles and missions that the United States is able to negotiate in the region?

In the first scenario, bases in Hawaii, Guam, Japan, and Diego Garcia (with a smattering of access agreements and hardware pre-positioning) might be all the United States feels that it would need in a post-Korean unification environment, given developments in America's long-range strike capability. In the latter case, Washington might try to line up as many security partners as it can, despite some overlap and limited versatility, on the theory that redundancy is a worthwhile strategic asset and that the process of building a broad network of security relationships in and of itself contributes to regional stability and serves U.S. interests. The final arrangement, now being pursued by U.S. negotiators from the State Department and OSD, could end up somewhere between these two extremes, and the details will largely determine what types of weapons systems the United States pursues in the future and how interoperable they must be with its allies' systems.

Consider a situation in which America's allies accept an arrangement (explicitly or implicitly) that has the United States providing certain power projection functions while the allies focus largely on coastal and border defense and logistical support operations. The United States would offer its expertise in long-range reconnaissance and strike capability, distant sea lane protection, and access to certain military technologies, possibly keeping the allies under its nuclear umbrella. In return, the ROK and Japan would provide for their own defense, achieve sufficient interoperability to support allied sea and air missions in the region, and contribute to the intelligence-gathering process. The combination would be extremely powerful and provide a strong deterrent to potential enemies, but it could also be reassuring to neighbors because of the high political threshold necessary to exercise that power (two democracies must support a military move in order for it to be triggered). Korean and Japanese power projection, therefore, is largely outsourced to the United States and "bolted on" to domestic capabilities under certain circumstances.

In addition to being an efficient use of resources (less redundant investment in carriers, airlift, submarines, and so on), this arrangement has the added benefit of allowing the ROK and Japan to provide for their own defense in a manner that does not

POTENTIAL REGIONAL SECURITY BURDEN SHARING APPROACH BETWEEN THE UNITED STATES & ITS ALLIES

threaten others or stimulate an arms race. In this situation it might also be possible to encourage a higher level of specialization with effective trilateral coordination, for example if Japan were to develop relatively more robust rear-area logistical support capabilities while Korea could be more flexible to support, or even participate in, certain off-peninsula combat operations.

Some U.S. military planners might question the benefit of aligning so closely with both the ROK and Japan in this manner, since each alliance will still require a significant amount of tailored investment and maintenance. Others could take issue with the emphasis on developing tightly interdependent synergies with other nations in the name of maximizing efficiency. The result could be to concentrate America's weapons research and procurement budgets on a narrow spectrum in which it holds a comparative advantage, such as long-range reconnaissance and strike capability. Military historian Frederick Kagan makes this argument in one article. "Above all, the U.S. must avoid the search for 'efficiency' in military affairs. Redundancy is inherently a virtue in war...America should continue to try to build armed forces that are the best in every category and have the latent capabilities to meet challenges that cannot now even be imagined."[6]

His article is primarily an attack on the application by OSD of a 1990s-era business model exalting specialization, but his criticism naturally extends to how this kind of transformation influences the nature of America's alliance relationships. Kagan specifically questions a premise of transformation enthusiasts that says, "It was no longer necessary to concentrate forces... [since] it would not be necessary to move many forces around, only to ensure that they were within a 600-mile range of their proposed targets."[7]

The potential emphasis in the United States on military specialization and alliance interoperability has important implications for the complexity of managing each alliance. Interoperability is an efficient and attractive concept, but at times it has been attacked by critics in host countries as a code word for limiting independent national action and restricting their procurement options to primarily U.S.-made weapons systems. A good example of the tensions this can cause occurred in 2001 and 2002, when South Korea was looking to buy about forty new F-X fighter jets, valued at around $4 billion. Bidding for the project were America's Boeing Corporation (F-15 division), France's Dassault Aviation, and Russia's Sukhoi. South Korea ended up choosing the more expensive Boeing F-15K, an improved version of the F-15E multi-role fighter, after a long and hotly contested evaluation process, which Dassault claimed was rigged in favor of the ROK's alliance partner.

The United States applied significant political pressure on the ROK to choose the American aircraft. Top U.S. officials, including President Bush, Secretary of Defense Rumsfeld, and Secretary of State Colin Powell, reportedly pushed for the Boeing selection during meetings with South Korean leaders, emphasizing the need for interoperability. Moreover, a leaked memo showed that the Pentagon told ROK military officials that the United States might not be able to integrate certain U.S. weapons systems on non-U.S. aircraft.[8] After factoring in "political and strategic considerations," South Korea chose Boeing, and Dassault subsequently opened a legal battle against the ROK government to either block the contract or be compensated for some of its bidding expenses. To make matters worse, as a matter of policy the United States would not allow the F-15K to be equipped with the most current "friend or foe" identification systems used on the newest NATO fighters. Critics in South Korea argued that the country ended up paying more for a less capable weapon, and the whole experience contributed to the swell of anti-Americanism in mid 2002. Interoperability can have both positive and negative implications when it comes to alliance management.

Of course, it is important to note that U.S. and ROK forces have already achieved a significant level of interoperability, driven largely by the fact that the two armies must fight as one if they were ever called upon to repel an invasion from the North. The combined command structure of the USFK and ROK forces places a premium on well-coordinated command, control, and communication abilities, though there is always room for improvement. In recent years, the South Korean military began developing its own communications systems that proved to be incompatible with the U.S. system. The Pentagon called attention to this issue in a report to Congress in 2000. "Secure telephone and data encryption, interoperability of command post systems, and electronic interface of automated intelligence systems are all major improvements needed for interoperability in the command."[9] This development underscores the difficulty of achieving "jointness" in combined military operations, even with a combined command structure and a clear, imminent threat. Possible changes in command structure, however, are another aspect of the discussions regarding military transformation and USFK realignment, which could ultimately influence the future direction of the U.S.-ROK alliance.

The Debate over Command Structure

Debates in the United States about military transformation and USFK realignment inevitably lead to the issue of reforming the military command structure, both around the region and on the peninsula. The regional aspect refers to how the U.S. armed forces and PACOM tinker with the command and control apparatus in PACOM's area of responsibility in response to transformation. Pentagon officials are discussing how they might take advantage of new technologies to streamline the regional command while at the same time accommodate possible changes to the size, composition, and missions of various forward deployed assets. Such adjustments will likely impact the USFK's relationship with PACOM and possibly even its relationship to USFJ. Indeed, one plan being considered at the Pentagon would disband the separate military commands in South Korea and Japan and put them under one commander, presumably in Hawaii (or perhaps Japan). There are other command structure issues, however, that are unique to South Korea, and these issues are more closely linked to the broader debate about the future of the U.S.-ROK alliance.

The legacy of UN involvement in the Korean War means that a United Nations Command (UNC) remains in South Korea. The UNC is responsible for upholding the terms of the Korean War Armistice Agreement and coordinating the military efforts of the ROK, the United States, and other UNC member countries in response to a North Korean attack. At the same time the U.S.-ROK Combined Forces Command (CFC) manages the practical operation of the U.S.-ROK defense system and takes over in a wartime scenario. The CFC is commanded by a four-star U.S. Army general, who concurrently heads the USFK and reports to the national command authorities of both countries. The CFC deputy commander is a four-star ROK Army general. In a war-time scenario, the CFC commander generally reports through PACOM, but in some instances he reports directly to the Joint Chiefs of Staff in Washington. On the ROK side, the CFC commander reports via the Permanent Session of the ROK-U.S. Military Committee, which includes the ROK Joint Chiefs of Staff.

There is a close relationship between the UNC and the CFC. Because the UNC has no forces of its own, it delegates the warfighting role to the U.S.-ROK combined forces. Moreover, the CFC commander plays a dual role as the UNC commander, and some of the CFC staff members also serve on the UNC staff. It is important to remember, however, that the two commands are legally separate organizations. The CFC was established under a bilateral agreement between South Korea and the United States, while the UNC was formed under an international agreement. All the commands (the UNC, CFC, and USFK) are currently located at Yongsan Garrison in Seoul, which is slated for relocation south of the capital as early as 2006 as part of the USFK force realignment and the FOTA discussions (see chapter 8 for details of FOTA negotiations).

The military command structure on the peninsula has evolved over the years, and it is appropriate to consider changes during this period of transformation, particularly if the allies are successful at diversifying their security relationship. The CFC was established in 1978, and in 1994 the two countries adopted a policy whereby the ROK would exercise operational control over its forces during peacetime, though the American CFC commander would reassert control in the event of a war. The ROK government has publicly stated its desire to push for the transfer of war-time operational command from the CFC to the South Korean military, which could lead to a parallel command structure similar to that of the USFJ and Japan's Self-Defense Forces (SDF).

The issue of whether or not to perpetuate the UNC also comes up from time to time in both capitals, though the FOTA has not directly tackled either of these issues to date. There does not appear to be a clear consensus among U.S. officials about what would be an ideal arrangement from America's perspective, in part because the issue is inextricably linked to unanswered questions regarding the future of the peninsula, the U.S.-ROK alliance, and the USFK's relationship to the broader regional command structure. Some see the UNC as becoming obsolete in a reunification scenario, while others point out that it could be useful as an international monitor for some sort of interim peace regime, and it could also facilitate the UN's provision of humanitarian assistance and refugee relief operations.

Some U.S. military planners are arguing for an innovative plan to get ahead of the curve of transformation and possible alliance diversification, perhaps via a more regionally oriented U.S. headquarters structure. In this example, the new structure might be directly managed by PACOM, as the strategic-level command, with a reconfigured USFK becoming more like a subordinate, regional-level command charged with more functional tasks. Another alternative is to strengthen the command capabilities of USFJ and have a four-star general there assume responsibilities for a "Northeast Asian Command" that would include the USFK (probably commanded by a U.S. three-star general). This might involve Japan becoming the home to U.S. Army headquarters in charge of Asia and the Pacific (the army's I Corps), which is now located at Fort Lewis in the state of Washington. There is also the possibility of transforming the command structure on the peninsula into a CJTF-type of headquarters arrangement, focused principally on training and operational planning for regional and even extra-regional contingencies. Any of these arrangements would probably work in a diversified alliance scenario, though subordinating the USFK to a commander in Japan could raise questions of asymmetry between the two American security partners.

Improvements in communications and network technologies are enablers of change in these cases. One example is PACOM's expanded use of "split operations" in various training exercises, where fewer U.S. personnel are required to relocate from Hawaii to manage a forward air operations center or a similar facility because more of those functions can be executed from a centralized rear headquarters far removed from battle. Technological improvements are making it easier for military leaders to command operations farther away from the battlefield, though how much the Pentagon should take advantage of these technologies remains an open debate in Washington. Still, these kinds of technological developments are an opportunity for the U.S. military to engage in significant cooperation with allies while minimizing its forward presence.

Related to the issue of command structure and technological change are proposed changes to the size and number of U.S. military bases around the world. Further complicating the process of transformation is the fact that the Pentagon is preparing for another round of base realignment and closure (BRAC) evaluations, scheduled for 2005. The BRAC process has become an important part of the military's transformation efforts, as the Pentagon tries to eliminate excess capacity and infrastructure to free up funds for installations deemed more pertinent to the GWOT and future war-fighting scenarios. For the time being, the Pentagon has indicated that it intends to focus exclusively on rearranging the overseas footprint before it turns to specifics on the domestic front, but it will not be long before the Bush administration (if elected) asks for painful cuts at home.[10]

Regardless of what happens globally, OSD has indicated that it is still committed to reducing capacity in the nation's military infrastructure (domestically) by about 25 percent, so clearly some congressional districts are going to be hard hit economically as a consequence of local base closings. So, too, congressional pressures, arising either from a protracted BRAC debate or as a result of reactions to South Korean anti-Americanism (or just an apparent ROK indifference to U.S. security priorities), might drive Washington to the point where the entire U.S. presence on the peninsula is placed in question for cost reasons, especially in the absence of a North Korean threat and a continued strong (and relatively inexpensive) USFJ posture. Even though there is no apparent linkage between overseas bases and domestic bases (that is, closing one might save another), any new military facilities in Asia will likely be viewed critically by U.S. lawmakers looking to preserve bases in their home districts.

All or Nothing for the USFK?

Another issue of debate in the United States relates to the question of whether the U.S.-ROK alliance could be sustained without an attendant deployment of American forces on the Korean Peninsula. The American experience of losing its air and naval basing rights in the Philippines in 1991 is useful to consider when contemplating what a complete USFK withdrawal from South Korea might mean for the alliance, and it suggests that the future of U.S.-ROK security relations need not be cast in stark, all-or-nothing terms.

The United States established a significant naval presence at Subic Bay in the Philippines as early as 1904, and following the Second World War, Subic Bay Naval Base and Clark Air Base were two of America's largest and most important overseas military facilities. They served as staging areas, billeting, and supply and service depots during the Korean, Vietnam, and first Gulf wars. The United States and the Philippines signed a mutual defense treaty in 1952, and American forces carried out several defense missions for which the Philippine military was unprepared, such as twenty-four-hour air defense and patrolling of the country's maritime boundaries. American military assistance to the Philippines (through loans and grants) was estimated to account for roughly 90 percent of its spending on military operations and maintenance prior to the U.S. withdrawal.[11]

The long history of a permanent U.S. military presence in the Philippines came to an end, however, following the one-two punch of the Philippine Senate's rejection of a new base agreement in 1991 and a volcanic eruption of Mt. Pinatubo that damaged the base facilities. By the end of 1992, some fifteen thousand U.S. military personnel, three thousand defense civilians, and around twenty thousand dependents had left the country. The U.S. diplomatic mission in the Philippines also got smaller, as fewer military representatives were needed in Manila.

Although the United States tried to put on a brave diplomatic face, the withdrawal caused friction in the bilateral relationship. When U.S. forces left Subic Bay they took the dry dock equipment with them, prompting Filipino criticism that the Americans were "hardhearted," since the equipment was of little use at other bases. More tension arose when China began to assert its claim to Mischief Reef in the disputed Spratly Island chain in 1995 by building permanent structures that some observers suspected had military utility. The Philippine government was upset with the weak response by the United States and what it claimed were incomplete intelligence reports on activity around the reef, but Washington reminded Manila that it no longer had forces in the country to prevent such Chinese aggression. This is a story that former U.S. government officials have reportedly retold to ROK politicians in the past year.[12] Security relations hit another low in 1996 when Washington suspended all port calls by U.S. naval vessels, after the Philippine Congress closed a legal loophole that had shielded visiting U.S. military personnel from prosecution for local crimes. The annual U.S.-Philippine military exercises were also cancelled that year.

Despite these setbacks and continuous criticism from certain interest groups in both countries, some U.S. and Filipino officials kept working to maintain and diversify the bilateral security relationship. Philippine President Fidel Ramos, and later even President Joseph Estrada (who, as a senator, helped force the closure of the bases), expressed willingness to cooperate with Washington on a variety of security issues. The two countries signed a visiting forces agreement in 1999 that paved the way for the resumption of large-scale joint military exercises and visits by U.S. warships. The GWOT gave further impetus for stronger security ties, leading to a large increase in U.S. foreign military financing for the Philippines and then a mutual logistics support agreement (MLSA) in 2002. Over one thousand U.S. troops were stationed in the Philippines to work with their Filipino counterparts in a campaign against the Abu Sayyaf terrorist group in Mindanao. In 2003, Washington designated the Philippines as an MNNA.

Although the United States would obviously prefer to maintain a military presence in the ROK if the South Koreans are willing, the Philippine example demonstrates that a strong security relationship can survive the loss of a permanent base presence, as long as both countries can point to mutual benefits from cooperation. One lesson to take from this experience, however, is that it would be better for the allies to articulate the scope of their new relationship prior to any type of withdrawal, rather than hope for favorable circumstances to bring the partners back together at a later date. The other point to note is that the efforts of government officials, military personnel, journalists, and politicians were instrumental in recasting the security relationship.

An alliance must have advocates who are willing to speak up and press for closer cooperation.

The U.S.-Philippine experience demonstrates both the fragility and the inherent strength of any alliance. On the one hand, security ties in transition can easily fall victim to public whim or the prevailing political winds of the day. On the other hand, mutual interests and common threats can quickly override disagreements and revive interest in forging security relations. Avoiding the former outcome and promoting the latter scenario require active efforts on the part of both partners to prepare for a broad range of potential futures. Such a balancing act is equally applicable to the U.S.-ROK alliance. As noted above, it is far preferable for the United States and the ROK to maintain a forward leaning relationship (rather than a reactive one) that is capable of anticipating, tempering, and even preventing shocks to the alliance.

The need for a proactive posture is particularly urgent in this context because what happens to the U.S. military presence on the peninsula will almost certainly have consequences for, and spillover effects on, the U.S.-Japan alliance. For instance, the potential for a singularization phenomenon in Tokyo is among the least desirable results that could follow a messy and haphazard alliance breakup between Washington and Seoul in the post-unification era. In contrast, a successful and smooth transition in U.S.-Korean relations that either maintains a robust American military presence or leads to a gradual U.S. withdrawal would enable Japan to adjust adequately to changing strategic realities. In other words, whether the Japanese react favorably or negatively to the fate of the U.S.-ROK alliance depends in part on how well Washington and Seoul manage the transition to a new security bargain.

Looking beyond the transitional phase, there appears to be a general consensus among American officials that the United States needs to articulate a new regional security paradigm that is centered on a broader network of security ties, as opposed to a couple of strong, but separate, bilateral relationships, as discussed earlier. In this sense, there is general support in Washington for a "thickening" of diplomatic and other cooperative relationships among the major powers in Northeast Asia, parallel to any

U.S. efforts aimed at "thinning" its forward military presence. Such a thickening of regional security ties may well be based on current multilateral efforts to resolve the North Korean nuclear controversy, an observation that only goes to underscore the connection between initiatives aimed at finding a solution to the current nuclear problem and those targeted at restructuring or reinvigorating the U.S.-ROK alliance.

It is worth emphasizing that the trend toward a thickening web of regional relationships and the ongoing moves aimed at thinning the U.S. military presence are not mutually exclusive developments. The U.S. defense transformation will inevitably lead to reductions in American forward presence in Asia. At the same time, strengthening a more diverse range of bilateral and multilateral relations in the region might serve to offset the decreasing visibility of the U.S. military posture (even if the same capabilities are maintained). However, given the malleability of perceptions of U.S. security commitment (which is often wedded to troop levels) and the uncertainty of future relations with non-allied partners and great powers in Asia, Washington must ensure that efforts to readjust its military configuration do not move too far ahead of policies aimed at promoting a regional network of ties. In other words, the tradeoffs between the two trends are likely to occur only gradually through a careful balancing act and, more importantly, the United States needs to be prepared for the possibility that any proposed new security architecture might not adequately develop.

Election Year Politics

As the United States heads deeper into a presidential election year, foreign policy issues are likely to occupy a considerable portion of the public debate, and the Democratic and Republican parties have staked out significantly different positions with regard to how the United States should pursue its objectives in this area. During the Democratic primary, for example, many candidates suggested that they would open up direct negotiations with North Korea, as a supplement to the six-party talks, and try to reduce the strain on the U.S. military by internationalizing the stabilization mission in Iraq and handing off more authority to the UN. Democrats have also criticized the Bush administration policies regarding the ideal size and funding level of the U.S. military, international agreements, and the general conduct of foreign policy.

Though at the time of this writing President Bush's chances for reelection seem relatively good, it is difficult to gauge the potential effect of a serious national discussion about these issues on future Republican policy choices and cabinet appointments, in what could possibly be a close election. Both Secretary of State Colin Powell and National Security Advisor Condoleezza Rice have suggested that they would not serve beyond Bush's first term, and changes in other influential defense and foreign policy positions can be expected. What this means for the future direction of American foreign policy is unclear at this time, and it is precisely this uncertainty that could stymie bold progress in the FOTA talks or the broader process of military transformation.

Beyond the potential for policy inertia in this area, resulting from election year pressures or pending personnel changes, there is also the possibility that subtle, though important, policy shifts could take place. Chief among these is U.S. policy toward the PRC, which has been relatively cooperative and conciliatory during the GWOT but could easily become more adversarial, either through a change in circumstances (such as some type of conflict involving Taiwan or suppression of a democracy movement in Hong Kong) or because policy specialists who advocate a tougher line on Beijing gain influence in the next administration. The trend line of U.S.-PRC relations could be a facilitator of or an obstacle to diversification of the U.S.-ROK security relationship, and the future direction of this trend line is far from established at this point.

The administration's North Korea policy, too, is hardly assured with the coming election. The presumptive Democratic presidential candidate, John Kerry, favors at least bilateral negotiations with the North, if not fuller integration of the DPRK into the world community in exchange for a verifiably nuclear-free peninsula. This contrasts rather sharply with the Bush administration's insistence strictly upon multilateral negotiations and conflicting statements about "regime change" in Pyongyang. Should the North Korean stalemate fail to improve by the fall, the administration might feel pressure to adopt new tactics to resolve the situation or else face criticism from the Kerry campaign. Even if Bush wins a second term, changes at the State Department and the National Security Council could influence the short-term direction of North Korea policy, with a subsequent effect on U.S. relations with the ROK.

In addition, the economic situation in the United States during the run-up to the election could have important implications for both the domestic and foreign policy of the country. While the U.S. economy as a whole has grown stronger in the past year, the unemployment rate remains disproportionately stagnant, evoking references to the so called "jobless recovery" of the early 1990s that contributed to the senior George Bush's failed presidential re-election bid.[13] If this situation persists, the ever-widening trade gap between the United States and China, and the perceived exporting of American manufacturing and service jobs abroad, could take on a higher political profile in domestic policy debates and inject more tension in trade relations with the PRC or other trading partners in Asia. At the start of 2004, Washington placed South Korea on a special watch list of countries for intellectual property piracy (joining Taiwan, the Philippines, Indonesia, and others). The more serious and prominent these sorts of conflicts become, the greater the chance that trade and economic issues could spill into, and complicate, the security arena.

Domestic debates about military spending and troop levels are also likely to emerge in the election year. Driving the issue is the ballooning U.S. federal budget deficit, set to reach nearly $500 billion in 2004, along with the fact that U.S. spending on national defense (at $425 billion in 2003 and up from $335 billion in 2001) is now roughly equal to all other federal discretionary spending combined.[14] Military spending is expected to peak in 2004 at around $475 billion, and thus any calls for further increases to pay for transformation efforts (either in terms of new facilities or weapons systems) may be met with skepticism. Even with the appropriate funding, the conceptual notion of transforming the U.S. military into a leaner organization could face criticism as well. The roughly 130,000 troops committed to Iraq have forced significant deployment of U.S. National Guard and reserve units to combat operations, leading several lawmakers in Congress to press Defense Secretary Rumsfeld to consider increasing the number of military personnel.

Policy Differences over North Korea

The most important foreign policy issue for the United States in the context of U.S.-ROK relations is how to respond to North Korea's development of nuclear weapons and its withdrawal from the NPT. In many ways, the future of the U.S.-ROK alliance begins with successfully handling the North Korean WMD challenge in a coordinated fashion, and, in this sense, it is not a contradiction to talk about the long-term future of the alliance and at the same time discuss the immediate policy choices vis-à-vis North Korea. There is little hope for the alliance if Seoul is attacked and thousands (or possibly hundreds of thousands) are killed at the perceived provocation of the North by the United States. Similarly, the alliance will seem of little value to Americans if North Korea begins nuclear testing or if its plutonium starts popping up in terrorist training camps with only a tepid response from South Korea. Regardless of one's vision for the alliance's future, in the short term it depends on jointly and cooperatively dealing with the North, which is more easily said than done, given fundamental differences that exist in terms of the two countries' threat perceptions and policy priorities.

U.S. and ROK Perspectives

For the Bush administration, the threat posed by WMD and their proliferation to state and non-state terrorist actors is the most serious security challenge of the new era, and the DPRK has proven to be a notorious proliferator over the years. For the South Koreans, while there is concern in elite circles about North Korea's WMD capabilities, there is little awareness of, or interest in, the broader proliferation question. Furthermore, several American officials interviewed in the course of this project noted that while South Koreans are acutely aware of North Korea's military threat to Seoul and of the fact that KPA forces are equipped with chemical weapons targeted on the South Korean capital, there is a general sense of unreality when it comes to North Korea's nuclear threat.

In fact, among many South Koreans, especially those of the 2030 generation, there is a widely held perception that North Korea would never use its nuclear weapons against fellow Koreans in the South. They might use them, it is quietly implied by some, against Japan or the United States, but not against South Korea. Even among military professionals and others who know better, the onus for North Korea's recent behavior is often placed on the United States, with arguments that the emphasis on preemption in the Bush Doctrine leaves the DPRK with few options but to "go nuclear" as a way to guarantee its survival (ignoring the apparent fact that the North's highly enriched uranium, or HEU, program predates the Bush administration).

Even if a verifiable agreement not to proliferate could be reached with a nuclear North Korea (a very problematic proposition at best), the United States and other countries like Japan worry that the North's withdrawal from the NPT and its development of nuclear weapons could be a crippling blow to the global non-proliferation regime. The fear is that North Korea's behavior could increase proliferation incentives among other countries, just as Pyongyang itself benefited from Pakistan's nuclear development. North Korea might now perceive nuclear weapons as an essential means for thwarting a potential U.S. attack, and it is possible that other countries, such as Iran (which is trying to balance adherence to the NPT with its own nuclear program), will reach a similar conclusion and disregard the NPT, further extending this domino effect.

Within U.S. government circles and among the research community, there are clearly differing views about the nature of the North Korean WMD threat and how it should be countered. American intelligence services speculate that North Korea already possesses two or more nuclear devices, that it might soon have more, and that it could be close to developing the capability of mounting them on ballistic missiles. The choices for the United States and the rest of the world, therefore, boil down to either finding a way to live with a nuclear North Korea or developing strategies ranging from traditional non-proliferation mechanisms to coercive measures aimed at a rollback of that capability.

Among American officials, there appears to be a distinct divide between those who are more concerned with proliferation-related

issues and those who emphasize the potentially profound implications of North Korea's actions for regional stability and for the
role of the United States in the Asia-Pacific region more broadly. The officials who identify proliferation as the more serious
of these concerns are themselves conflicted, with some abjur-
ing any policies that would legitimatize DPRK nuclear weapons
development and others stressing that the United States must
contain North Korea's WMD export activities, even if to do so
means giving up attempts to roll back Pyongyang's nuclear capability. The tensions between U.S. non-proliferation proponents
and regional security experts have long been apparent, but, with
respect to North Korea, the conflicting endgames envisioned by
these two groups imply the need for a more concerted effort to
coordinate contrasting strategies.

Working Toward Rollback

Rolling back North Korea's nuclear capabilities is at best, difficult, and at worst, impossible short of war. It is, however, an appropriate place to start in addressing this challenge, and a priority
of some in Washington has been a "negotiated rollback" that provides incentives for a verifiable dismantlement of the DPRK's nuclear program. Other U.S. officials, however, deride the attempt
to negotiate with Kim Jong-il and advocate a type of "coercive
rollback" strategy. Coercive rollback could involve a variety of
military and non-military contingencies, from restricting foreign
currency inflows to an all-out military strike designed to degrade
North Korea's nuclear capabilities. In between these two courses
of action, there are, of course, other options, ranging from involving the UN or a coalition of countries in a ban on DPRK weapons shipments backed by interdiction, trade sanctions or a trade
embargo, or even covert actions to try and destabilize the DPRK
leadership. The truth, however, is that none of these options is
appealing, given the DPRK's unpredictable behavior and the vulnerability of thousands of American forces and their dependents
on the peninsula, not to mention forward deployed DPRK artillery positions and Seoul's proximity to the DMZ. Pyongyang likely perceives its WMD as the only credible tool for assuring regime
survival against internal and external threats, so even measured
efforts at coercing the North might lead the DPRK to react dis-

proportionately, including exercising military options, to outside pressure.

Increasingly few Americans believe that any kind of rollback is a viable option, even if the United States seriously contemplated surgical military strikes. Apart from the weapons complex at Yongbyon, U.S. intelligence about the DPRK's uranium-based activities is incomplete. With respect to Yongbyon itself, an unofficial U.S. delegation visit there in January 2004 determined that the nuclear fuel rods had been removed and that at least some reprocessing of spent fuel probably took place. No one in the West knows where the fuel rods are now. There are also some intelligence reports of a second, secret plan for producing weapons-grade plutonium.[15] Moreover, no North Korean HEU facilities have been located, though three suspect sites have been identified.[16] North Korea maintains an extensive array of underground facilities, and it has been exceedingly difficult to pinpoint locations (for targeting purposes) that are central to the DPRK's weapons proliferation activities. Then there is the possibility of retaliation by Pyongyang against South Korea, U.S. forces stationed on the peninsula, and/or Japan, if the regime in Pyongyang believed that a limited strike was really a prelude to an all-out U.S.-ROK invasion. On this basis, some American officials observe that North Korea's proliferation is really a fait accompli, and that in this sense it is simply a situation that the world will have to live with, and, optimally, contain, by keeping the number of nuclear weapons down, hopefully restricted to single-digit levels.

In general, South Korean officials are more optimistic about the prospects for a negotiated rollback, due to the longer time horizon with which they view the situation. Without the pressing worry about nuclear proliferation to terrorist groups and with their growing conventional military superiority over the North (at least in qualitative terms), many South Koreans believe that time is on their side in negotiations. In contrast to their American counterparts, ROK officials tend to be more pessimistic about the potentially benign nature of a coerced rollback approach and its chance for success. Despite all this, the Roh administration is willing to keep the pressure on and not simply accept a nuclear North Korea. President Roh was quite clear in his inaugural speech that North Korea has a clear choice between becoming a nuclear state or seeking economic engagement and assistance. He reiterated this message in a joint statement with President Bush at their May 2003 summit meeting, warning that they "will not tolerate nuclear weapons in North Korea." The ROK has since made it quite clear to the DPRK that economic cooperation will move forward very slowly as long as the nuclear problem remains unresolved, much to the irritation of Pyongyang.

Still, a complicating factor is that among a portion of South Koreans, particularly the younger generation, there is also a certain feeling of pride in North Korea's nuclear developments, notwithstanding their profound implications for ROK security planning. On this particular issue, there is a clear disconnect with the United States, especially among a segment of the ROK population (small as it may be) who advocate an eventual role for nuclear weapons to secure a reconciled/reunified Korea's future. The idea that the Korean nation has such a capability is a matter of pride for a larger percentage of South Koreans than Americans might wish to believe, and, for those ROK officials who seek over time South Korea's strategic independence from the United States, it amounts to a virtual capability that, in extremis, could even be invoked in certain scenarios against Japan, Russia, or China.

Anecdotal evidence suggests that certain ROK officials were privately elated when North Korea launched its *Taepo Dong* missile over Japan in 1998. The reaction reflected not only pride in the technical achievements of their northern brethren but also the belief that a united Korea might one day inherit such capabilities. That sentiment illustrates the way in which some in the ROK increasingly view the world, and, again, for U.S.-ROK relations (let alone U.S.-ROK-Japanese security cooperation), it is not an encouraging sign.

This is not to suggest that the Roh government fails to perceive a threat from North Korea. Many South Koreans, Roh included, do perceive a real threat from the regime in the North, but what worries them more is the prospect that the United States may act precipitously or that it will mismanage the current situation so that it triggers, even if accidentally, a conflict with the DPRK. Even though most would agree that U.S. and ROK forces would ultimately prevail in such a conflict, it could entail the destruction of Seoul, and this, in the view of South Koreans who actually feel threatened by the North, would be an unacceptable cost.

Crisis and Opportunity

Conflicting pressures face the Roh and Bush administrations on the issue of alliance relations. For its part, the Roh government appears to understand that it needs the U.S. security umbrella to enhance its bargaining leverage with North Korea. For example, the South was able to score diplomatic victories in negotiations with the North concerning transportation corridors through the DMZ in late 2002. Seoul was able to insist that issues related to delineating the road/railway connections and controlling the flow of traffic between the North and South had to be coordinated through the UNC. On the one hand, American backing provided South Korea with the diplomatic authority to stare down North Korea on the issue. On the other hand, and more cynically, Seoul was able to deflect pressure from Pyongyang by blaming Washington for preventing a compromise. To the extent that a visible U.S. presence lends weight to South Korean initiatives with the DPRK, or at least to ROK negotiating positions, it may be regarded by the Roh government as a good thing, despite the fact that Roh's domestic political interest to some extent lies in asserting the ROK's independent role in relation to that of its alliance partner.

For the United States, it is possible that it might someday reach a point where it believes that it must choose between the U.S.-ROK alliance and its own national security, for example, in the context of DPRK WMD development and proliferation. This would amount to a catastrophic failure of alliance management, however, and it could, in and of itself, significantly harm American national interests. Reaching such a conclusion would be a true crisis for the United States and South Korea. But there is still time before the United States reaches this critical juncture, and all efforts now must be focused on forestalling the need for such a choice.

If maintaining the alliance is a priority, then the United States and South Korea must move forward together and demonstrate (primarily to the ROK public and PRC leadership) that each incremental move vis-à-vis the North is appropriate and measured. The two allies must maintain agreement (or, at least, minimize disagreement) on their assessments of North Korea's capabilities and actions, and they should proceed with a negotiated rollback approach including, as necessary, "acceptable" levels of a coercive rollback strategy. "Acceptable coercion" in this case refers primarily to how U.S.-ROK policies are perceived by the South Korean public. It means that any DPRK reaction must be seen as a disproportionate response to U.S.-ROK policies. Perception is important. If there is to be conflict, the alliance will survive only if South Korea is perceived as being "attacked." The alliance could easily crumble if North Korea is seen as being "provoked."

Keeping the U.S.-ROK alliance so focused on the North Korean issue in the short term presents certain dangers as well as opportunities. Invariably such preoccupation with the military threat from the North means that a North-South reconciliation scenario will require a more drastic and difficult shifting of gears. The absence of a strategic stalemate on the peninsula would bring into sharp focus the end to the alliance's central rationale. More concretely, U.S. ground forces would lose their primary mission virtually overnight once inter-Korea peace prevails. Moreover, because the two countries' threat perceptions have begun to differ more markedly, especially since the GWOT, the prospect for dissonance in the relationship after peace comes to the peninsula is real and growing. It is not unthinkable for either side to succumb to temptations to declare an early end to the alliance. Indeed, without preparations for equipping the alliance to cope with a new strategic environment, the disappearance of the North Korea threat could inflict irreparable harm to bilateral security ties.

The danger of rapid obsolescence during or after reconciliation is being compounded by increasing ambiguity surrounding the definition of success for the alliance. In very narrow terms, as defined by the defense treaty, the security relationship has been an unqualified success. The alliance has successfully provided for the defense of the ROK and served as a deterrent against North Korean aggression. During the Cold War, the alliance allowed South Korea to function as a strong anti-communist partner, while the U.S. military protection afforded the opportunity for Seoul to develop into a modern nation.

However, as the relationship matured over the decades, the purpose and value of the alliance changed. As a result, the measure of a successful alliance has also changed, and bilateral security ties increasingly mean different things to different people. Some believe that the alliance enables the two partners, alone or in conjunction, to 1) pursue dialogue with Pyongyang; 2) contain and pressure North Korea; 3) change the DPRK's behavior; or 4) at the extreme, break the ruling regime in Pyongyang. However, others are equally convinced that the alliance heightens the security dilemma for the North by (unnecessarily) elevating the DPRK's sense of vulnerability. The resulting insecurity, this argument goes, has compelled Pyongyang to adopt hostile or intransigent policies, including the pursuit of WMD, in order to safeguard its survival. In the end, according to this line of thought, U.S. military power on the peninsula is simply prolonging the inter-Korea division.

The arguments set out above and throughout this discussion demonstrate the scope of disagreement around the purpose, value, and necessity of the alliance. These basic differences could widen further if the dialogue between and within the two allies is not handled carefully. The proposed USFK realignment, however, is an example of the opportunity that exists to bridge the gap from a North Korea-centered alliance to a more versatile partnership by moving forces from a one-dimensional posture to a more flexible arrangement. The USFK deterrence capability will be as strong as it is today, if not stronger, as U.S. troops will be in a better position to counterattack more quickly and with more of their force strength intact. The plan will also help reduce the USFK's footprint in the crowded Seoul area, which can only help to limit the number of potential accidents. Moreover, the plan is accompanied by a significant investment by both partners in better equipment and more training.

An additional result will be improved capabilities for the allies to operate off-peninsula if required to intervene in a crisis or provide a stabilizing force. In this sense, the alliance should be more physically prepared to undertake a broader range of missions should the countries' leaders request such action. This was not necessarily the main driver behind the USFK realignment plan – there were broader global and technological reasons at work as well – and the move does create a certain amount of friction in the process, but it could be a blessing in disguise for the alliance as it ponders a new future.

In addition, the shift of the USFK to south of the Han River has the psychological advantage of removing them from a position where they can be seen as physically dividing North and South. If and when a North-South reconciliation process is initiated, the alliance can probably delay the question of what to do with the USFK since they will not necessarily be "in the way." Last but not least, the North Korean crisis and the plan for USFK realignment have led to a frequency and level of bilateral communication not seen in years, which can only improve mutual understanding and lay the groundwork for more effective cooperation.

There are many reasons to think that the proposed realignment will make a positive contribution to the alliance, but the United States must also recognize that some South Koreans will complain (and not without some legitimacy) that the net effect will simply be higher taxes and a U.S. force less dedicated solely to the defense of the ROK. Why should South Koreans embrace this change? In theory, the answer lies in enhanced indigenous defense capabilities and greater independence in a more mature partnership with the United States. The goal for the United States and South Korea should be to deliver on this promise of a stronger, better balanced, and more stable alliance.

Notes for Chapter Five

1   Kurt M. Campbell and Celeste Johnson Ward, "New Battle Stations?" *Foreign Affairs* 82, no. 5 (September/October 2003).

2   The Defense Policy Review Initiative was launched at the U.S.-Japan Security Consultative Committee meeting on December 16, 2002. For the joint statement from that meeting, section 10, see *Japan Ministry of Foreign Affairs Official Web Site*, http://www.mofa.go.jp/region/n-america/us/security/scc/joint0212.html. The committee convened several times in 2003 to discuss such issues as bilateral roles and missions, forces and force structures, and bilateral cooperation in facing regional and global challenges.

3   Linda Sieg, "Okinawa's Strategic Value to Grow – Top U.S. Marine," Reuters, June 20, 2003.

4   Masami Miyashita, "U.S. Pacific Fleet Planning to Relocate Intelligence Center From Hawaii to Misawa; North Korea in Mind," *Mainichi Shimbun*, June 21, 2003.

5   *Mainichi Daily News*, "U.S. to Close Yokohama Post, Relocate to Northern Japan," June 7, 2003.

6   Frederick W. Kagan, "The Art of War," *The New Criterion* 22, no. 3 (November 2003).

7   Ibid.

8   Bradley Perrett, "U.S. Tilting Korean Fighter Competition – Europeans," Reuters, August 7, 2001.

9   Department of Defense, "2000 Report to Congress on the Military Situation on the Korean Peninsula," *United States Department of Defense*, September 12, 2000, http://www.defenselink.mil/news/ Sep2000/korea09122000.html (December 15, 2003).

10 Sergeant 1st Class Doug Sample, "U.S. Will 'Reposition' Overseas Footprint before BRAC Cuts at Home," American Forces Press Service, October 7, 2003, *DefenseLINK*, http://www.defenselink.mil/ news/Oct2003/n10072003_200310072.html (December 15, 2003).

11 Renato Cruz de Castro, "Adjusting to the Post-U.S. Bases Era: The Ordeal of the Philippine Military's Modernization Program," *Armed Forces and Society* 26, no. 1 (fall 1999): 119.

12 When MDP Chairman Han Hwa-gap visited Washington early in 2003, he was reportedly reminded of the Mischief Reef story by former Secretary of State James A. Baker III, who added, "The same applies to Korea," if Seoul goes for U.S. military pullout. *Chosun Ilbo*, January 26, 2003, cited in Kim Byung-Kook, "To Have a Cake and Eat it Too: The Crisis of Pax Americana in Korea" (paper presented at the International Conference on East Asia, Latin America, and the "New" Pax Americana, sponsored by the Weatherhead Center for International Affairs, Harvard University, February 13-15, 2003).

13 At an annualized rate, GDP grew by 4.1 percent in the fourth quarter of 2003, but the unemployment rate for December of 2003 remained steady at just under 6 percent.

14 See *Center for Defense Information*, http://www.cdi.org/news/mrp/ discretionary-graph.pdf, for a graph on FY2003 fiscal spending based on U.S. Office of Management and Budget statistics.

15 David Sanger, "North Korea Hides New Nuclear Site, Evidence Suggests," *New York Times*, July 20, 2003, p. 1.

16 Phillip C. Saunders, "Military Options for Dealing with North Korea's Nuclear Program," *North Korea Special Collection*, January 27, 2003, Monterey Institute of International Studies, http:// cns.miis.edu/research/korea/dprkmil.htm.

CHAPTER SIX

Possible ROK Complications & Incentives *for* Alliance Diversification

As described briefly in chapter 2, South Korea is experiencing several domestic political and demographic transitions that are complicating efforts to strengthen and diversify the U.S.-ROK alliance. Whether one tries to label the underlying trend (either a cause of societal change or an effect) as a rise in anti-Americanism, a decline in pro-Americanism, or more generally a rise in nationalism is largely beside the point. The important issue is that the United States must try to recognize and understand what is happening in South Korean society and then devise a strategy for adapting to these transformations. This is, of course, more easily said than done. A roomful of South Korean scholars, student activists, business and labor leaders, and housewives would, themselves, be hard pressed to agree upon the precise nature and source of societal change in the country, let alone what it means for their future. But this does not obviate the need for Americans to listen carefully to that debate, if only for the self-serving purpose of designing effective foreign and security policies. As one U.S. analyst noted, "The only thing worse than overreacting to this phenomenon [of so-called anti-Americanism] would be to ignore it completely in hopes that it would somehow go away. Given the critical role that public opinion plays in determining national policies within vibrant democracies – which the United States and ROK clearly are – we ignore such sentiments only at our peril."[1]

At the same time, the South Korean economy has undergone some important transitions of its own. In the last decade, ROK trade with, and investment in, the PRC has risen dramatically, and some observers suggest that stronger ROK-PRC economic ties could result in a zero-sum weakening of the U.S.-ROK alliance. Indeed, many opinion polls show that younger South Koreans see their country's future as more dependent on good relations with neighboring China than with the United States. Still, economic relationships with the United States and Japan remain vital to national prosperity, and South Korea's near total dependence on imports for its energy needs, which can only be secured (at least for the foreseeable future) by U.S. naval superiority, is another important factor to consider when pondering the ROK's future strategic calculations underlying its foreign and national security policies.

Anti-Americanism or Nationalism (or Both)

Concern in the United States over what many perceive as a troubling rise in anti-Americanism in South Korea reached a high point toward the end of 2002, when strong ROK nationalist sentiments fanned by World Cup success coincided with disputes with Washington over North Korean policy and the USFK accident that killed two Korean school girls, culminating in an emotional and closely fought presidential election. To make matters worse, a large number of South Koreans, correctly or not, believed that the Republican Bush administration favored the more conservative GNP candidate in the election, and that it was thus disappointed with Roh's success.

It was against this backdrop that the FOTA was established, and U.S. government officials recognized that the volatile political climate in Seoul would not make their job of USFK realignment any easier. In fact, a few in South Korea interpreted the tough opening stand by American FOTA negotiators in April 2003, including a tight timetable for base realignment and mission transfer, as a form of punishment (or at least disappointment) regarding the ROK government's failure to rein in anti-American protesters the previous winter. Perhaps in an effort to strip some of the emotion from the issue, U.S. officials seemed to go out of their way to emphasize that the motivations behind realignment were being driven by global priorities and had little if anything to do with Washington's views of the ROK's domestic political developments. The United States found itself in a no-win situation, however, since the resultant focus on technical and logistical details left many in South Korea with an impression that certain unique aspects of their situation were not being considered and addressed by the negotiations.

The tensions in bilateral relations were evident in a rise of negative perceptions of the alliance, revealed by recurrent public opinion polls in South Korea throughout the latter part of 2002 and early 2003. During this time, roughly half of polled respondents indicated a negative or unfavorable perception of the United States.[2] While policy elites in Seoul continued to recognize the importance of the U.S.-ROK alliance for South Korean security planning, in broader public opinion the United States seemed to become a scapegoat for all manner of ROK policy ills; it was seen, for example, as the source of South Korea's economic troubles and its inability to attain reciprocal commitments from the North Korean leadership in terms of a return summit visit and substantive movement on the family exchanges and other CBMs on the peninsula.

Related issues of concern included South Korean complaints about the Status of Forces Agreement and the lack of ROK jurisdiction over U.S. soldiers in certain criminal cases, host-nation support expenditures for the USFK, and a perceived lack of American respect for the Korean justice system. Amongst the political elite, a growing number began demanding changes in the CFC to give the ROK military operational control of ROK forces in a crisis, and, where appropriate, even over USFK units, similar to the way U.S. forces can deploy under non-U.S. commanders at lower levels of NATO's Allied Command Operations. The ROK government has stopped short of demanding such a change, but it has stated that it plans to push in this direction in the future.[3] In the past two years, these issues have often been linked in the United States to what it perceives as a rise in anti-Americanism among South Koreans.

A thorough analysis of anti-American sentiments in South Korea is beyond the scope of this book, but it is worth noting here that the broader phenomenon is not new or specifically tied to recent events. Some degree of anti-Western feeling emerged soon after Europeans and Americans first arrived in the region in significant numbers as far back as the 1800s. Before that time, anti-foreign demonstrations were largely directed at the Chinese. One Korean scholar described these feelings as "an expression of a deep-seated sense of anxiety regarding Korean identity...or another chapter in their history where Koreans are forced to adapt to a new civilization," such as they did in the past during encroachments by China and Japan. "It is not so much America per se, that is the object of nationalist sentiment. It is just that America happens to be the hegemon of the time and the possessor of the 'global standard' that Koreans are forced to adopt."[4]

Even if "anti-American" is too strong to describe the feelings of most South Koreans, there is relatively broad resentment in the ROK that Americans frequently see themselves as exempt from certain rules and restrictions that apply to others, and this perception of American "exemptionalism" contributes to weaker U.S.-ROK ties. Moreover, one can argue that anti-Americanism strengthened following the 1980 Kwangju uprising, in which about 240 protesting civilians were killed by ROK military and police forces. Although the United States had no part in the violence, critics accused America of varying degrees of complicity.[5]

Over the years, discontent with the United States has ebbed and flowed. The growth of American economic and military power coincided with a flowering of South Korean democracy and digital connectivity, ensuring that anti-Americanism would become increasingly politicized and more easily vocalized and disseminated, even if by a minority of citizens. In addition to USFK issues, there were some who blamed the havoc caused by the Asian financial crisis in the late 1990s on U.S. policies or hedge fund companies, for example, and who saw the International Monetary Fund's assistance, with strings attached, as an extension of American influence.

More recent frustrations stem from disagreements with policies of the current Bush administration toward North Korea, Iraq, international treaties, the ICC, and international trade negotiations. In one extreme and symbolic example of discontent, a fifty-five-year-old South Korean farm union leader publicly committed suicide at the WTO ministerial meeting in Cancun, Mexico, in September 2003, to protest proposed trade rules that would lead to cuts in domestic agriculture subsidies. His followers hailed him as a patriot and a hero.[6] As one Korean scholar explained, "Korea is going through an historic process of political self-cleansing and moral soul-searching…as all forms of repressed energy and grievances, boosted by Internet connectivity, gush out to the surface all at once, brilliant ideas and dazzling creativity get mixed up with dangerously wishful thinking. There is not one area in South Korea's national life these days where consensus can be easily attained."[7]

Still another South Korean scholar saw a silver lining in the anti-American activities in 2002 and 2003 in that they generally reaffirmed a strengthening bond of democratic values between the allies. "The series of recent anti-U.S. activities," he wrote, "were by no means a rejection of U.S. values. On the contrary, the main purpose of protest was to disclose the failure of the United States to act according to its official ideology of democracy, human rights, legal justice, and environmentalism. Criticism centered on the hypocrisy and double standards of the United States as it departed from what it purported to enshrine."[8]

In the end, there may be little the United States can do on its own to dampen anti-American sentiment or promote empathy. To be sure, it can try to take South Korean public sentiment into account when crafting or implementing certain policies, and it can work harder to engage ROK citizens in explaining its policies and listening to public opinion. Now that South Korea is a more vibrant democracy, the United States can legitimately reach out to key opinion makers of the country just as others have done in Washington. It may be prudent for U.S. policy makers to forge closer ties with leaders of political, business, and grass roots organizations as channels to convey America's perspectives and to measure the pulse of the Korean public. There is still a large, though relatively less vocal, number of South Koreans who support the alliance and strong economic ties with the United States that Washington can tap into as a source of support. Evidence of this was confirmed by a poll in early 2004 that indicated roughly 60 percent of South Koreans favor a continued USFK presence on the peninsula.[9]

The U.S. government could also go so far as to establish some sort of fund or foundation that would be dedicated to promoting friendship and mutual understanding (not unlike the Japan-U.S. Friendship Commission or the German Marshall Fund), but at best these efforts would only improve the situation on the margins. While it is important for the United States to make these efforts, ultimately the roots of resistance to enhancing the partnership with America lie within South Korea itself and reflect broader, societal changes underway in the country that are not quickly or easily countered. As another South Korean scholar noted, "To a certain extent, the enormous perception gap which separates the younger from the older generation, and in particular the manifestation of unwarranted anti-American sentiment, is a consequence of the failure of our educational system to provide clear factual knowledge concerning the real situation in North Korea, [and it can also] be seen as a reflection of the success we have achieved in democratizing our political system and developing enough self-confidence to let out passions and sentiments which had long been repressed."[10] It seems clear that the job of making a strong case for the alliance and responding to America's critics will require actions by both governments.

What matters most to U.S. policy makers, however, are not vague implications of an intangible force called "anti-Americanism," but rather how these sentiments are manifested in the political process in South Korea. On this front the outlook is not bright for U.S.-ROK ties, due in part to a deep-seated suspicion held by young ROK voters about America's commitment to South Korea's long-term interests and U.S. intentions with regard to USFK realignment. As touched upon earlier, although ROK democracy is probably stronger today than it has ever been, the political leadership and political parties are exasperatingly weak and fractured. In this situation, it is difficult for politicians to lead on sensitive issues.

The debate in the second half of 2003 over whether or not to send additional ROK troops to assist in Iraq's reconstruction was a case study in political indecision and policy drift. The GNP and the business community generally wanted South Koreans to make a strong stand with the United States and send upwards of ten thousand military personnel to serve in Iraq, but Roh, the MDP, and most of the voters favored either a scaled-down force or no involvement at all. What made matters worse was a series of confusing and conflicting statements from various "government sources" about how many troops might be deployed and when. American military planners eventually gave up the idea of counting on a specific number of ROK soldiers and began making arrangements to call up more U.S. reserves as a hedge against an unfavorable ROK response. South Korea eventually agreed to send a relatively large troop contingent of close to three thousand to Iraq, but the way in which this issue was handled (both between the allies and within the ROK) added to bilateral tensions and undermined American confidence in Roh's leadership. An underlying public mistrust of the United States in South Korea combined with domestic political weakness is a poor recipe for effective alliance management and will complicate efforts to diversify alliance functions.

ROK Attitudes and the USFK

Even if U.S. and South Korean negotiators are able to successfully conclude the FOTA discussions and agree upon a schedule and cost-sharing arrangement for USFK base relocation, there are significant domestic political challenges to smoothly realizing the realignment. If the experience of USFJ base relocation in Okinawa is any indication, local opposition to property procurement, facility construction, environmental impact, and planned training activities in the Osan-Pyongtaek area could delay the move for several years and harden criticism of the alliance. The United States and Japan, for example, agreed in principle in 1996 to relocate the assets of Marine Corps Air Station Futenma to another part (or other parts) of Okinawa within five to seven years, but because of local opposition to building a new permanent base near the preferred site, that deadline has already passed without a start in construction. Whenever (or if) construction does begin in Okinawa, it will probably take an additional nine years to complete the facility. In many ways, building a new, overseas U.S. military base in a developed, democratic country has become about as simple and quick as putting up a nuclear reactor near a major U.S. city. No one wants it in their back yard, even if they understand the need.

In the South Korean case, the issue of base relocation has generated a mixed response from the public. Generally speaking, army camps are less disturbing to a neighborhood than air stations, and towns around Osan and Pyongtaek (the most often discussed destination for the new bases) should benefit economically to some degree. In part for that reason, local officials and business groups have embraced the possibility of a new base, and the Pyongtaek representative in the Kyonggi Provincial Assembly added, "It's more than about economics. We realize the USFK's significance on the peninsula and want to contribute to their mission by hosting the USFK headquarters."[11]

But the potential for a significant USFK expansion around Osan has others up in arms. "Unacceptable," says the local leader of an opposition movement. "I will lie in front of the bulldozers when the day comes."[12] Moreover, there is a history of local mobilization against erecting new USFK bases in the area. South Korean and U.S. officials originally agreed in 1990 to a partial relocation of the Yongsan Garrison south to Osan-Pyongtaek, but the deal fell through in 1993 because of disagreements over how to share the relocation costs. Before the plan collapsed, however, local opponents organized themselves to fight the relocation, and it has been relatively easy for this lobbying group to reconstitute itself in opposition to the new plan. Though Washington and Seoul might succeed in completing the realignment within a reasonable timeframe, history shows that these types of adjustments are often fraught with delays and political compromises. The ambiguous future of the U.S.-ROK alliance makes the task significantly more difficult.

With this as background, there is a growing feeling, at least in ROK academic and policy circles, that unless the U.S.-ROK relationship improves, the alliance is likely to become increasingly irrelevant to the future of ROK security planning. In this context, it is worth considering that, from a U.S. perspective as well, the entire concept of an "alliance" is changing, and that even if the United States and South Korea are able to sustain some type of political connection, security cooperation is bound to suffer if the relationship is devoid of a specifically defined security component. Thus, fundamental to this discussion is a consideration of whether the alliance can survive in the absence of U.S. forward deployed troops on the Korean Peninsula.

Some South Koreans believe that it can, and have argued that advances in technologies and U.S. military transformation, more generally, should be regarded as providing options to offset an American troop withdrawal. In defense parlance, the tradeoff between manpower and technology has been termed a "virtual" presence. In other words, regular rotations of U.S. forces through small bases on the peninsula and the region, along with over-the-horizon capabilities, would be sufficient to substitute for the physical presence of American troops. Some Americans, however, are skeptical, and as one senior military official pointed out, "Virtual presence is actual absence." The level of allied interaction and the frequency of U.S. troop rotations would have to be high in order to preserve alliance cohesion in this scenario.

That said, it is important to point out that in the face of the current unfolding situation with North Korea, official ROK government sentiments about the alliance and the stationing of American troops on Korean soil have become less negative since the 2002 presidential election. At least for the moment, talk of encouraging an American troop withdrawal has diminished in official circles. If anything, America's announced plan to realign its footprint and to redeploy forces south of the Han River has been met with some resistance, due to fears that the transformation of the USFK might diminish its capacity to act as a "tripwire" force. The fear is that this could undermine the ROK's deterrent posture and, at the same time, create new ROK concerns about opening up more options for unilateral U.S. initiatives, including preemption against the DPRK.[13]

The United States is pressing ahead with USFK realignment, and though few in official ROK government circles support U.S. troop relocation during this time of tension with the North, South Korea increasingly recognizes that this move is part of a broader, global U.S. strategy, and that it is in its own best interest to work cooperatively with the Americans on this process. Moreover, there is a belief that over the long term the transformation of the American military presence on the Korean Peninsula is a foregone conclusion anyway, so the ROK might as well proactively participate, manage the pace of change, and allow for a smaller American footprint to survive, probably with existing air bases and residual ground forces deployed away from Seoul. This would correspond to the Roh government's view that "American transformation or even disengagement" must not be precipitous.

Other South Korean voices, however, are far less certain that even this type of residual presence would be acceptable to the Korean people, contending that the USFK serves to reinforce the Cold War division of the peninsula. From this perspective, the only way that U.S. forces could continue to be welcomed on the Korean Peninsula would be in the context of some type of multilateral arrangement, perhaps in the context of modernizing the UNC to focus it on regional security issues. This presents other problems, however, in that, theoretically, the UNC is slated to dissolve once the armistice is replaced by a North-South peace treaty, which has been a publicly enunciated objective of the Roh administration. Even if the UNC did not dissolve, the transformation of the UNC and its multilateralization for planning off-peninsula security activities could open a more fundamental debate on whether the U.S.-ROK alliance, as a distinct and separate entity, would or should survive.

Trade and Economic Considerations

It is more than just political and demographic issues that could frustrate U.S. and ROK attempts to broaden their security relationship. Trade and economic factors are important as well, and in this are both positive and negative developments. South Korea's economy rebounded relatively quickly and strongly after suffering severe shocks from the Asian financial crisis of the late 1990s, and by 2000 South Korea was experiencing nearly double-digit growth in its gross domestic product (GDP). The economy has been significantly cooler in the last three years, however, reaching a low point in the second quarter of 2003, with less than 2 percent growth for GDP and negative consumption growth (the latter of which continued into the third quarter). Although 2004 looks a bit more promising, thanks to a recent pickup in exports, political paralysis and uncertainty over the North Korean situation cast a pall over the country's economic prospects. Indeed, in February 2003, Moody's downgraded South Korea's sovereign credit ratings and overall economic outlook in direct connection with the nuclear crisis following several years of favorable assessments.[14] The Bank of Korea also warned in late 2003 that the nation's economic growth potential for the next decade will fall below the 5 percent level, the first time the central bank has announced the possibility of a falling potential growth rate.[15]

The South Korean unemployment rate of 3.5 percent (end of 2003) is relatively low by global standards, but it is on the higher end compared to the last few years, and the Roh administration continues to face significant labor unrest in key industries such as the rail and automotive sectors.[16] The government has resorted to deficit spending in an effort to spur the economy, and future spending plans could make it difficult to bring the roughly $100 billion per year budget back into balance. Most notable of these is an ambitious plan to build a new administrative capital in the central Chungcheong area at an estimated cost of over $38 billion, though this is by no means certain to go forward. If the government wants to bring the budget back into balance, it is easy to see how fiscal constraints can complicate efforts to increase the defense budget (already boosted over 8 percent in 2004 to about $16 billion), not to mention pressures to cover at least part of USFK relocation costs, estimated at anywhere from $3 billion to $15 billion (depending on who is estimating and what they include). U.S. policy makers should anticipate a rise in opposition to alliance adjustments based purely on real and opportunity costs to the South Korean taxpayer, and they should be prepared to answer critics with an explanation of how the alliance continues to serve both countries' interests in an economical manner.

An analysis of recent trends in ROK foreign trade flows, trade composition, and investment patterns, however, reveals a mixed and less pessimistic picture with regard to future U.S.-ROK economic relations. Much attention has been directed to the fact that China (including Hong Kong) overtook the United States as South Korea's largest trading partner in 2003. This is an important development considering the fact that ROK exports of goods and services accounted for about 40 percent of its GDP in 2002

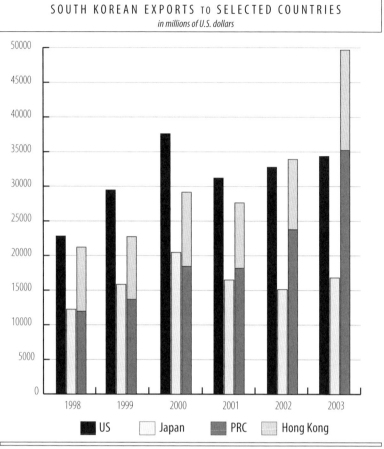

SOUTH KOREAN EXPORTS TO SELECTED COUNTRIES
in millions of U.S. dollars

■ US   □ Japan   ■ PRC   ▦ Hong Kong

(compared with about 9.5 percent for the United States). China now represents over 19 percent of South Korea's total trade, while the United States accounts for around 16 percent.[17] Adding Japan to this equation provides a more complete view of South Korea's trade picture. Together, these three countries buy more than half of South Korea's exports in value terms.

In terms of foreign direct investment, the PRC became the ROK's most important destination for outflows in 2002, edging out the United States, and this trend continued in 2003. Of all overseas investments by South Korean companies, more than three-quarters were funneled into the PRC in the first nine months of 2003. With regard to ROK inward direct investment, however, the United States and Japan remain the largest sources by far, at 54 percent and 17 percent respectively. In terms of portfolio investment, American investors own almost a quarter

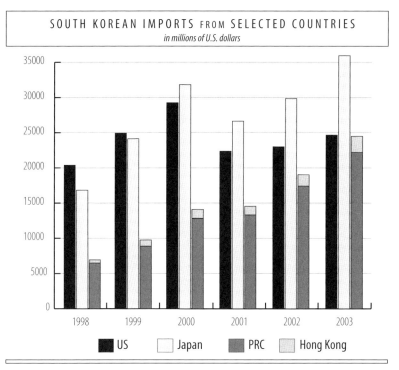

SOUTH KOREAN IMPORTS FROM SELECTED COUNTRIES
in millions of U.S. dollars

of South Korean equities. The next-largest foreign portfolio investor is the United Kingdom, holding a little under 5 percent of the ROK market. There is no doubt that China is becoming an increasingly important economic partner for South Korea, and this will certainly inform its future foreign policy calculations, but the United States and Japan will continue to provide vital markets and investor funds for at least the next few decades. Moreover, the increased investment flow into China from the ROK has the potential to arouse concern among South Koreans about the potential for a "hollowing out" of its less sophisticated manufacturing industries.

A review of South Korea's trade composition also underscores the importance of its economic relationships with the United States and Japan. Americans buy half of the cars produced by the ROK's automobile industry, which employs the most manufacturing workers in the country and is the largest exporter in value terms. The United States is also the biggest purchaser of the ROK's second largest export, electronic integrated circuits, absorbing about 20 percent of those shipments. On the import side, South Korea buys a large amount of high-value integrated circuits and data processing machines from the United States, its second and fifth largest imports respectively. Korean trade with Japan is strikingly similar, except that instead of automobiles Japan buys about 40 percent of the ROK's refined petroleum exports. Overall, ROK trade with the United States (and Japan, for that matter) is characterized by a high degree of intra-industry trade in some of South Korea's most valuable industries.

ROK trade with China and Hong Kong, however, cuts across a wider variety of less connected and relatively less valuable products. The largest ROK export item to China is refined petroleum, which is the ROK's fourth most valuable export. The second largest export item is televisions and cameras (the ROK's fifth most valuable export); next on the list is cathode tubes and valves (number eight). Main imports from China include computer parts and accessories (the ROK's sixth most valuable import), simple semi-conductors (number ten), basic electronic parts and equipment, and coal.[18]

The rise in economic activity between South Korea and the PRC since normalization in 1992 has certainly been dramatic, and current indications are that this trade and investment rela-

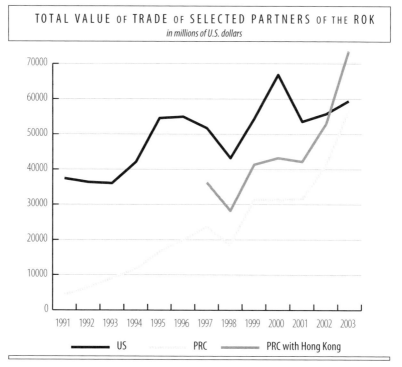

TOTAL VALUE OF TRADE OF SELECTED PARTNERS OF THE ROK
in millions of U.S. dollars

	TOP TRADING PARTNERS *Estimated for 2003*		
	1ˢᵗ	**2ⁿᵈ**	**3ʳᵈ**
ROK	United States	PRC	Japan
PRC	Japan	United States	ROK†
Japan	United States	PRC	ROK
United States	Canada	Mexico	Japan

Hong Kong is excluded from this calculation. If it were included, it would replace the ROK as the PRC's third largest trading partner.
† *The ROK and Taiwan are virtually equal.*
Source: Central Intelligence Agency, The World Factbook 2003 *(November 26, 2003).*

tionship will continue to grow over time. Still, the importance to Seoul of good economic relations with the United States and Japan will not diminish quickly, based on the relative size of U.S. and Japanese investment in the country and on the value of those export markets. Moreover, it should be noted that although the PRC is becoming one of Seoul's most valuable economic partners, the reverse is not necessarily true. PRC exports to the United States are almost five times what they are to South Korea. For Washington, however, South Korea remains a relatively more important export and investment market than the PRC, suggesting more balanced and reciprocal economic ties between the two allies.

More broadly, it seems clear that the U.S.-China-Japan triangle of economic relationships will remain critical to South Korea for many years, and Seoul cannot afford to curry favor with one at the expense of another. In fact, the trading patterns of these four countries are quite tightly intertwined. The rankings shown in the table above are roughly estimated, since in some cases they are so close that technical differences in the way the figures are calculated could alter the position. Regardless of the precise order, the overall dynamic is clear: for each of these leading Northeast Asian economies, the trading relationship among the three, and with the United States, is vital to their individual economic strength.

Underlying this regional trade picture is the single most valuable South Korean commodity import, crude oil. While the oil to fuel South Korea's economy does not necessarily come from

one country, it does come predominately from one region, namely the Middle East. Thus, trade in energy inputs and the pursuit
of energy security are the other major pieces in the puzzle of
South Korean international economic relationships. An analysis
of these issues suggests that the ROK, or even a unified Korea,
cannot escape a heavy dependence on oil shipped through the
Strait of Malacca, or on coal and uranium purchased from Australia and North America.

Factoring in Energy Security

While it is highly desirable for an alliance to gain normative
acceptance irrespective of the national interest calculations
underpinning its formation, the foundation of any bilateral
relationship is the vital national interests that the alliance is
geared toward promoting or protecting. In the context of regional energy security, even a cursory examination of South Korean
demand and supply patterns clearly indicate that considerations
of access to energy inputs will exert a strong influence on South
Korea's foreign policy in the foreseeable future.[19] A diversified
U.S.-ROK alliance, supplementing ROK defense with off-peninsula contingencies, such as the safeguarding of vital shipping
lanes and strategic chokepoints in the South China Sea used to
transport oil from the Middle East to Asia, should be appealing
from South Korea's perspective.

South Korea, like Japan, has relatively few fossil fuel resources and is almost entirely reliant on energy imports to support its
economy, mostly in the form of crude oil from the Middle East.
In 2002, the ROK's energy import reliance ratio was 97.1 percent, with petroleum representing 49 percent of total primary
energy consumption, followed by coal (24 percent), nuclear energy (14 percent), and liquefied natural gas (LNG, 11 percent).[20]
South Korea imported approximately 2.2 million barrels per day
(b/d) of crude oil that year, with Saudi Arabia responsible for 30
percent of the total, followed by the United Arab Emirates (13
percent), Kuwait (7 percent), and Iran (7 percent).[21] South Korea
was the world's sixth largest oil consumer and the fourth largest oil importer in 2001, and 77 percent of its oil came from the
Middle East, up from 72.3 percent in 1999.[22]

The ROK will remain heavily reliant on oil as an energy input in the future, with an expected oil dependency ratio in 2020 of 45 percent. The remaining share of primary energy consumption is expected to come from bituminous coal (21 percent), nuclear power (17 percent), and LNG (15 percent). Nuclear power is particularly important for generating electricity, accounting for 40 percent of the primary fuel in this case, followed closely by bituminous coal (37 percent).[23] Like oil, both bituminous coal and uranium must be imported. The former comes predominantly from China, Australia, and the United States, while uranium comes mostly from Canada and Australia.[24] As of March 2004, South Korea had eighteen nuclear reactors, with another ten expected by 2015, at which time nuclear energy is expected to supply 45 percent of the country's electricity.[25]

Clearly, prudent planning compels South Korea to seek alternative sources of oil in an effort to reduce its reliance on petroleum from the turbulent Middle East, perhaps from sources in Russia and Central Asia. The prospect of significant new supplies over land from Russia to a reunified Korea seems particularly appealing, but a number of factors suggest that South Korea's heavy dependence on Middle Eastern oil will not soon diminish, with or without reconciliation or even reunification with the North.

To begin with, the infrastructure necessary to transport sufficient quantities of crude in a cost-efficient manner from the Russian Far East to the Korean Peninsula simply does not exist, nor is it likely to in the near future. Large-scale Russian oil exports to Northeast Asia are limited by the lack of export facilities in the Russian northeast, along with inadequate investment in exploration, production, and infrastructure in eastern Russia.[26] Only oil from Sakhalin Island, where current estimates place reserves at 600 million barrels and peak total production at 240,000 to 300,000 b/d, is expected to reach Northeast Asia before the end of this decade. A consortium led by Exxon Neftegaz started drilling in May 2003, and after 2005 plans to ship Sakhalin crude westward to De-Kastri on the Russian mainland by underwater pipeline, from which point it could then be exported to Asia. Yet such low levels of production, combined with competition from other energy-hungry countries in the region, indicate that export volume from Russian oil fields will be insufficient to displace South Korean imports from the Middle East.

Central Asia does have the potential to become a major player in world petroleum markets, with exports expected to reach 4 million b/d in 2015 (up from 1.4 million b/d in 2001).[27] But such export figures pale in comparison with those from the Middle East (18.8 million b/d), and the options for transporting crude are either not cost effective (due to the need for lengthy, overland pipelines via Kazakhstan and China) or defeat the initial purpose of relying less on the Persian Gulf region (since the oil would still end up being shipped from there after passing via pipeline from Central Asia to Iran). Thus, South Korea will not be able to replace Middle Eastern oil in significant quantities with Central Asia crude.

With regard to natural gas, the ROK recently entered into a $17 billion project with Russia and China to transport natural gas by pipeline from the vast Kovytka gas field near Lake Baikal to the ROK through China and the Yellow Sea.[28] The deal could bring to the ROK around 10 billion cubic meters annually of natural gas over a thirty-year period, beginning in 2008. While this represents (theoretically) a near 40 percent increase in available supply, these shipments are more likely to displace other sources of natural gas than they would oil or other sources of primary energy. Such prospects for supply and demand indicate that South Korea will continue to rely heavily upon Middle Eastern oil passing through the South China Sea.

More broadly, the Asia-Pacific region currently imports approximately 11 million b/d of oil, or 59 percent of total consumption, and with expected production decreases in Australia, Malaysia, and Indonesia combined with increases in region-wide demand, the import figure could reach as much as 14 million to 15 million b/d by the end of the decade (about 65-69 percent of total consumption).[29] The Middle East supplies over three-quarters of Asia's oil imports, and will continue to play a dominant role in fueling the region's economic growth and development.

Furthermore, South Korea must vie for resources with traditional, large-scale oil importers like Japan, along with up-and-coming importers such as India and China. In early 2004, International Energy Agency figures showed that China, at 5.46

million b/d, overtook Japan as the world's second largest consumer of crude (after the United States) in 2003. China, itself a large petroleum producer with production levels at nearly 3.5 million b/d in 2002, became a net importer of oil in 1993. Both China and India currently consume less than 0.005 b/d per capita (South Korea's figure is approximately 0.05, Japan's is 0.04), and both countries alone are expected to account for 50-55 percent of the region's consumption growth of crude over the period 2002-2015.[30] Furthermore, North Korea, like its counterpart to the south, has relatively few indigenous energy resources. Thus, given the extraordinarily low level of energy use in the North today, the energy demands of a future, reunified peninsula can only result in greater weight attached to energy security issues in the formation of a unified Korea's foreign policy.

Under all realistic future scenarios, it is apparent that either a reunified Korea or simply its southern half will remain heavily dependent on Middle Eastern oil passing through key chokepoints, such as the Strait of Malacca, for the resources needed to power its economic growth and development. In addition, the reliance on maritime trade for the importation of energy inputs will only be exacerbated by the planned expansion of nuclear power plants and the concomitant need for greater amounts of Australian uranium. Given this structural reality, one can expect that South Korean diplomats will maintain a world vision in which they continue to look southward for the country's energy supply, despite mediating factors related to a possible reunification with the North and overland access to continental energy supplies.

In addition, given America's naval dominance stretching from the Persian Gulf to the western Pacific, South Korea will continue to rely (or free-ride, however indirectly) on U.S power projection to ensure its energy security. Further, since the United States faces no credible peer competitor on the high seas across this oceanic arc, at least in the near to medium term, Seoul will clearly benefit from Washington's ongoing security commitments. Because ensuring the unimpeded flow of trade through Southeast Asia is clearly a vital national interest for South Korea, one could expect that policy makers in Seoul might be receptive to sharing the burden with the United States of responding to various off-peninsula contingencies involving the policing of critical sea lanes and protecting this vital trade from potential disruptions.

More broadly, South Korea today already possesses all the attributes of a maritime nation that may become even more evident after unification. Geopolitically, if China gradually assumes a dominant position on the eastern end of the Eurasian landmass, then a relatively fixed balance of power to Korea's north and west would emerge. In other words, as the regional center of gravity shifts toward Beijing, interstate interactions – particularly in the absence of Russian resurgence – will tend to conform to China-centric interests. At the same time, South Korea's trading patterns noted above suggest that Seoul will continue to look to the south and east (trade with the United States, Japan, and the Middle East) for its economic vitality. Thus, the only geopolitical and economic space in which Korea could expand in the future will be oceanic in nature (much as the same conditions propelled Spain and Portugal from the Iberian Peninsula centuries ago). Over the longer term, these maritime drivers could lead either to a convergence or a potential conflict of naval interests with the United States, which is itself a product of naval/oceanic imperatives. Enhancing security and economic cooperation today is a way to help solidify the path of convergence.

Notes for Chapter Six

1   Ralph A. Cossa, foreword to *Anti-Americanism in Korea: Closing Perception Gaps*, Issues and Insights, vol. 3, no. 5 (Honolulu: Pacific Forum CSIS, July 2003).

2   May 2003 Pew Global Attitudes Survey, Pew Research Center for the People and the Press, http://people-press.org. In the 18-29 category, those with an "unfavorable" opinion of the United States reached 71 percent.

3   Kim So-young, "Seoul Lays out Security Goals," *Korea Herald*, March 4, 2004.

4   Hahm Chaibong, "Anti-Americanism, Korean Style," in *Anti-Americanism in Korea: Closing Perception Gaps*.

5   The accusation of American complicity centered initially on the CFC's release from its command (i.e. with the approval of a U.S. general) of two elements of the ROK 20th Infantry Division that were sent to Kwangju to retake the city after the outbreak of conflict, though this decision was made in part to avoid the inde-

pendent dispatch of ROK special forces units that had a reputation for ruthlessness. Some South Koreans were further angered when incoming President Ronald Reagan warmly welcomed ROK President Chun Doo Hwan at the White House in February 1981, even though a primary American motive for this visit was to secure the commutation of a death sentence for Kim Dae-jung, a leading political dissident at the time. Residents of Kwangju have long claimed that the death toll in the incident far exceeded the 240 figure later released by the ROK government. See Don Oberdorfer, *The Two Koreas: A Contemporary History*, rev. ed. (Indianapolis: Basic Books, 2001), 124-38.

6   James Brooke, "Farming is Korean's Life and He Ends it in Despair," *New York Times*, September 15, 2003.

7   Lee In-ho, "Historic and Cultural Roots of Anti-Americanism in Korea," in *Anti-Americanism in Korea: Closing Perception Gaps*.

8   Bong Youngshik, "Anti-Americanism and the U.S.-Korea Military Alliance," *Confrontation and Innovation on the Korean Peninsula* (Washington, D.C.: Korean Economic Institute, 2003).

9   Yoo Dong-ho, "Six in Ten Koreans Back U.S. Military Presence," *Korea Times*, February 23, 2004.

10   Lee In-ho, "Historic and Cultural Roots of Anti-Americanism in Korea."

11   Seo Soo-min, "Expansion Plan for Osan Base Sparks Controversy," *Korea Times*, April 28, 2003.

12   Ibid.

13   The United States has often disputed the characterization of USFK troops deployed along the DMZ as a "tripwire" force, as if somehow American resolve to defend South Korea from attack by the North required early and substantial USFK casualties. American officials would probably argue that there was a time, given then-available military technology and prevailing military strategy, when forward deployment along the DMZ was the most effective deterrent, but that developments in both factors (combined with increased ROK capabilities) mean that deployment farther south would be a superior tactical approach. The United States insists that it would respond to a North Korean invasion as if a tripwire were in place, no matter where the USFK is stationed, in part because North Korean missiles now threaten U.S. bases anywhere in South Korea and Japan.

14   Andrew Ward, "Agency Downgrades S Korea Outlook as Nuclear Crisis Grows," *Financial Times*, February 12, 2003.

15   Kim Jae-kyoung, "BOK Warns of Falling Growth Rate," *Korea Times*, December 17, 2003.

16   For example, on November 12, 2003, the Korean Confederation of Trade Unions called a nationwide strike of 150,000 members, 38,000 of whom work at Hyundai, halting production at Korea's sec-

ond largest auto manufacturer. That was the 305th labor dispute of the year.

17 Christine P. Brown, "Korea's Trade: Increasingly Looking to Asia," *Korea Insight* 5, no.11(Korea Economic Institute, November 2003).

18 Trade composition data from the ROK Ministry of Finance and Economy.

19 Energy security is defined as the securing of access to sufficient supplies of energy, along with the unimpeded transport to its final destination.

20 Korean National Statistical Office (KNSO), http://www.nso.go.kr/eng/index.shtml (November 25, 2003). The reliance ratio is derived by dividing total energy imports by total energy demand, with both variables measured in terms of tons of oil equivalents (TOE). Primary energy refers to energy embodied in natural resources (coal, oil, natural gas, sunlight) that has not undergone any form of artificial conversion or transformation. Secondary energy, such as electricity, refers to the energy obtained from the transformation of primary energy sources.

21 KNSO.

22 Ministry of Commerce, Industry and Energy (MOCIE), http://www.mocie.go.kr/english/policies/toward/default.asp (November 25, 2003).

23 Korea Electric Power Corporation (KEPCO), *Information Center*, http://www.kepco.co.kr/kepco_plaza/en/e/e1/e2_01_06.html (November 26, 2003).

24 Uranium Information Centre, "World Uranium Mining," Nuclear Issues Briefing Paper, no. 41, June 2003, http://www.uic.com.au/nip41.htm (November 26, 2003).

25 Uranium Information Centre, "Nuclear Power in South Korea," Nuclear Issues Briefing Paper, no. 81, November 2003, http://www.uic.com.au/nip81.htm (November 26, 2003); and Uranium Information Centre, "World Nuclear Power Reactors 2002-04," March 17, 2004, http://www.uic.com.au/reactors.htm (March 18, 2004).

26 Jeffrey Brown and Kang Wu, "Asian Oil Market Outlook: Role of the Key Players," AsiaPacific Issues, no. 70 (Honolulu: East-West Center, October 2003), 10.

27 Kang Wu and Fereidun Fesharaki, "Managing Asia Pacific's Energy Dependence on the Middle East: Is There a Role for Central Asia?" AsiaPacific Issues, no. 60 (Honolulu: East-West Center, June 2002). Central Asia is defined here to include Armenia, Azerbaijan, Georgia, Kazakhstan, Kyrgyzstan, Tajikistan, Turkmenistan, and Uzbekistan.

28 "Giant Russian Gas Pipeline to China, South Korea gets Green Light," Agence France-Presse, November 14, 2003.

29 Brown and Wu, 7.

30 Ibid., 3.

CHAPTER SEVEN

Perspectives from Around the Region

The preceding chapters illustrate an increasingly complex bilateral security relationship that features both diverging and converging interests and threat perceptions between Washington and Seoul. The two sides have exhibited varying degrees of disagreement and harmony over the future size, basing arrangement, and operational role for the USFK in the ROK, as well as on the basic policies and coordination efforts toward North Korea that could have direct implications for the future of the alliance. Moreover, the level of accommodation toward (and resistance to) recasting the partnership in the near to medium term to meet the challenges likely to arise during and after the inter-Korean transition could prove just as decisive in determining the vitality of bilateral security ties.

It is equally clear, however, that Korea's geopolitical future does not rest on the evolving dynamics of U.S.-ROK relations alone. Indeed, any analysis of Korea's alternative futures in the context of the alliance would not be complete without incorporating the views and potential positions of the two major regional powers in Northeast Asia, namely China and Japan. From a historical perspective, they have both been the key arbiters of Korea's destiny. Today, each could in its own way contribute to the pace of reconciliation, ensure stability and peace on and around the peninsula, and constrain U.S. policy options. In other words, depending on how Washington handles its regional relationships,

Beijing and/or Tokyo could either facilitate or hamper the pro-posed diversification agenda for the alliance. Washington cannot, therefore, expect to effectively address the challenges and op-portunities of the peninsula during and after the reconciliation era in the absence of a clear understanding of the enduring and emerging interests of China and Japan. The following is an over-view of the strategic perspectives vis-à-vis the Korean Peninsula from the vantage point of these two countries.

China-North Korea Relations

Among the regional players of Northeast Asia, assessments by China with regard to the Korean Peninsula's future are perhaps the least well understood by the United States and its allies. Giv-en the complexity of China's relationships with North and South Korea, discerning the multiple, and often contradictory, motiva-tions behind Chinese policy is a difficult task. Moreover, not only are Beijing's intentions difficult if not impossible to discern, its behavior often appears to belie familiar official statements em-phasizing peace and stability. Yet, because China's decisions and actions regarding the two Koreas today could prove decisive for the longer term, deciphering Beijing's interests is becoming an increasingly urgent policy priority.

To begin, China's posture regarding the two Koreas should be understood in the broader context. The geopolitical centrality of the Korean Peninsula is hard to understate for Beijing. Surround-ed by China, Russia, and Japan, the peninsula is the geographic epicenter of Northeast Asia. A power vacuum on this land bridge between the Eurasian landmass and the Pacific Ocean has invari-ably drawn in one of the regional players, and in the last century, the United States. Reflecting this importance, China has histor-ically sought to retain and exercise its traditional influence over the Korean Peninsula and has vigorously defended the fate of Korea, including during the 1950-53 Korean War, well into the twenty-first century. The peninsula's proximity to the industrial centers of China's northeastern region also means that stability there has significant geo-economic implications.

Beijing's current Korea policy can be best described as a del-icate balancing act that reflects the sharp contrasts in Chinese interests between the North and the South. China must contend with its longstanding obligations – that have proved increasingly burdensome – as a fellow communist ally to Pyongyang, while at the same time maintaining access to the irresistible economic opportunities offered by Seoul. The problem is that the two policy priorities are closely interrelated for Beijing. For example, if China is unable to rein in the North's challenge to the NPT, a major political or military crisis on the peninsula could seriously disrupt the South's economic well-being, which would have a direct impact on China's own economic health. As the uneasy stalemate between the two Koreas continues to unfold in unpredictable patterns, several core interests will inform the Chinese calculus toward the DPRK and the ROK.

China's immediate and primary focus still centers on North Korea because Pyongyang poses a set of thorny dilemmas that could unsettle Beijing's economic modernization plans and its broader political aspirations in the region. Above all, China must ensure that North Korea, which has been on the economic brink over the past decade, does not collapse precipitously. Regime survival is important to Chinese national interests as a way of preserving Chinese influence on the peninsula and avoiding the shock of a humanitarian and refugee crisis on its border. From a realpolitik perspective, keeping an unfriendly neighbor – or one aligned to a potentially hostile power – away from its doorstep has long been a mainstay of Chinese foreign policy. In general, Beijing continues to perceive the North as an important geopolitical buffer against the United States, though this view is not as pervasive today as it was in the past. As with America's security commitments to its allies and friends, China believes the degree to which it can defend North Korea's vital national interests is a measure of its own credibility in the region. Also, symbolically, the collapse of North Korea would further underscore the bankruptcy of the communist ideology, for which Beijing has yet to find an acceptable alternative.

From a socio-economic perspective, the failure to sustain Pyongyang could incur high costs and entail unacceptable risks. The flood of refugees into northeast China that would surely follow regime implosion could easily overwhelm China's fragile health services and other public welfare infrastructure. Moreover, the chaos ensuing from a refugee crisis could plant the seeds of social unrest in China's high-unemployment, rustbelt region of the northeast. In the short term, the costs associated with providing humanitarian relief to those displaced inside China and along the Sino-Korean border could be prohibitive. Allowing the UN or foreign governments into China to help mitigate the crisis is unpredictable and undesirable from Beijing's perspective.

In the longer term, the reconstruction of a devastated North could also require substantial and sustained financial commitments from China (if it wants to maintain its influence there) at the expense of its own internal economic development. Furthermore, a significant amount of South Korean investment, now funneling into China, would likely be diverted to what was North Korea. The short-term costs of collapse would likely outweigh whatever longer-term benefits might result from an uncertain reconstruction process. To preclude these highly undesirable outcomes, China has been the primary supplier of food and energy aid to the impoverished North.

Beijing has also sought to encourage North Korea, with dubious success, to embark on a path of socio-economic reforms resembling China's experiments in the last two decades. It believes that gradual reforms may be able to rescue the DPRK's moribund economic system, based on the ill-founded ideology of *juche* (roughly, self-reliance), which proved to be utterly disastrous in terms of its human toll. Presumably, an economically viable North Korea could gradually wean itself from its dependence on Beijing and would no longer have to fear internal collapse. It is hoped by the Chinese leadership that bottom-up reforms may some day spawn a more market-oriented system, one over which China would have substantial influence. Increasing mutual economic benefits could also help Beijing defray the costs accrued from supporting the North over the years. These hopes are not completely unfounded, as North Korean experiments with administrative and economic reform since the late 1990s have yielded some (albeit modest) positive results, including joint North-South business ventures and limited free markets selling food, tobacco, and Chinese light industrial goods.[1]

In the meantime, propping up the Kim Jong-il regime has produced vexing liabilities. From a purely economic perspective, the life-support system that Beijing runs to keep Pyongyang afloat incurs draining opportunity costs. Politically, particularly in the past decade, China has had to come to terms with a range of North Korea's erratic and often embarrassing behavior. Beijing has learned to live with the reality that associating with an international pariah and, now, a charter member of the "axis of evil," often involves unsavory responsibilities. More recently, heightened expectations, especially from the United States, that Beijing should maximize the apparent leverage it enjoys to sway Pyongyang from its nuclear weapons ambitions has placed yet another burden on the Chinese leadership. The reality is that Chinese influence may be limited, and what leverage it does possess must be used selectively to be effective. The PRC and DPRK political and economic systems have drifted far apart over the last two decades, and in that time each side has become increasingly ambivalent about the other. Indeed, Beijing now has more interests in common, at least in economic terms, with Seoul than with Pyongyang. In the latter half of 2003 and early 2004, China has acted as the key interlocutor with Pyongyang, and it is engaged in active shuttle diplomacy to try to keep the six-party process moving toward some kind of settlement.

It is clear from the analysis above that coping with the declining benefits and increasing costs associated with Pyongyang is the defining parameter of Beijing's North Korea policy. In the short term, sustaining the North Korean regime together with restraining the most destabilizing aspects of Pyongyang's behavior, particularly those related to its nuclear weapons program and proliferation issues, remains China's most important policy priority. Thus far, Beijing has not favored some of the hard-line approaches, including embargoes, sanctions, and other punitive responses, that have been proposed by the United States. Instead, China has insisted on a softer diplomatic and economic route that contains Pyongyang, while inducing and rewarding cooperative behavior from the North. Beijing justifiably fears that a deliberate attempt to dictate terms to Pyongyang could push the regime, already teetering on the brink, over the edge. Alternatively, undue international pressure might further radicalize the calculus and behavior of a desperate Kim Jong-il, leading either to even riskier brinkmanship or to dangerous moves that accelerate regime instability or adversely affect the region in some other way.

However, as the cost (or the probability of failure) of engaging North Korea increases, especially if Pyongyang flouts demands for constraining its nuclear ambitions, China may take on a harder line with the North. China almost certainly wishes to ensure that the North does not become an overt nuclear weapons power, given that the potential regional realignments that might result from such nuclearization on the peninsula would threaten Beijing's geopolitical interests. In particular, a nuclearized North Korea could have the cascading effect of causing South Korea, Japan, and perhaps Taiwan to feel compelled to pursue their own security hedges, including the acquisition of nuclear weapons. In addition, Chinese officials are increasingly concerned about the potential for North Korean nuclear weapons material to fall into the hands of terrorists, including Uighur separatists in China. The problem is compounded by the fact that the more Beijing tries to pressure Pyongyang's leadership, the more likely it is that Pyongyang will determine that the PRC has abandoned its old ally, and the less inhibited North Korea might feel to engage in profitable proliferation activities.

There are also economic dimensions to nuclear proliferation on the peninsula that Beijing must consider. The perceived failure of China to exert decisive control over the DPRK could harm Beijing's overall economic ties with Washington, Tokyo, and Seoul. Over the horizon, should Pyongyang's nuclear maneuvering trigger a wider nuclear breakout and a prolonged arms race in Northeast Asia, the regional instability and rivalries likely to ensue would fundamentally undermine China's overarching goal of steady modernization and development.

The choices that China has to make with regard to Pyongyang have been stark. Beijing can choose to pressure the North in order to resolve the nuclear stalemate at the risk of regime collapse or war on the Korean Peninsula. Alternatively, the Chinese leadership can passively witness the dawning of the second nuclear age in Asia while rupturing relations with China's major trading partners. This dilemma is perhaps why China has thus far chosen a middle path that delays either outcome for as long as possible. It has been in the interest of Beijing to prevent unilateral, regional, or international measures that might corner Pyongyang and leave little maneuver room except for further escalation. At the same time, Beijing has sought to promote negotiations that might produce at least a stopgap measure, such as a successor to the now defunct Agreed Framework.[2] This tactic is sustainable so long as the Chinese side believes that the North still serves Beijing's long-term geopolitical interests. However, if defending Pyongyang leads to developments that ultimately undermine China's position, particularly its economic development, Beijing may opt to endorse, implicitly or explicitly, coercive strategies to rein in the North.

China-South Korea Relations

In contrast to the turbulence and uneasiness that characterize Sino-North Korean ties in recent years, China's relations with South Korea have become among the healthiest and most vibrant in Northeast Asia. Since the normalization of ties in 1992, China has actively sought to deepen and expand its ties with the South across the board. The transformation from an ideological rivalry to a robust bilateral relationship reflects the deep convergences of mutual economic and geopolitical interests in the aftermath of the Cold War. From the Chinese perspective, fostering good relations among its neighbors is consistent with its need to develop internally within a peaceful international environment. Moreover, recent gains in China's comprehensive national power have increased Beijing's confidence to exert its influence and heighten its activism along the continental periphery (to include South Korea). These strategic incentives have thus compelled China to forge a tight bond with the ROK. This new partnership's emergence as an additional element in regional dynamics will likely bolster China's ambitions in the future and perhaps complicate America's security strategy in Asia.

Most significantly, Beijing has encouraged trade with, and investments from, Seoul in order to further facilitate its economic development strategy and to accelerate major technological transfers critical to China's long-term well-being. As a result, the volume of two-way trade is already surpassing that of other regional trading partners that have long dominated the South Korean market (see chapter 6 for details). Geographic proximity, cultural affinities, and historical interactions further cement the economic ties. Indeed, the PRC-ROK linkages now provide far more tangible benefits for China than the troubled PRC-DPRK relationship. In this economic context, China would not likely tolerate any short-term, reckless North Korean behavior that could jeopardize the fruitful partnership with the South. Along with economic activities, both sides have engaged further on the diplomatic and political fronts, including presidential and ministerial visits. Moreover, military-to-military ties have deepened significantly to include regular high-level exchanges.

Interestingly, the generational shifts and, to a lesser extent, changes in political culture in South Korea noted earlier in this study have also reinforced the positive trends in PRC-ROK ties. In the past few years, the two sides have seen favorable domestic public opinion emerge for each other. In particular, many South Koreans now nostalgically think well of China based on cultural and historical ties, and younger Koreans increasingly view China in a better light than the United States. Abstract notions of "China" have become so trendy in South Korean popular culture that one scholar described the phenomenon as "China fever."[3] Whether this public mood, an inaccurate barometer in a democracy, will become a more permanent feature of South Korea's regional outlook remains debatable.

There is always a possibility that closer economic integration will lead to increased tension, such as trade disagreements or worries in Seoul that ROK investment in the PRC will result in a hollowing out of its basic industries and exacerbate unemployment. Moreover, the wrath of Korean nationalism has not been limited to Japan and the United States. Public sensitivities to China's historical dominance over the peninsula remain palpable. The widely publicized and highly controversial dispute in early 2004 between China and South Korea over the ethnic origins of an ancient Korean kingdom (extinguished more than thirteen hundred years ago) exemplified the complex historical relationship between the two countries.[4] There have been economic clashes as well, evidenced by protests in Pyeongtaek when a Chinese company, China National Bluestar, bought a controlling stake in Ssangyong Motors, proving that South Korean sensitivity to foreign investment is not limited to purchases by Westerners or Japanese.[5] It remains to be seen, therefore, how far China can exploit this outpouring of goodwill in the South to Beijing's advantage.

In aggregate, the PRC-ROK relationship has moved forward in leaps and bounds since the early 1990s. Beyond the socio-economic and political benefits that Beijing enjoys from robust ties with Seoul, China believes that the successes in bilateral ties with South Korea can be exploited for broader geostrategic purposes. In the near term, collaboration with the South enhances Beijing's leverage to manage or constrain North Korean behavior. China and the ROK can present a credible united front to prod the DPRK to behave responsibly. China may also be hoping to cultivate or reinforce views in South Korea that are more aligned with or amenable to Chinese policy toward the North. For example, both sides at present appear to prefer a less confrontational stance toward Pyongyang than does Washington. In this sense, Seoul can serve as a (admittedly limited) proxy to slow certain U.S. policy initiatives that Beijing might find objectionable. To a much lesser extent, China's good standing in the South's public eye serves as a potential wedge between South Korea and the United States, particularly when U.S.-ROK ties are strained or are in a crisis.

China's South Korea calculus also involves longer-term strategic considerations. Beijing perceives potential challenges and opportunities in Seoul's alliance relations with Washington and its growing closeness with Tokyo. The U.S.-ROK alliance in particular could stand in the way of China's broader regional aspirations, especially if Chinese ambitions clash with American interests in East Asia or if broader Sino-American relations deteriorate in the future. Beijing's embrace of Seoul may therefore serve to offset America's diplomatic, military, and economic weight on the Korean Peninsula and in Northeast Asia more broadly. To a lesser degree (given the current shallowness of Japan's ties with South Korea), the same logic holds for Chinese intentions to counterbalance Tokyo's willingness and capacity to assert its interests related to Korean and regional affairs.

Looking ahead, robust bilateral ties could increase China's ability to exercise its influence over the longer term on the Korean Peninsula. Beijing is no doubt casting an eye toward the prospect of a united Korea. In this context, the growing closeness with Seoul reflects in part the sober recognition in Beijing that the South will inherit the northern half of the Korean Peninsula in all of the plausible scenarios of reconciliation/unification. China no doubt accepts the reality that in the event of a gradual and peaceful integration process, all the roads leading to economic development and political influence will run through the ROK. Given these prospects, fostering interdependence with Seoul is a prudent investment for Beijing and reflects the expectation that South Korea will emerge as the "winner" in this anachronistic Cold War contest.

China's Long-Term Perspectives

The brief overview of PRC-ROK and PRC-DPRK relations logically leads to an assessment of China's integrated strategy toward the Korean Peninsula as a single unit of analysis. Ultimately, a Korean reconciliation process that could open the way for unification is an assumed eventuality that China cannot ignore. As noted in the bilateral analyses above, Chinese interests and policies toward the DPRK and the ROK stem from Beijing's longer-term desire to exert China's traditional sphere of influence over key regions along its periphery. Indeed, the Korean Peninsula's geostrategic importance compels China to assume a major, if not dominant, role. A common theme that looms large in the formulation of Chinese policy regarding the two Koreas is the need to ensure permanent participation in any process related to the future of the peninsula.

In terms of China's policy agenda with respect to unification, Beijing is primarily guided by the formula of how best to maximize its influence at lowest risk and cost. As noted previously, China needs the status quo or some version thereof so that it can concentrate on internal development. It is not surprising, then, that a top priority for the leadership is a smooth, gradual transition involving a negotiation process in which China plays an indispensable part. In contrast, prolonged instability, war, and/

or a power vacuum on the Korean Peninsula are the least desirable outcomes for China, because each would entail huge costs that Beijing remains unprepared to cover. Driven in part by a zero-sum game mentality, the worst-case scenario for Beijing is probably that other regional powers with the financial resources and political clout (that is, the United States and Japan) might intercede and undercut China's long-term influence.

Perhaps the best method for understanding the Chinese perspective is to assess Beijing's optimal objectives in order to better appreciate the constraints and opportunities that China must confront. A useful question would be, what are the conditions under which China would deem reconciliation and unification ideal? First, China would prefer North Korea to function as a viable negotiating entity and partner in the process. Should Pyongyang survive and, even better, its dependence on Beijing continue, then the North would be the most effective vehicle to represent China's interests. Thus, keeping Pyongyang afloat is not only an immediate consideration, but also a long-term security hedge. Normalization of North Korea's relations with both the United States and South Korea, as well as with Japan, would be critical to carrying out this strategy. This in part explains China's efforts to mediate as flexibly as possible between Pyongyang and Washington.

Second, China would oppose any hasty process that could bring about upheaval and instability, envisioning instead a gradual, phased integration of the two Koreas. It is noteworthy that the regional players with a stake in the Korean Peninsula, particularly South Korea, concur and support a peaceful reconciliation. The German experience and the more recent, chaotic reconstruction of Iraq underscore the difficulties inherent in the transition of a highly centralized and authoritarian state. In addition to the potential physical and political turmoil that could erupt from an ill-conceived plan, China fears that the runaway costs of rebuilding the North could undermine its own primary economic interests. It is likely that the economic giants of the region, the United States, Japan, and South Korea, would share the majority of the costs, with expectations that Beijing's contribution be commensurate with its status. While this would not bankrupt China, the financial resources of the other economies (particularly the

ROK), whose health are crucial to Beijing's own development strategy, could be stretched to the limit. These considerations underscore the need for China to ensure that the costs of integration and unification be kept manageable. The best way to avoid a major financial burden would be for North Korea to help itself out of its state of destitution. DPRK regime reform, therefore, is seen by Beijing as a key ingredient to help strengthen the infrastructure for reconstruction.

Third, China hopes to accrue veto power over as much of the transition process as possible. In other words, Beijing hopes that it might be able to accumulate sufficient influence in both the South and the North to preclude outcomes unfavorable to its long-term geopolitical position. In particular, China would likely seek to block U.S.-led initiatives (related, for example, to the future of America's forward military posture in region) that could undermine Beijing's influence. A worrisome proposal, according to some policy specialists in Beijing and Shanghai, is the potential USFK relocation to the Pyongtaek area, near a sizable ROK port on the Yellow Sea just across from Qingdao, which is

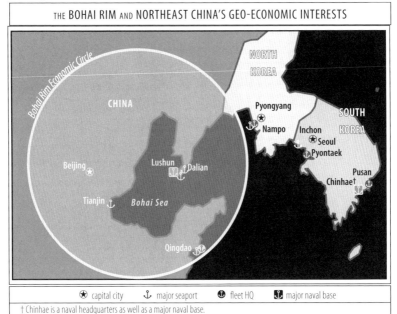

THE BOHAI RIM AND NORTHEAST CHINA'S GEO-ECONOMIC INTERESTS

✪ capital city   ⚓ major seaport   ⊕ fleet HQ   ⚓ major naval base

† Chinhae is a naval headquarters as well as a major naval base.

In 2003, China became the largest handler of seaborne containers in the world with a record-breaking 48 million TEUs (twenty-foot equivalent units) that year. In northern China, Qingdao, Tianjin, and Dalian ports are the largest and busiest container hubs. They collectively provide critical services to the Bohai Rim Economic Circle, one of the largest industrial zones in China. The Bohai Rim, which stretches from the Shangdong and Liaodong Peninsulas to inner Mongolia, accounts for 12 percent of China's territory and 20 percent of the country's population.

home to the Chinese headquarters of the North Sea Fleet and a major naval base. The Chinese understandably fear that such a presence could serve as a strategic chokehold near China's northernmost access points to the sea, including the major port at Tianjin, the naval base at Lushun, and the large-scale shipyard at Dalian. Policy makers in the PRC recognize that the primary motives for USFK realignment are not related to containing China, but they are concerned nonetheless about the erection of a new, large U.S. base near a major sea lane of communications. They would therefore prefer to have more dialogue with U.S. officials regarding the planned move.

Clearly, the reality on the ground strongly suggests that China has little hope of achieving all, or any, of its goals. A significant obstacle for China is its limited influence over the North Korean regime, which, as noted above, is deeply paranoid and has undergone a gradual ideological estrangement and socio-economic divergence from China. Recent diplomatic efforts to cajole more cooperative behavior from Pyongyang reveal that, short of blunt economic tools of coercion (such as economic and energy supply cutoffs), Beijing has little leverage to dissuade the DPRK from its course, and its leverage weakens the more it is used. The dilemma is that an "effective" coercive strategy might trigger a backlash from a desperate North.

Thus, even if the DPRK survives, the regime may still not act in ways amenable to Chinese interests. Given the inherent suspicions that Pyongyang harbors of the outside world, the types of negotiated threat reduction and CBMs being bandied about by analysts might not resonate with the regime. Moreover, Kim Jong-il likely fears that reforms intended to restore health to the economic system might slip out of his control once they are unleashed. Beijing must therefore prepare for a collapse scenario, however unpalatable such an outcome may prove to be. In this sense, strong patterns of regional cooperation involving the PRC can be an attractive hedge against a North Korean collapse.

The other major component to this analysis, without which China's long-term perspective would be incomplete, involves conflicting U.S. and Chinese interests. Whatever the interests that now shape China's longer-term designs for the peninsula, these will likely contend, if not collide, with U.S. interests in Northeast

Asia. In particular, a key issue that will shape China's strategy is the future of the U.S.-ROK alliance during and after the expected unification process. To date, Beijing has not directly challenged this security partnership, recognizing that any objections would be ignored. Moreover, Beijing fears that overt opposition to the U.S. military presence would arouse suspicions among South Koreans about China's intentions regarding the future of the Korean Peninsula. There is also the less openly stated Chinese acknowledgement that U.S. alliances and forces in the region have benefited China, and Asia more generally, since the postwar period. American military presence on the peninsula has 1) been instrumental in preventing another military adventure by North Korea; 2) curbed possible imprudent South Korean actions; and 3) promoted stability that has led to prosperity in the region. China also appreciates the reality that any sudden American departure or large reduction in forces could bring on crisis or regional instability – such as a major increase in Japanese military capability or a confrontation on the Korean Peninsula.

Yet, the forces of change that are emerging have modified the Chinese calculus. China correctly perceives the looming transition on the Korean Peninsula as a period that could either bolster or erode the U.S. alliance system in East Asia. On the one hand, the end of the North Korean threat and accumulated frustrations in the ROK over the U.S. presence could alter South Korean perceptions of America's military utility on the peninsula. On the other hand, regional anxieties about instability on the peninsula might draw in the United States still further. It is this latter outcome that most troubles Chinese leaders. Beijing certainly will not endorse an unending and unlimited U.S. military presence in a united Korea over the long term. Chinese leaders understandably fear that such an extension of permanent American power in Northeast Asia might undermine China's own interests there. Additionally, there are widespread suspicions that Washington's alliances could in the end be used as a broad geopolitical instrument to hem in China. Thus, Beijing has an interest in weakening U.S. security ties in the region in the hopes that the Americans will eventually depart.

However, recognizing the continuing benefits of U.S. security commitments in the region, Chinese leaders may not reject out of hand a reconfigured American force posture on the peninsula as a stopgap during the transition period. For example, China might agree to a modest air and naval presence limited to the south as a security hedge against Japan and as a reassurance measure for the neighborhood. But this acquiescence should not obscure the reality that China's willingness to tolerate expanded U.S. military presence, particularly an extension to the northern half of the peninsula, is very limited. Such consent should be properly viewed as an effort by Beijing to free-ride on American power while it accumulates influence to be able to challenge the United States in the future. It is important to note that the Chinese vision of regional security for the coming decades of the twenty-first century does not feature lasting U.S. security alliances. Indeed, many of the Beijing-led initiatives on the Korean Peninsula noted above have been intended to prepare the way for China to challenge, if not replace, the United States as the pillar of regional security.

Beijing's evolving attitudes on this matter will no doubt be critical in determining its negotiating position regarding the future of a reconciled or reunified Korea. In the final analysis, however, China has no veto on the presence of U.S. forces, and Washington would be wise to underscore the notion that whether or not those forces in Korea are ever used to constrain Beijing will depend solely on China's own long-term path. As noted already, Beijing is probably prepared for an outcome in which Seoul will determine the future of a united Korea. But at least for the moment, China is not likely to actively or independently facilitate any reconciliation in the near term, fearing unintended consequences. Beijing would be content with a very slow reconciliation and gradual reunification process from which a stable Korea emerges, one that it hopes will have closer ties to China.

Japan and the Korean Peninsula

Japan's security posture toward the Korean Peninsula remains one of the most underrated and underappreciated in Northeast Asia. This phenomenon can be attributed in large part to the fact that Japanese regional policy has often been overshadowed by the activism of the United States in Asia. Given Japan's post-World War II reluctance to exercise "hard power" and its preference for "soft power," such as economic leverage, it is widely assumed that Tokyo invariably follows Washington's lead when it comes to security-related concerns in Asia. Of course, unresolved disputes in the region about Japan's past aggression also constrain Tokyo's options. However, closer examination suggests that assumptions of Japanese passivity and deference to the United States do not always hold true. Indeed, enduring geopolitical and socio-economic interests as well as more contemporary policy imperatives have compelled Tokyo to assume a more proactive stance in recent years.

In terms of long-standing interests, the most obvious one is the geographic proximity of Korea to the Japanese home islands. Any major strategic reverberation on the peninsula would almost invariably have a bearing on Japan's vital national interests. Indeed, Korea has been described negatively as a dagger pointed at the heart of Japan. Second, the history of the twentieth century weighs heavily on Japan and Korea. During Japan's rise as a new imperial power, the peninsula became a geostrategic and colonial prize, and many Koreans suffered greatly under Japanese occupation. To this day, Japan's annexation and occupation of Korea from 1910 to 1945 remains a stubborn and enduring scar, and contested interpretations of the past continue to animate Japanese-Korean relations. In the early years of the Cold War, the Korean War propelled Japan to become a bulwark against communist expansion, and although South Korea and Japan eventually became de facto allies in the process, the northern half of the peninsula remained a bitter enemy of Japan. Since then, the uneasy peace between the two Koreas has long preoccupied strategists in Tokyo.

Third, less visible but no less important are the socio-economic links that tie Japan to the Korean Peninsula. Strong interdependencies have developed after decades of close economic cooperation between Tokyo and Seoul. The combined economic health of Japan and South Korea ensures that the Asia-Pacific region remains a major engine of global economic activity. There is also an often ignored domestic dimension to Japan's connection with Korea. Korean residents in Japan, who have lived there for generations, are the largest non-ethnic Japanese population in the country. Many of these ethnic Koreans are openly sympathetic to the regime in Pyongyang and have provided crucial hard currency to the North through remittances. It is against this backdrop of geography and history that Japan confronts the more pressing dangers of the divided peninsula.

Japan and the DPRK

For Japan, stability and threat reduction are the two primary interests driving Tokyo's policy objectives toward North Korea. The DPRK poses a threat not only to regional stability but also directly to Japan's national well-being. Obviously, a war on the peninsula or the North's collapse would create havoc on the regional order upon which Japan's economic health rests. In the event of conflict, it is widely accepted that military bases and civilian centers in Japan would become targets of missile attacks by the North, especially since the United States would most likely move substantial military reinforcements through Japan. The expected devastation of Seoul from a conflict would plunge Japan, a major trading and investment partner with South Korea, into financial crisis. In a collapse scenario, the resulting chaos, including a region-wide refugee crisis, would be equally unsettling for Japan. With an economy only now beginning to recover from over a decade of recession or near-zero growth, the financial burden of rebuilding a devastated Korea, either from war or regime implosion, could strain even Japan's large economy. Thus, at least in the short term, Japan seeks to sustain some form of the status quo, where the North remains a viable but contained entity.

The prevailing situation, however, poses its own set of worrying security challenges that contribute to Japan's threat perceptions. First, North Korea's existing arsenal of medium-range *No Dong* ballistic missiles, which number in the hundreds, can reach most parts of the Japanese home islands. Japan rightfully fears that those missiles could be launched against U.S. bases in Japan, Japan's SDF bases, and key civilian as well as economic targets in times of crisis or war on the Korean Peninsula. Indeed, the very threat of their use could serve as an effective instrument to coerce Japan and, in the process, drive a wedge in the U.S.-Japan alliance. Longer-range capabilities, as exemplified by the surprise launch of a *Taepo Dong* intermediate-range missile over the home islands in 1998, further fuel public anxieties.

Second, the potential of a nuclear breakout in North Korea is another major source of concern that has come to the forefront since late 2002. The nuclear crisis on the Korean Peninsula highlights both the difficulties in halting the DPRK's nuclear program and the relative ease with which the North could amass a nuclear stockpile. Moreover, the threat of nuclear proliferation to third parties is a serious global problem that Japan cannot ignore. More directly related to Japan, should Pyongyang demonstrate the ability to place nuclear warheads atop its ballistic missiles, Tokyo could be vulnerable to nuclear coercion or blackmail. All of this underscores a serious worry among Japanese policy makers that the global nuclear non-proliferation regime is slowly breaking down, and that the five permanent members of the UN Security Council are not able to protect peaceful, non-nuclear weapons states. Japan is being confronted with several difficult (though not mutually exclusive) choices. Japan can choose to 1) do nothing and remain under America's nuclear umbrella; 2) pursue missile defense options more aggressively with the United States; and/or 3) develop its own nuclear deterrent.

Third, the North's past unpredictable behavior has unsettled Japan's sense of security. In addition to a series of provocative ballistic missile tests in the past decade, Pyongyang has on several occasions directly intruded into Japan's territorial seas. One such incident in December 2001 led the Japanese maritime authority to sink a suspected North Korean spy ship. More recently, Kim Jong-il's admission that the North had kidnapped Japanese citizens in the 1970s and 1980s created a diplomatic crisis and an obstacle to further efforts at normalizing bilateral ties. The admission to the kidnappings has heightened fears that the North might employ fifth-column agents to attack Japan's critical infrastructure during a crisis or conflict on the Korean Peninsula.

In dealing with the challenges emanating from the North, Tokyo has had to strike a balance between engagement and deterrence. In other words, Japan has operated on the principle that its efforts to induce cooperative behavior from Pyongyang must be backed by a credible capacity, primarily based on U.S. military power, to deter North Korean aggression or intimidation. On the one hand, the policy of engagement reflects Japan's realistic acceptance that money is its only real lever with Pyongyang, and that there exist implicit but nonetheless strong expectations that Tokyo must pay some form of compensation to North Korea to atone for its past aggression (as it essentially did for South Korea in the form of economic aid in the 1960s and 1970s). Thus, Japan has willingly accepted its roles as a major donor of food aid to the North and as a key financier of the weakened Korean Peninsula Energy Development Organization (KEDO). In addition, it is likely that whatever successor agreement emerges from the rubble of the largely discredited Agreed Framework, Japan will be a key diplomatic player and financial sponsor of the new project. The underlying rationale for Tokyo's generous financial support is that such rewards might dissuade Pyongyang from risky actions and thereby ease the military threat to Japan.

On the other hand, Tokyo relies on the politico-military muscle of the United States to serve as a credible deterrent against North Korean aggression and as the basis for negotiating from a position of strength. Japan plays host to forty-seven thousand U.S. troops that are forward deployed largely for a Korean contingency. Moreover, the alliance revitalization process that began in the mid 1990s has enhanced Japan's military capacity to provide rear-area support in the event of crisis or conflict on the peninsula. Thus far, Japan does not possess the military capabilities or the constitutional and legislative maneuver room to respond to all forms of North Korean adventurism. However, a gradual shift of Tokyo's strategic outlook (as described below) may to a lesser extent bolster its political and diplomatic clout in the coming years.

Yet, the delicate balancing act between engagement and deterrence is itself indicative that Tokyo's policy options toward the North are still limited. Japan does not have the same economic leverage that China and South Korea enjoy over the DPRK. Moreover, not only does Japan lack the military capabilities that the United States boasts in the region, but the potential use and threat of force against the North are contingent more on U.S. interests than on Japan's needs. As a result, the inducements to encourage certain outcomes and the disincentives to deter destabilizing behavior that Japan can bring to bear on the North are not as compelling. Given Tokyo's relative inability to directly affect North Korea calculations, Japan fears both abandonment and entanglement in the context of the U.S.-Japan alliance. There are persistent anxieties that Washington might cut some sort of deal with Pyongyang without adequate consultations or Tokyo's acquiescence. Worse still, Japan has learned from previous experiences – especially from the 1994 nuclear crisis that ended with the Agreed Framework – that Tokyo may end up with the financial burden of an agreement with the North even if it was not party to the negotiations. The converse is equally true. Japan is wary that a more aggressive U.S. posture toward the DPRK and expectations in Washington that its allies should form a united front might drag Tokyo into a dangerous confrontation. For these reasons, Japan is guided as much by its concerns over the health of its alliance relations with the United States as by the North's security challenges.

From a domestic perspective, the sharp increase in threat perceptions of the North has strengthened the voices of those in Japan advocating a new approach to the nation's security posture. Defense Agency Director General Ishiba Shigeru's public statements regarding Japan's right to attack North Korea in self-defense if Tokyo detected a missile launch (or imminent launch) against Japan point to the gradual shifts in the Japanese mindset.[6] Perhaps the most striking aspect about the assertion was the relative lack of backlash from the public, suggesting that a subtle, but deeply significant, evolution in Japanese strategic thinking has indeed emerged and taken root. The Japanese government's deliberations on its responses to North Korea's brinkmanship are likely to push forward many broader debates about Japan's global responsibilities and roles, as reflected in the 2004 deployment of SDF personnel to Iraq. Indeed, if the situation on the Korean Peninsula deteriorates further, it is entirely possible that Tokyo may accelerate its reassessment of Japan's peace constitution and the country's defense needs and security obligations.

Japan-ROK Relations

Tokyo's relationship with Seoul is marked by an intriguing contradiction: it has evolved and matured into a dynamic partnership at the same time that it remains stuck in the past. As major engines of growth in the region, Japan and South Korea maintain strong economic ties (as noted in chapter 6). In addition, since the ROK's democratization process in the 1980s, both countries increasingly share common political values rooted in democratic institutions. More recently, the surge in cultural links and exchanges, including the co-hosting of the 2002 soccer World Cup, have bonded the two peoples together to an unprecedented degree. From a security perspective, Japan and South Korea, through their security ties with the United States, are allies by association, or "virtual allies." Given that Tokyo will play a crucial support role to Washington in most conceivable crisis/conflict contingencies on the peninsula, South Korea is an integral part of Japan's security and vice versa. So, too, both countries have engaged in high-level military-to-military exchanges as well as in joint exercises. As a byproduct of this virtual alliance, Tokyo, Seoul, and Washington consult closely with each other on their respective North Korean policies within the TCOG, and their collective involvement in the regular TCOG meetings has helped institutionalize policy coordination.

Even as ties have deepened, diplomatic disagreements arising from historical animosities remain and could still hamper meaningful interactions between Tokyo and Seoul. These irritants have complicated efforts by Japan to participate in developments on the Korean Peninsula in a consistent and constructive manner. Many South Koreans continue to believe that Japan has failed to address certain sensitive aspects of Japan's wartime past adequately. Japan's behavior (including Prime Minister Koizumi's repeated visits to the controversial Yasukuni shrine) and public gaffes by high-ranking officials have certainly not helped to dispel those negative perceptions. In short, historical memories could still obscure the more important strategic dimensions of the current bilateral relationship. Furthermore, each side continues to harbor anxieties about the other. Japan's recent efforts to increase its political profile in the region and to pursue a more independent defense posture have been met with suspicion in the

South. Japan, for its part, monitors closely South Korea's military modernization plans that increasingly emphasize power projection – that could focus on Japan – beyond the peninsula. As a consequence, the Japan-South Korea axis remains the weakest link in the virtual trilateral alliance.

As Japan navigates between the push of progress and the pull of history in its relationship with the ROK, Tokyo must also seek to coordinate and, to the extent possible, align policies with the South towards the North. Clearly, it is in Japan's vital national interests to derive as much leverage as possible through a concerted diplomatic effort with Seoul and Washington. That said, the motives and drivers behind the policies of the three capitals are far from congruent. As a consequence, Japan faces two major dilemmas.

First, Tokyo could fall victim to policy divergences between Seoul and Washington toward Pyongyang. Japan risks alienating Washington or Seoul or both, whether it chooses one side over the other or sits on the fence. Second, the fear of abandonment and entrapment noted above applies equally in this context. Policies pursued by South Korea that either leave Japan behind or force Tokyo to adopt positions that it is unwilling or unable to assume are obviously undesirable. Indeed, Japan's active involvement in multilateral approaches toward the DPRK partly serves as insurance that neither the South nor the United States moves hastily ahead on initiatives with the North that either exclude or harm Japan's interests. Haste should not be confused with urgency in this matter, however, since Japan is perhaps the most desirous of a quick resolution to the nuclear standoff among the countries involved, primarily because of its vulnerability to North Korea's missiles and its dependence on the global non-proliferation regime.

Japan's Integrated Long-Term Strategy

Long-term stability on the peninsula is of primary importance to Japanese security. As a consequence, Tokyo has actively attempted to influence events, to the extent that it could, so as to render shifts in the status quo more compatible with its own well-being. As a policy principle, Japan seeks a gradual and peaceful integration between the two Koreas. A gradual reconciliation process that yields some type of unification would serve to ensure regional stability. Short of this ideal outcome, Tokyo's most realistic hope is for a soft landing by the North that avoids the chaos that would surely result from a sudden and complete collapse.

Whatever the reconciliation scenarios, Japanese strategists, like their counterparts in Beijing, almost uniformly recognize that the South would become the successor regime, and Tokyo expects the close policy coordination with Seoul today to bear fruit in terms of influence and leverage tomorrow. In this context, the bold but ultimately abortive bid by Koizumi to normalize ties with the North in 2002 should be viewed in part as an interim measure intended to stabilize relations with Pyongyang for the coming transition. One part of the deal under discussion between Japan and North Korea before the breakdown of talks reportedly involved an enormous aid package from Tokyo in return for normalization and other concessions from Pyongyang. Japanese officials hoped that the financial largesse would ease the North into an economic soft landing.

Over the horizon, Japan's longer-term interests center on potential opportunities and challenges emerging from the Korean Peninsula itself, as well as from future regional security dynamics more broadly cast. First, Tokyo has much to gain from a united Korea that is aligned with Japan both politically, as democratic nations, and economically, as economic powerhouses. To a certain extent, the common values and interests cultivated between Japan and the ROK in recent years could in fact translate into a "unification dividend" for Tokyo.

Second, on the challenging side, the prospect of a united Korea with substantial resources and military capabilities no doubt worries some Japanese observers. There are genuine concerns that a more powerful Korea, driven by unity and associated nationalistic fervor, might seek to settle old scores or disassociate itself from Japan and/or the United States. How to avoid such a security dilemma and potential arms race between Tokyo and Seoul remains a vexing question.

A third, and closely related, issue for Japan is the prospect of the South's inheriting Pyongyang's WMDs and the associated infrastructure that would remain in the North. The fact that some South Koreans privately took delight in the 1998 *Taepo Dong* missile test did not escape the notice of Japanese policy makers. Most importantly, Japan must seek to preclude the nuclearization of the peninsula (which of course depends on how the current nuclear crisis unfolds) that could initiate serious vertical and horizontal proliferation problems in Northeast Asia.

Finally, a composite outcome of the above points could be a unified Korea that chooses far more independent options than previously assumed. Seoul could seek to become a non-aligned, medium-sized power in the region with its own nuclear and conventional deterrent (similar to that of France during the Cold War). This would of course involve jettisoning its alliance relations with the United States and thus indirectly abandoning a security hedge with Japan.

Beyond the peninsula, Tokyo's long-term policy priorities will be driven by the future role of China and the fate of the U.S.-Japan alliance. As noted in the previous section, China has compelling strategic interests in maximizing its influence over the Korean Peninsula. Tokyo recognizes with growing apprehension that Beijing's broader regional ambitions may not be compatible with its own vision for Northeast Asia. Indeed, some dispirited strategists, especially in light of Japan's relative economic decline in the past decade and more recent Tokyo-Beijing trade spats, have concluded that the two powers might eventually become peer competitors in both the economic and security realms sooner rather than later. In this context of pessimistic expectations, a united Korea's place in the regional order could have more ominous geopolitical portent for Japan. Tokyo worries that Seoul might reach an accommodation with Beijing that could radically change the regional balance of power to Japan's disadvantage.

This fear in part motivates Tokyo's enhanced activism with regard to the two Koreas and the region more broadly. Indeed, Japan perceives its balanced policies toward Seoul and Pyongyang as setting the stage for a strategic alignment with a united Korea in order to counter-balance a rising China. Furthermore, the anxiety that a more powerful China might flex its military muscles and try to dominate interactions in Northeast Asia, particularly given the 1996 Taiwan Strait missile crisis precedent, has already compelled Japan to embrace a more robust security posture in conjunction with the United States.

Transition on the Korean Peninsula will also have a direct and major impact on the U.S.-Japan alliance. Clearly, a shift in the U.S.-ROK alliance, both in terms of rationale and force posture, will have spillover effects on Tokyo's security partnership with Washington. Two radically divergent outcomes are possible. As noted in chapter 5, a more pessimistic assessment posits that a "singularization" phenomenon will emerge. Under this scenario, the central purpose for the U.S.-ROK alliance vanishes either quickly, as a result of war/collapse in the North, or gradually, through a peaceful integration process. In the absence of a compelling rationale to maintain its forward presence, and under increasing demands for force reductions from a united Korea, Washington could drastically cut down or completely withdraw its military forces from the peninsula. Such an outcome might prove untenable for Japan if it finds itself serving as the last remaining military outpost for U.S. forces, as long as Korea-Japan relations are positive and stable. Tokyo might then come under domestic pressure to request reductions in the U.S. military footprint. In such a scenario, Japan might choose to pursue an independent military path, possibly including nuclear capabilities, or, less likely, a condominium with China.

An optimistic perspective argues that the U.S.-Japan alliance will become more relevant and vital in the process and aftermath of unification (with or without a residual USFK). This school of thought contends that the alliance renewal effort since the mid 1990s, aimed in large part at coping with contingencies on the Korean Peninsula, has prepared Japan and the United States to absorb future shocks to the alliance. As Japan retools its security and defense postures to meet regional and extra-regional challenges beyond its shores, Tokyo's responsibilities will widen and depend less on the exigencies of the peninsula. Indeed, the dispatch of naval forces to the Indian Ocean for counter-terrorist activities in Afghanistan and the deployment of the SDF to Iraq appear to confirm this trend. In this outcome, Japan becomes a major regional operating hub in support of U.S. military forces for a broader range of missions.[7] The extent to which these changes would further strengthen the trilateral security relationship between Washington, Tokyo, and Seoul remains to be seen. Nevertheless, a scenario that bolsters Tokyo's regional security profile in conjunction with a robust U.S.-Korea alliance is desirable because it avoids all the negative developments that could follow the singularization path. Thus, this alternative view asserts that it is in the interest of the security partnership to seize the opportunities that the transition on the Korean Peninsula could offer to benefit and reinforce the alliance's long-term health.

As the analysis above demonstrates, far from being a player sidelined and eclipsed by other great powers in Northeast Asia, Japan's vital national interests will ensure its active role in the developments of the Korean Peninsula. Japan's interlocking ties with the South and North through both bilateral and multilateral contacts, together with its standing as America's primary ally in the region, make Tokyo an indispensable partner in the reconciliation process and in the shaping of regional security relations after reunification.

Implications

The analysis above demonstrates that the Korean Peninsula's fate will be inextricably linked to the broader regional dynamics of Northeast Asia. The evolving calculus of Tokyo and Beijing will almost certainly shape strategic interactions on and surrounding the peninsula, with potentially decisive consequences for regional cooperation or competition. This complex web of interlocking (and often historically troubled) ties among the two Koreas and their neighbors undoubtedly presents an additional complicating factor to U.S. policy. Moreover, the United States, a relative newcomer to the scene compared to Japan and China, will have to navigate carefully around deeply embedded sensitivities that Washington does not always fully appreciate. Against this backdrop, several themes can be discerned.

China and Japan obviously have tremendous stakes and interests vested in the Korean Peninsula, and both recognize that the promise of dramatic strategic change in the future there could either benefit or severely undermine the geopolitical position of either player (perhaps at the expense or to the benefit of the other). The two powers are therefore understandably wary of the range of negative processes and consequences of reconciliation that could prove detrimental to regional stability. Beyond the self-interested preference (or perhaps wishful hope) for the status quo, both strongly desire changes to the existing order that ultimately prove to be smooth, gradual, and, at the very least, not too disruptive. This emphasis on stability is perhaps the only substantive common ground shared by all the major actors involved, and suggests that Beijing and Tokyo will likely display varying degrees of resistance to change. Given China's acute sensitivities to geopolitical shifts along its periphery, it would likely adopt a more rigid position on the future of the peninsula than Japan, which may be resigned to embrace a new regional order. So, any drastic realignment for the U.S.-ROK alliance during the transitional period will require explicit and implicit assurances to Korea's neighbors that the relationship will be geared toward ensuring stability and broader institutional collaboration in the region.

Yet, there is an inescapable reality for China and Japan that the likelihood for disruption, if and when a united Korea emerges, will be rather high. The stalemate on the peninsula, whereby the North and South focused exclusively on each other, in effect eliminated Korea as a unitary entity – and its geopolitical impact on the region – for the past fifty years. Consequently, the emergence of a united Korea will introduce an entirely new dimension to the strategic dynamics of Asia. Indeed, the region would witness the rebirth of a sizable, medium power wedged between two continental states (China and Russia) and two naval powers (the United States and Japan). In the absence of a highly institutionalized regional mechanism (akin to NATO) to manage such a tectonic geopolitical shift, there is little reason to expect "the day after" to be either smooth or comfortable for any power. From this standpoint, perhaps no amount of reassurance from the United States will sound convincing, particularly to Beijing.

Consequently, Washington must also recognize that there will be limits to its ability to assuage the fears and anxieties of its allies and fellow great powers alike. In this context, the United States must maintain its resolve to articulate and act upon a persuasive vision that precludes the patterns of great power competitions of the past, which left behind lasting scars on interstate relations. Moreover, even if historical rivalries prove to be irreversible or irresistible to those involved, the United States should be prepared to undertake postures that dampen the effects of such struggles.

The dichotomy between the hopes for a "soft landing" on the peninsula and the sense of inevitability that reconciliation could bring unwelcome news among the regional players is one of the major policy challenges confronting the United States. Can Washington promote the former and avoid the latter? If so, how can the United States assuage and persuade nations in this complex region? To resolve this apparent twin problem, this study proposes a dual policy of active assurance and assertive persuasion. More concretely, Washington should seek to assuage regional powers to the extent possible that a strong U.S.-Korean alliance in the post-unification era will benefit Northeast Asia (and possibly beyond). Perhaps more importantly, the United States needs to underscore its willingness to push forward its agenda if certain Asian capitals either opt out of a new regional architecture or seek overtly to constrain U.S. options.

To be sure, the current USFK realignment and the possible diversification of the alliance in the future must take into account regional perspectives. Washington must recognize that Japan will seek to ensure that it is a part of any process that would inform the structure of the emerging order in Northeast Asia, while China, for its part, will push an agenda that would preclude the future formation of a regional block intended to blunt its ambitions. Given these contending concerns, proposals to reshape the U.S.-ROK alliance for the future must contain strong elements of stability that alarm neither China nor Japan unnecessarily and avoid isolating one or both of them from any emerging regional security architecture.

At the same time, Washington must insist that there is a limit to how much Chinese interests can be taken into account in the alliance diversification process. While the United States should recognize that China could make life very difficult if Beijing chooses an obstructionist path toward a new regional order, Washington cannot permit the Chinese to wield a veto over U.S. decisions. Implicit in this posture is a hedge against the uncertainty of China's future, in which China could, in the worst-case scenarios, emerge as an anti-status quo, revisionist power in the region or fracture into an internally weak and chaotic state as it has in the past.

Looking beyond the horizon, American efforts to forge a tighter trilateral security dialogue among Japan, South Korea, and the United States are bound to run into difficulties. For instance, the strengthening of Korean nationalist sentiments, in conjunction with Seoul's historic enmity toward Japan, could undermine American efforts and even move South Korea closer to China. The implications of a tighter Sino-ROK relationship for America's relations with South Korea may not necessarily result in a zero-sum game, but clearly there are likely to be consequences – consequences that could affect the U.S.-ROK alliance quite directly, and not necessarily for the better (such as a de facto Chinese veto on a long-term USFK presence near Pyongtaek). Given the potential for such chain reactions, the regional powers will be watching the evolution of the U.S.-ROK alliance closely, and how Washington and Seoul manage this process will likely have far-reaching ripple effects throughout Northeast Asia and beyond.

Notes for Chapter Seven

1   See, for example, Senate Committee on Foreign Relations, "North Korea: Status Report on Nuclear Program, Humanitarian Issues, and Economic Issues," staff trip report, 108th Congress, 2d sess., February 2004, Committee Print 40.

2   The 1994 Agreed Framework was a negotiated settlement between the United States and the DPRK that sought to freeze, and ultimately dismantle, the DPRK nuclear weapons program. As a part of the agreement, Pyongyang consented to shut down its plutonium-producing capability and submit to international monitoring in return for a steady supply of heavy oil, a mutual commitment to pursue normal relations, and the eventual construction of two light-water nuclear reactors in the North by an international consortium.

3   David Shambaugh, "China and the Korean Peninsula: Playing for the Long Term," *The Washington Quarterly* 26, no. 2 (spring 2003).

4   A public uproar erupted in South Korea when a Chinese government-sponsored study claimed that the ethnic origins of the Kingdom of Goguryeo were part of ancient China. See Anthony Faiola, "Kicking Up the Dust of History," *Washington Post,* January 22, 2004, p. A15.

5   David Murphy, "When the Big Stars Venture out of China," *Far East-ern Economic Review,* February 5, 2004.

6   See, for example, the *Kyodo News* report of Ishiba's remarks to the House of Representatives Committee on Security, "Japan Should Consider Offensive Capabilities: Ishiba," March 27, 2003.

7   For details see Charles Perry and Toshi Yoshihara, *The U.S.-Japan Alliance: Preparing for Korean Reconciliation and Beyond* (Herndon, Virginia: Brassey's, 2003), 104-15.

CHAPTER EIGHT

Options *for a* U.S. Military Transition *on the* Peninsula

Planning for a U.S. military transition in South Korea is already underway, mostly as a result of the ongoing FOTA discussions. This planning, however, has been limited by the initially narrow scope of the FOTA, and only in the last half of 2004 will it consider in earnest the potential for a fundamentally different U.S.-ROK security relationship. It is unlikely, therefore, that the FOTA will be able to lay the groundwork for alliance diversification in the five or six months it has left, and therefore follow-on discussions regarding the alliance's future will need to be picked up from where the FOTA leaves off. At the same time, ROK military planners are pressing ahead with a modernization program and adjustments to the country's defense posture that will increasingly focus on a wider array of less traditional security missions (such as anti-terrorism, counter-WMD operations, and the protection of sea lanes, energy supplies, and the environment). These missions are not necessarily DPRK-focused and they will likely emerge as more important for Seoul as the North and South move more decisively toward reconciliation and eventual unification. Over time, this could either reinforce or undermine alliance diversification depending on how "independent" a defense capability the ROK pursues.[1]

Working with the assumption that alliance managers are able to direct bilateral talks toward consideration of a new security relationship, this chapter outlines three alternative end states of the alliance that can help negotiators envision some of the options available to them and the variables that can constrain their choices. Each of the end states, which would be reached during and after a reconciliation scenario, is based on certain assumptions about the nature of reunification and the prevailing regional security environment, as well as a particular division of potential roles and missions. As a result, each alternative yields a different set of outcomes in terms of force structure, command structure, and weapons procurement. This analysis makes it easier to understand in concrete terms what a diversified alliance might look like, and it leads to the conclusion that a regional/hemispheric posture is potentially achievable and desirable from both a U.S. and an ROK perspective.

U.S.-ROK FOTA Negotiations

Before examining the potential options for military transformation and alliance diversification, it is important to understand recent developments regarding the allies' discussions on these issues. These discussions have been conducted primarily under the auspices of the FOTA, which was established in December 2002 during the thirty-fourth annual U.S.-ROK Security Consultative Meeting (SCM). Seven FOTA meetings occurred from April 2003 to February 2004, four in Seoul and three in Honolulu, and additional meetings are planned until the process officially ends at the fall 2004 SCM, which will involve U.S. Defense Secretary Rumsfled and his ROK counterpart. Key participants in the FOTA have included Mr. Richard P. Lawless, deputy assistant secretary of defense for Asia-Pacific affairs, and Lieutenant General Cha Young-Koo, MND deputy minister for policy. Officials from other agencies and departments also participate, on the U.S. side from the State Department and DoD, and on the Korean side from the MND and the Ministry of Foreign Affairs and Trade (MOFAT).

The FOTA was largely an American invention, and it was meant to provide the allies with an opportunity to finalize and implement a restructuring of the USFK (and its relationship to ROK forces) that had been talked about for several years but never carried out. The desire to realign the USFK strengthened as it became intertwined with a global realignment of U.S. forces as part of military transformation. The FOTA talks, therefore, have focused on a variety of issues pertinent to transformation, including mission transfer, the realignment of U.S. forces, the re-location of the Yongsan Garrison in Seoul (which houses the UNC and CFC functions), U.S. investment in the USFK, and minor alterations in command relationships. The discussions, at times laborious and contentious, produced agreements on a number of issues. Three memorandums of understanding (MOUs) are planned for signing in 2004: 1) on mission transfer; 2) for the Yongsan Garrison relocation; and 3) an amended land partner-ship plan (LPP) that relates mostly to moving the U.S. 2^{nd}Infantry Division south of Seoul to the Osan-Pyeongtaek area.[2]

U.S. officials hoped to handle these realignment arrangements relatively quickly in 2003, and thus free up time in 2004 to discuss more fundamental changes to the sharing of roles and missions, as well as develop a new rationale for the alliance that political leaders could explain to their constituents. For this reason, the FOTA was essentially divided into two parts, with the first being short-term alliance adjustment (centered around USFK realign-ment) and the second being a discussion about a new vision for the long-term future of the alliance. A major problem, howev-er, has been slower than expected progress on ironing out the short-term issues, which has crowded out discussion about the long-term future and made it difficult for ROK officials (and the ROK public) to perceive the FOTA as anything but focused on near-term logistics related to a U.S. policy objective. As a result, the FOTA has an image problem in South Korea that can proba-bly only be remedied by extending the discussion of the alliance's future in a new, follow-on set of talks after FOTA concludes.

From the start, U.S. officials were intent on relocating and consolidating the USFK in a two-phase process, with U.S. forc-es north of the Han River consolidating in the Camp Casey and Camp Red Cloud areas during the first phase, followed by a final redeployment to one of two hubs, the central Osan-Pyeongtaek area, home of Osan airbase, or the southeastern Taegu-Pusan area, which includes Camp Hialeah. Although ROK negotiators generally agreed to this relocation plan, some South Korean of-ficials expressed concern regarding the proposed abandonment of the "tripwire" positioning of U.S. forces in the DMZ, a move they viewed as potentially destabilizing at a time when the DPRK nuclear issues remained unresolved. As a result, Washington offered a concession in which U.S. forces would maintain a rotational presence north of the Han even after the completion of the second phase.

As a sweetener, U.S. officials also decided to invest $11 billion over four years on around 150 enhancements to the USFK. These enhancements will include, among many other steps, the deployment of new or upgraded *Apache* attack helicopters (already being undertaken) and a gradual phase-in of additional PAC-3 anti-missile capabilities among *Patriot* batteries on the peninsula. Overall, these investments are intended to increase the mobility of USFK forces, bolster their military intelligence capabilities, and strengthen their overall capacity to cope with asymmetric threats (such as ballistic missile and WMD strikes from the DPRK). U.S. government officials have indicated that some of the upgrades will result from a reallocation of assets from other theaters, while others may require new monies and, consequently, future congressional approval.

Both sides also agreed on the transfer of certain military missions from the USFK to ROK forces. Focused specifically on countering the DPRK threat, these missions include, among others, guarding the joint security area (or the JSA, an area along the DMZ jointly controlled by the UN and the DPRK),

PLANNED MISSION TRANSFERS FROM THE USFK TO ROK FORCES

2004
- Rear-area decontamination
- JSA security (United States retains command in near term while ROK role expands and eventually oversees the JSA)

2005
- Mine emplacement
- Air-to-ground range management
- Counterfire headquarters (begin evaluation of ROK capability in 2005 before deciding whether to go ahead with the transfer)

2006
- Maritime counter-special operations forces interdiction
- Search and rescue
- Close air support
- Weather forecasting

laying minefields, decontaminating biochemical and radioactive materials in rear-echelon areas, search and rescue operations, counter-battery operations, and the deterrence of naval infiltration from the North, along with a greater role for ROK forces in missile defense and in protecting against the DPRK's special operations forces. Seoul initially wanted to delay the transfer to 2009, but was persuaded to accept 2006 as the target.

Both sides also agreed to evaluate command relationships and make recommendations consistent with the proposed mission transfers, with the results to be presented during the 2005 SCM. Lastly, Seoul agreed to Pentagon plans to expand the responsibilities of U.S. troops in the ROK to encompass off-peninsula contingencies, provided that these alterations do not disturb the two countries' joint defense capabilities, that ROK forces are not used in contingencies unrelated to South Korea's defense, and that Seoul be consulted before the dispatch of troops from the peninsula to foreign locations.[3]

Thus, to some extent, the FOTA meetings have begun to yield a possible future vision of the alliance in which USFK forces increasingly handle off-peninsula, regional contingencies, while assuming a reduced, yet equally effective, deterrence role on the peninsula in conjunction with ROK forces. At the same time, the South Korean military gradually would assume greater responsibility for national defense in advance of, and during, a reunification scenario, slowly preparing itself for a truly independent defense capability. In this context, Seoul may also gravitate toward a more regional, off-peninsula focus, but in a more limited fashion and with respect to a narrower geographic framework than that of the USFK.

As visions of the future go, however, this is only a sketch, and it has been drawn largely to accommodate the short-term needs of the U.S. military without discussing important issues such as whether and how ROK forces could be integrated in off-peninsula missions. It is almost as if U.S. and ROK negotiators are trying to build a house by picking up materials lying around and discussing (sometimes arguing) where each piece should go, rather than poring over a set of building plans together ahead of the construction project. Moreover, despite Seoul's tentative agreement so far, South Korea does not appear sufficiently enthusiastic about this new vision to expect quick and smooth implementation without more dialogue.

Some mission transfers, for example, have been delayed, and others might be, given tensions in the current security environment and depending on the modernization of ROK forces. During the FOTA talks, South Korean officials raised concerns regarding the transfer of the USFK from the DMZ due to persistent tensions with the DPRK, and both sides agreed to postpone U.S. troop withdrawals from the JSA until 2006, as opposed to 2004, the initial withdrawal date. Current plans have the United States reducing its troop strength in the JSA from 179 soldiers to around 40 by 2006, when the first stage of the 2nd Infantry Division's relocation is expected to be completed. During the second phase of the relocation, the remaining U.S. forces will be removed and responsibility for policing the JSA will be handed over fully to ROK forces.[4] In a separate mission area, by 2005 a joint ROK-U.S. team would evaluate whether the ROK had the independent capability to run the headquarters set up to prepare for a DPRK long-range missile attack. If this capability were found lacking, further evaluations would be held every six months.

Perhaps the most contentious issue discussed during the FOTA talks involved the relocation of the Yongsan Garrison out of the densely populated Seoul area, an issue that some thought was settled over a decade ago. As the FOTA talks proceeded, differences arose regarding the terms of the relocation. Two agreements from 1990, an MOU and a memorandum of agreement (MOA), governed the terms of the Yongsan relocation, though neither document was ever submitted to the National Assembly, since portions of them were viewed as "unfair" and "unrealistic" by some South Korean politicians and interest groups. Specifically, many ROK officials were displeased with provisions that placed explicit responsibility on the ROK for the reimbursement of losses incurred by businesses on the Yongsan base following relocation, while also failing to hold the U.S. government liable for any environmental damage at USFK bases. Furthermore, ROK officials also balked at U.S. requests to provide new in-base housing for the remaining U.S. forces.

A related point of disagreement involved the amount of land to be reserved for a reduced Yongsan Garrison. ROK officials initially offered only 139 acres for the Yongsan garrison (and later increased the offer to 164 acres), while Washington sought either to maintain a third of the current garrison (about 228 acres) or leave the city entirely. Politicians in Seoul, however, feared that giving in to the U.S. demand would further inflame anti-U.S. sentiments in the country and hurt their domestic standing.[5] These numerical differences were never bridged, and thus in January 2004 ROK negotiators agreed to the relocation of all seven thousand U.S. troops in Seoul, including the CFC and UNC headquarters, to a new base in Pyeongtaek by 2007. The agreement, once the new MOU is signed, has to win the approval of South Korea's parliament before it can be implemented.

In deciding an appropriate Yongsan policy, Seoul was essentially forced to balance opposing political forces. While the maintenance of the garrison in the capital was desirable in order to placate conservatives and others who wanted to keep some U.S. troops stationed in Seoul as a symbol of U.S. deterrence, others, particularly the constituency that voted President Roh into office, undoubtedly viewed the continued stationing of U.S. troops at Yongsan as emblematic of an asymmetric alliance that continues to account inadequately for the ROK's enhanced status. It should also be noted that Yongsan ties up a significant and valuable piece of prime real estate in downtown Seoul. Thus, ROK officials only offered the amount of land that they considered was consistent with a smaller and less visible U.S. presence in the capital. Impasses in the FOTA negotiations can be viewed as essentially reflecting divergent preferences, along with jockeying for a more favorable distribution of the costs and benefits associated with both the global and local dimensions of the alliance.

As discussed earlier, the U.S.-ROK alliance is in part experiencing growing pains that are due to the U.S. strategy of transforming its global military footprint to respond to the anticipated threats to U.S. interests and security. The realignment of forward deployed forces in South Korea is one such aspect of the envisioned transformation. In this context, American military planners increasingly view the tripwire concept and forward positioning of U.S. forces near the DMZ as technologically and strategically obsolete. The USFK's current configuration, charged with only one mission, is viewed as well as an inefficient use of manpower and resources, especially since their deterrence and war-fighting capability were based on an unbalanced capital-to-labor ratio that did not adequately reflect advances in high-tech warfare. For U.S. policy makers, a more efficient deterrent capability could be provided by a greater reliance on lighter, more agile ground forces and advanced naval and air assets, as opposed to the comparatively static, heavy, and single-focus American ground force units traditionally deployed along the DMZ.

Global structural changes and technological improvements are not the only independent variables influencing USFK realignment. Politically, it has become more difficult for U.S. leaders to justify the expenditures of national treasure and, potentially, American lives in implementing the tripwire concept, when decades of ROK economic growth have given South Korea greater capacity to provide for its own security in conjunction with a reorganized, yet equally effective, American role. Neither do American policy makers accept the argument that realignment signals a reduced U.S. commitment to South Korea's defense, since the USFK would respond to a DPRK attack regardless of the number of U.S. troops stationed north of Seoul. Indeed, it can be argued that U.S. forces redeployed to the Osan-Pyeongtaek area would be among the first targets struck, for example, by North Korean missiles in the event of open hostilities, thereby guaranteeing a U.S. counterstrike on the DPRK.

Undoubtedly ROK policy makers will face challenges in explaining the realignment to the ROK population, whose sense of security over the past fifty years has rested upon the presence of forward deployed U.S. troops near Seoul and the DMZ. It is a rather quick turnaround for ROK politicians to say to their constituents that USFK forward deployment, which was so vital and effective for decades (despite occasional indignities and hardship), is suddenly not that important anymore. Moreover, it is unlikely that U.S. assurances will remove lingering suspicions among a few South Koreans that USFK realignment is intended to give U.S. policy makers greater freedom of action in terms of launching a pre-emptive attack on the DPRK, since the abandonment of USFK forward positioning arguably means that they are no longer "hostage" to North Korea retaliation (in the form of artillery and shorter range ballistic missile barrages) in the event of a U.S. first-strike scenario.[6] The FOTA, therefore, has already been dealing with many of the same complicating factors that could stymie alliance diversification.

Despite the focus on pedestrian details, the political hurdles, and the outstanding disagreements over some aspects of America's USFK realignment agenda, FOTA has made important progress on several issues long considered untouchable. The fact that the allies are moving forward with a substantial USFK realignment away from the DMZ at the same time that North Korea has withdrawn from the NPT and is overtly pursuing nuclear weapons is a sign of how confident and secure the ROK and the United States feel about their deterrent capability. In this sense, now is a fortuitous time to pursue alliance diversification. With a relatively small amount of tinkering, the FOTA process could easily be built upon to take on more ambitious consultations regarding the future of the alliance.

"Fight Tomorrow Morning?"

USFK realignment will necessitate reforms of ROK force structure and require greater defense spending by the ROK government. The USFK's motto has long been "fight tonight," underscoring its frontline status and extremely high level of readiness. Shifting more U.S. troops to the south and transferring certain missions to the ROK military will alter the USFK's traditional posture and place an additional burden on indigenous forces, for which the ROK government has been slowly preparing. Over the next few years, the "fight tonight" slogan will apply more and more to ROK forces, even though the USFK will always have an important role in the initial stages of repelling a North Korean attack. More broadly, these developments underscore a form of ROK military transformation that began in the mid 1990s and has the potential to accelerate quickly if North-South reconciliation moves forward.

In general, the realignment of the USFK and the evolution of the ROK military bode well for alliance diversification, primarily because they create momentum toward a more mobile USFK and multi-functional ROK military that will enable a range of off-peninsula missions, should that capability be desired. Not many years ago it was commonly thought that USFK restructuring and a pull-back from the DMZ would only take place toward the *end* of a North-South reconciliation process. Instead, a USFK pull-back is *preceding* movement toward reunification. It is the FOTA that has put these wheels in motion, and there now exists an opportunity to redefine the U.S.-ROK security relationship before a peace regime is established.

Today, the ROK armed forces are dedicated to defeating any threats directed against the ROK or its interests. Its primary focus, in conjunction with assistance from the USFK (and further add-on U.S. forces), is deterring and defending against the full range of DPRK conventional and non-conventional threats. The DPRK maintains one of the largest militaries in the world, with approximately one million active duty soldiers, an air force of over sixteen hundred aircraft, and a navy with more than eight hundred ships. Seventy percent of its active force, bolstered by eight thousand artillery systems and two thousand tanks, is stationed within one hundred miles of the DMZ, with much of this force protected in underground facilities. It is clear that the North Korean threat cannot be ignored.

Despite the seriousness with which Seoul views the North Korean threat, the ROK government has been planning for several years to move away from a defense concept that identifies a specific enemy and to seek a defense capability that can counter an attack from any trajectory. The Blue House decision in 2004 to drop the term "main enemy" as a description of North Korea from its National Security Council white paper is illustrative of this trend, but the roots of a broader, capabilities-based approach go back at least to the ROK's Force Improvement Plan (FIP) of 1996.[7] At that time, the MND was looking to invest more in improved intelligence and early warning systems, command and control platforms, air strike and missile systems, and enhanced transport and sea lane protection assets (involving larger and more capable destroyers and submarines, as well as an amphibious/aviation vessel that can carry around ten helicopters and seven hundred marines).

By 2000, ROK defense officials were reevaluating all prospective defense procurements, based on a matrix that identified each program as contributing to defense against the existing North Korean threat, future regional challenges, or both. Although the matrix was heavily weighted toward the North Korean threat and the "both" category in 2000, by around 2025 it was expected to swing dramatically to the "regional stability challenges" column. This brightened the prospects for some of the programs noted above, but it led planners to question the value of investing in new systems with more limited applicability, such as a new anti-tank helicopter (HX). Tight government budgets and a lack of progress toward a peace regime with the North have

STRUCTURE OF MILITARY FORCES ON THE KOREAN PENINSULA			
		North Korea	South Korea	USFK and Area U.S. Forces
Troops	total	1,082,000	686,000	61,110[1]
	army	950,000	560,000	31,460
	navy	46,000	63,000[2]	20.230[1]
	air force	86,000	63,000	9,420
Principal Force Capabilities	tanks	3,500	2,390	116
	armored vehicles	3,000	2,520	237
	field artilleries	10,400	4,600	45[3]
	multiple launch rocket systems	2,500	185	[3]
	surface-to-surface missiles	300	12	0
	surface combatant vessels	313	123	0[4]
	submarines	26	20	0[5]
	fighters	525	468	84[6]
	bombers	80	0	0[7]
	attack helicopters	24	117	100

(1)   *Figure includes the 19,750 USMC troops stationed at Yokosuka Naval Base in Japan.*

(2)   *Marine Corps (28,000) included in naval troops statistics.*

(3)   *Figure includes multiple launch rocket systems.*

(4)   *While no U.S. surface combatant vessels are stationed in South Korea, 19 surface combatant vessels, including one aircraft carrier, are available from bases in Hawaii and Japan.*

(5)   *While again, no submarines are based in South Korea, 22 are based in Hawaii, any number of which could be patrolling near the Korean Peninsula at any given time.*

(6)   *Additional aircraft available from at least five fighter wings based in Alaska, Hawaii, and Japan.*

(7)   *The first three of six B-52 bombers were recently deployed to Guam to reinforce U.S. long-range bombing capabilities in the Pacific. Other bombers can be launched from bases in Alaska or other parts of the United States.*

Source: The Military Balance *103 , no. 1 (2003 - 2004), The International Institute for Strategic Studies, London.*

slowed some of the more omni-directional procurement programs, but a few new systems have been delivered and more are
in the pipeline.

These investments are providing the ROK with a more comprehensive defense capability and will eventually allow it to project
limited power around the region to look after its interests. In 2004,
South Korea's defense budget is set at around $16 billion, which
represents an 8 percent increase from the 2003 level and com-
pares to only a 2 percent increase for total government spending
this year. In this sense, the defense budget received a significant
boost in 2004, but it is less than the MND hoped for and does
not return military spending to the same levels (as a percentage
of the economy) that it experienced in the 1980s and 1990s. Although ROK defense outlays account for roughly 15 percent of
the central government's annual budget, they have been less than
3 percent of GNP since 1998 and now hover around 2.8 percent
(compared to 3.5 percent in 1993 and 4.2 percent in 1988). As a
result, the MND has been able to move forward with some, but
not all, of its procurement priorities.

High on the list of priorities in the 2004 defense budget are
many of the same systems and programs that have been promoted in recent years. The $5.2 billion acquisition budget includes
installments for new aircraft (the F-15K and others), the KDX-
II and KDX-III destroyer program, an eighteen-hundred-ton
class submarine, and an amphibious/aviation vessel (the LPX).
There will also be investments in improving the armed forces command, control, communications, computers, intelligence,
surveillance, and reconnaissance (C^4ISR) capability. Other programs that defense officials were hoping to slide into the 2004
budget were an aerial refueling tanker, joint direct attack mu-
nitions (JDAMs), air/missile defense upgrades, and an AWACS
capability.

ROK military investments in the near term suggest that the
country will be able to handle a wider variety of missions more
effectively, consistent with its stated goal of pursuing a more
independent defense capability and in response to some American requests for ROK forces to take over certain tasks currently
handled by the USFK or other PACOM assets. The ROK military
believes that even if its forces are not able to fully compete head-

on with the forces of regional powers in a future major crisis or, worse yet, outright war, they should have the ability to inflict "unacceptable damage" on adversary forces – that is, to destroy or cripple up to 60 percent or 70 percent of a potential adversary's forces in an actual assault. One way to view the ROK's military investments, therefore, is that it is looking to develop a "porcupine strategy" and to deter would-be intimidators from encroaching on Korean interests.

Certain aspects of South Korea's modernization plan, however, are designed to project power off-peninsula and therefore have a dual-use character, because they could support a defensive posture or offensive operations. This has the potential to stimulate a procurement competition with Japan and China, and some of the same systems have prompted critics to complain that precious funds are being diverted from more immediate and peninsula-focused defense needs. The submarine program is most commonly noted in this regard, and the ROK's plan to launch two amphibious vessels (or light aircraft carriers) by 2010 is attracting attention in the region. A mid-air refueling capability would also fit into this category, when it is funded. U.S. defense officials would probably rather the ROK put less emphasis on developing a blue-water navy at this time and spend more money closer to home on C^4ISR technology and the SAM-X missile defense system, but this is what comes from a more balanced relationship.

Looking ahead, what will matter most to the U.S.-ROK alliance and other Asia-Pacific nations is the future trend line of ROK military investments and how officials in Seoul perceive their nation's security needs. If South Korea develops an increasingly potent power projection capability, Japan and China might feel obligated to counter those weapons systems with investments of their own, unless Seoul's plans are seen as sufficiently integrated with (or at least tethered to) the U.S.-ROK alliance and/or a regional coalition that blunts the threat potential. An arms race serves no country's interests, and this is generally understood in the region. As part of its military modernization, however, South Korea (and eventually a unified Korea) will undoubtedly develop a stronger offensive and defensive capability that must be absorbed into the regional security order. What kind of military posture a unified Korea eventually adopts will depend on several factors, including the prevailing security environment during and following reunification, the manner in which reunification is realized, and the strength and nature of the U.S.-Korea security relationship.

Looking to Future Alternatives

The preceding analysis demonstrates that the U.S.-ROK alliance has entered a period of transition containing strong elements of both continuity and change. The current doctrine and force structure – including the U.S. forces based in Japan – that underwrite contingency plans on the peninsula are geared primarily for a single threat from North Korea, but this situation is changing, and it could look very different ten years from now. Current developments, including the FOTA negotiations and new patterns of ROK acquisition hinting at power projection, suggest that both Washington and Seoul are eyeing a future that deviates (perhaps substantially) from the peninsula-focused status quo. Yet, even while the two sides emphasize their commitment to each other and acknowledge that change is both inevitable and desirable, it remains unclear how the alliance will adjust its posture. While uncertainties surround the future peace on the peninsula, and the fluid regional dynamics obscure what alliance structures would best serve the United States and the ROK in the long term, preparations can and should be made in the next few years to maximize the alliance's flexibility ahead of expected (and unexpected) changes.

One analytical method for determining how Washington and Seoul should prepare for the potential shifts flowing from new regional developments and global trends is to project the range of possible future contours of the alliance and end states of the security relationship. Admittedly, this approach is not new. Some analysts have already examined this issue by producing shorter-term projections of the North Korean threat while others have assumed the demise of the Pyongyang regime as a key planning parameter (see the literature review in chapter 3 for details). This study relies on the latter form of analysis to generate a set of alternative security structures for the alliance. More specifically, the assessment below seeks to answer a central question: What might the U.S.-ROK alliance look like leading up to and following some type of reunification process?

The timeframe for analysis looks out to the next five to fifteen years. Of course, inter-Korean reconciliation and reunification, as well as many of the factors posited below, may or may not happen within this timeline. However, given a conclusion that the status quo is no longer tenable, it is almost certain that major changes – both anticipated and unexpected – in the region and on the Korean Peninsula will fundamentally reshape the outlook and structures of the U.S.-ROK alliance. Thus, a timeframe that allows for bold predictions provides a useful planning parameter with which to compare the present to the future. It also underscores the need to broaden and deepen the allies' formal discussion about their future security relationship as soon as possible, since negotiating and implementing substantive changes can take several years.

Several compelling rationales underpin this forward-looking methodology. First, the premise of the post-unification argument ensures that the analysis is not tied to a constraining timetable, especially since the North's fate has consistently eluded predictions. Second, a long-term framework frees the assessment from the exigencies of the fluid and unfolding realities on the ground. Third, looking beyond the horizon enables the study to incorporate assumptions about regional and global security trends that are not directly and specifically linked to the North-South dynamic. Fourth, some aspects of the end states discussed below are already evident in the planning and deliberations at the highest levels of the U.S. government (and in South Korea).

Given that the outright collapse of the alliance would leave little room for analysis, this study assumes that some form of alliance structure survives the next decade and the shocks of a unification process (or, at least, the initiation of such a process). It is reasonable to expect that Seoul will want to maintain the alliance in the near term to allow for maximum maneuver room and reassurance during a period of uncertainty. The security alternatives for the U.S.-ROK security relationship assessed below are by no means exhaustive or mutually exclusive. They are deliberately cast in rather stark terms in order to illustrate distinct characteristics of potential alternative alliance postures, and certain aspects of each scenario could easily co-exist alongside each other. The core purpose of this exercise is to use these alternatives as a framework for selecting the most plausible and desirable outcomes to inform ongoing and future policy choices.

A few words on the variables used to determine the alternatives are in order. First, core assumptions about the future security environment serve as the starting point for each scenario. Clearly, a destabilizing regional security dynamic would produce very different planning parameters compared to a peaceful and benign one. Second, these broader considerations then determine the roles and missions that the military leadership from the U.S.-Korea alliance might adopt. To be sure, a diverse range of potential roles and missions could be developed to cope with each of the embedded assumptions. Conversely, somewhat divergent assumptions could also conceivably produce a common set of roles and missions. However, to ensure brevity and analytical clarity, each scenario focuses on the most plausible and reasonable roles and missions for the U.S. and Korean militaries at the broadest level.

Based on the two planning variables mentioned above (that is, the security environment and roles and missions), two additional components to the proposed scenarios can be determined. The first relates to the force structures and command structures that would be needed to fulfill the proposed strategic and operational requirements, and the second considers some key modernization, acquisition, and procurement priorities needed to sustain the force posture.

These four factors provide an organic, integrated framework for projecting future alternative security postures for the U.S.-ROK alliance. The following analysis focuses on three distinct alternatives: 1) a recessed security posture; 2) a naval and air power posture; and 3) a regional/hemispheric posture.

Alternative 1: Recessed Security Posture
The key assumption in this scenario is that a benign and peaceful security environment emerges (or shows strong signs of emerging) in Northeast Asia. The reconciliation and reunification processes produce a stable, democratic, and united Korea

that is satisfied with the status quo both because of its near exclusive focus on closing the North-South socio-economic gap and the absence of a credible external threat to its security. As a more inward looking orientation takes hold, Seoul sees disentanglement from great power politics of the past as the most attractive strategic option. In such an environment, Korea might pursue more neutral or independent (though non-hostile) foreign and security policies, premised on regional collaboration and the promotion of multilateral institutions, which adroitly navigate among the major regional players. It is conceivable in this scenario that Seoul renounces indefinitely the possession of WMD and declares the peninsula a nuclear-free zone (if it has not become free of nuclear weapons already as part of the reunification process), as long as Korea can obtain adequate security assurances from the regional powers.

Insofar as broader regional trends are concerned, a powerful and confident China integrates further into the international community and embraces the emerging regional order. In particular, cross-strait relations enter a period of accommodation. Equally significant, as Korean and Japanese ties deepen and mature, mutual hostilities based on historical memories fade sufficiently to give way to a more cooperative (but perhaps still prickly) relationship. Moreover, the evolution of Japanese strategic and political thinking increases Tokyo's assertiveness and willingness to assume regional, if not hemispheric, security responsibilities in a non-threatening manner alongside the United States. Russia's recovery from the implosion of the Soviet Union progresses, but not sufficiently for Moscow to influence events in the Far East significantly.

America's global security commitments, which reached a zenith during and after operation Iraqi Freedom, ease over time with notable successes in the GWOT and the stabilization process of Iraq. Buoyed by these positive developments, the United States reaps a peace dividend akin to the years following the Soviet Union's dissolution. Given that no apparent rationale for continued presence exists without a threat from the North, the U.S. public loses its appetite for a major military commitment on the Korean Peninsula. As a consequence, the U.S. military draws down substantially from Korea and withdraws all major ground and air components. The U.S. military maintains an over-the-horizon capability based primarily in Japan, which continues to serve as a hub of regional security. Given the absence of a clear and present danger to Korea, the language of the 1953 U.S.-ROK Mutual Defense Treaty (particularly Article 3) is probably broad enough to continue to define sufficiently and sustain Seoul's security relationship with Washington. Furthermore, if the regional powers and Korea consummate a nuclear-free zone on the peninsula, the United States might even retract its extended nuclear deterrence guarantee. In sum, the alliance takes on a far more political character than the current orientation toward security and military issues.

Roles and missions. In this scenario, a united Korea would bear entirely the primary responsibilities for its security and defense. Once the threat vector to the north disappears, Korea could assume a more modest and omni-directional security posture, something for which it is already preparing. If Seoul makes sufficient progress in the absorption of the North, the Korean public might even acquiesce to certain off-peninsula peacekeeping and nation-building missions similar to those that the South was (and still is) involved in, such as those in East Timor and Iraq. In this alternative future, the United States effectively ends its involvement in the day-to-day management of Korea's security affairs (once its reassurance and assistance role during the early stages of unification is complete). However, both sides undertake regular joint training and exercises in Korea and in the continental United States as an interface to familiarize each other with evolving doctrines and capabilities. Access, joint training, and pre-positioning agreements provide the only vehicles for U.S. military visibility on the peninsula.

Force structure. The peace dividend permits Korea to draw down its military posture across all of the services, but the most substantial cuts are felt in the army. Seoul is almost certain to downsize its active force levels that today stand at nearly seven hundred thousand troops and reduce the large reserve force. Similar to the defense reforms undertaken by several NATO countries in the late 1990s, Korea might opt to abolish the conscription system and adopt a smaller, professional military better suited to the relaxed security environment. More mobile and lighter, deployable forces, including those capable of performing constabulary missions abroad, would replace the current emphasis on heavy armor, artillery, and mechanized infantry units. Preparation for peacekeeping and humanitarian operations could also lead to a stronger emphasis on strategic airlift and sealift assets, such as heavy transport aircraft, mid-air refueling capability, and the LPX amphibious transport ship, though the airlift function in particular could be provided by the United States under an updated MLSA.

For its part, the United States would reduce its military footprint on the peninsula to a minimum. Under a phase-out plan, the U.S. 8th Army would withdraw completely and all ground-force bases and installations south of Seoul would be turned over to the Korean authorities. The 7th Air Force would also pull out of Korea. However, under a new access agreement, Seoul might permit U.S. Air Force access to Osan airbase, where air expeditionary force units could be deployed on a regular rotational basis for training and exercises, as well as for signaling and reinforcement during crises and contingencies. The U.S. military could also maintain a skeletal crew in and around key access points and pre-positioning sites, including Pusan and other naval bases for regular port calls, to sustain operations and maintenance.

Command structure. In this case, the USFK, the CFC, and the UNC would be dissolved after peace on the Korean Peninsula. A newly organized combatant command based in Japan would thereafter make all strategic and operational decisions regulating U.S. forces operating in and around Korea. The new regional command (perhaps called Northeast Asia Command) serves as a sub-regional component command of PACOM. Its area of responsibility, as a part of PACOM's mandate, would roughly replicate the geography of Northeast Asia, including China, Japan, Korea, Taiwan, and the Russian Far East. Logically, following such a shift, Korea's MND and armed forces would be solely responsible for plans and operations concerning peninsula defense and the disposition of ROK forces. Under this new arrangement, the degree of command integration and coordination between a Japan-based Northeast Asia Command and ROK forces would likely be significantly reduced, but it would be helpful to preserve the practice of joint planning as much as possible.

Acquisition and procurement. The peace dividend enables Korea to delay or cancel certain defense items for its ground, air, and naval forces. Plans to buy additional main battle tanks, self-propelled howitzers, and similar army equipment might be the first acquisitions canceled. Moreover, the costs of absorbing and integrating the DPRK, not to mention the requirement to demobilize, disarm, and retrain large segments of the North's million-man army, impose serious budgetary constraints on the united Korea. In this scenario, Korea would rely primarily on its legacy systems for defense, particularly for its ground components. Seoul would selectively and narrowly focus on C^{4}ISR technologies and limited offshore air and naval power projection. It is even possible that Korea would use procurement as a political-diplomatic tool rather than for pure war-fighting purposes. Thus, Seoul could import a mix of capabilities from European countries and possibly from Russia and China to curry political favor and to garner a more visible standing in the international arena. Moreover, given the separation of command noted above, interoperability with U.S. forces would become a secondary, if not a negligible, defense priority.

While the U.S. defense industry would still lobby hard to sell equipment to Korea, the absence of an "interoperability" argument would substantially erode its leverage in negotiations with Seoul. However, the shift in Korea's modernization priorities would not likely disrupt long-term U.S. defense acquisition, at least as envisioned by Defense Secretary Rumsfeld's transformation plans. Indeed, the U.S. focus on long-range, precision, and mobile capabilities might even dovetail with Korea's more modest plans for power projection and a recessed U.S. posture on the peninsula.

Alternative 2: Naval and Air Power Posture

In many ways, this scenario is the converse of the assumptions laid out above. In general, Northeast Asia remains a potentially dangerous region fraught with risks and uncertainties. The Korean unification process, whether through collapse and absorption or peaceful integration, proves to be a difficult and tortuous process. The socio-economic and cultural chasms between the North and South are so wide that full reconciliation seems a distant proposition. Though perhaps unified on paper, the peninsula remains divided as the North's population becomes frustrated and isolated, dependent on aid that is managed by what it perceives is a dubious coalition of southerners and outsiders. The costs of rebuilding and rehabilitating the economy and the infrastructure of the northern regions are prohibitively high and require substantial foreign assistance and financial aid, particularly from the United States, Japan, and possibly Europe.

These internal problems and the potential for domestic upheaval spark insecurities among Koreans about the nation's long-term future. Indeed, such weaknesses heighten paranoia and evoke memories of past episodes of internal weakness and foreign domination by its neighbors. The increasing loss of public confidence engendered by such conditions convinces the political leadership that the fate of the Korean Peninsula is precariously balanced. Ironically, the atmospherics in this unification scenario recall the darker days of the divided peninsula, when each side perceived a threat to its existence from the other.

Given this acute sense of vulnerability, the united Korea looks decisively to the United States as its security guarantor and main economic lifeline. The real and perceived threats to Korea's national interests, such as the possible collapse of reconciliation or potential Chinese encroachment, reinforce the national consensus that the country must subordinate nationalistic sentiments and the desire for full independence of action to its more vital interests of safety and stability in the region. Moreover, the high political and economic costs of developing a nuclear security hedge as an ultimate means of protection compel Seoul to reject an independent nuclear deterrent and to continue to rely on America's extended nuclear guarantee. Hence, the U.S.-Korea alliance remains the bedrock of Korea's security and well-being. Similar to the original rationale for the security partnership aimed at a singular North Korean threat, Seoul's security agenda is once again motivated by a narrow set of national interests, focused on national survival.

For the United States, its various global missions stemming from the anti-terrorism campaign and the consequences of the wars in Afghanistan and Iraq continue to preoccupy U.S. policy makers. Regionally, the overall picture remains unpromising.

In a classic replay of great power politics, China's rise as a major economic and military player fuels anxieties among its neighbors. Beijing adopts an increasingly assertive foreign policy that more directly challenges U.S. interests in Asia as a whole, including its alliance structures with Korea and Japan.

China's posture pushes Korea to reassess its ties with Beijing, and it takes precautionary politico-military measures to hedge against a potential Chinese threat. While certain aspects of Japanese-Korean relations, such as economic ties, continue to improve, differences over the past still animate bilateral ties. Moreover, in the absence of a North Korean threat, a united Korea fixes its gaze on Japan (apart from China) as a likely security challenge. The lack of significant breakthroughs in the Japan-Korea relationship causes mutual suspicions to intensify between Tokyo and Seoul. While Moscow periodically engages in diplomacy in the region, Russia, still focused on political developments in Europe, remains primarily on the sidelines.

For the United States, the world in this scenario looks much the same as it does today. The persistence of global and regional challenges requires the U.S. military to retain the capacity to project power to far corners of the world. Washington is thus compelled to retain its global military infrastructure, albeit reconfigured for a wider range of missions and contingencies and in concert with advances in technology. Moreover, the fragility of post-unification Korea means that the United States will sustain a restructured presence on the peninsula. Indeed, ongoing tensions between Korea and Japan, as well as uncertainties surrounding China's future, expand America's defense commitment to the peninsula to include a greater reassurance role, in addition to classic deterrence and defense. Thus, Washington ends up playing a balancing and mediating role to ensure that none of the Northeast Asian states triggers a conflict emanating from the unresolved security dilemmas in the region.

While Korea would serve partly as a base from which America might carry out its global and regional responsibilities, the conditions noted above force both sides to adopt structures intended to reflect a new geopolitical environment on and around the peninsula. The U.S.-ROK defense treaty in force today, which focuses on a singular threat from the North, and such other documents as the status of forces agreements that underwrite the alliance, would be amended and adjusted to suit the strategic situation for a reconciled Korea. For instance, additional language (similar to Article 6 of the U.S.-Japan Treaty of Mutual Cooperation and Security) might be needed to empower Korea to assist the United States in limited operations surrounding the peninsula.[8] To reflect the new military requirements more accurately, the United States and Korea undertake a major re-posturing of their forces. In the absence of a DPRK military threat, the current emphasis on ground forces recedes to the background, and a new emphasis on air and naval power comes to the forefront. In sum, Washington and Seoul focus on elements of power projection that serve Korea's more immediate security needs and, to the extent possible, America's broader regional and extra-regional missions.

Roles and missions. In this scenario, then, the two sides share responsibility for Korea's security and defense. The alliance still exhibits elements of asymmetry that exist today, given the continued heavy reliance on the United States as an ultimate security guarantor. The insecurities that dominate strategic thinking in Korea within the context of a difficult North-South integration process compel Korean planners to place the defense against domestic instability and potential encroachment by its neighbors during a prolonged period of internal weakness as the top priorities. In this scenario, though Korea's defense policy is fundamentally capabilities based (as opposed to threat based), the outward looking aspect of its strategy, centered on air and naval power, is intended primarily as a defense against Japan and China. Seoul would need military capabilities for its immediate surrounding environment (akin to the Russian notion of the "near abroad") to counter-balance both Tokyo and Beijing. Practically speaking, however, Korea relies largely on the United States for these missions, because of the time and money necessary to build up its own independent capabilities.

In return for American support during this uncertain time of reconciliation, Korea remains a partner in fulfilling America's broader security agenda in the region. Since Korean security planning is still tied to the defense of the peninsula under this scenario, Seoul would not likely be willing or able to contribute directly (or substantially) to America's extra-regional missions, except in very select circumstances. In this sense, Korea participates in a regional security coalition (like the one described in chapter 4), but it is not a core member and maintains a relatively low profile in security and humanitarian missions. Consequently, the peninsula serves as an important operational air and naval hub for projecting American military power in the region, with only limited Korean support in the short term. In the longer term, as Korea stabilizes and grows stronger, this kind of security relationship could evolve into a situation not unlike the next scenario, where off-peninsula activities dominate the alliance and U.S. forces largely disengage from Korean defense.

The United States, for its part, continues to take an active part in the major decision making processes related to the defense of the Korean Peninsula. Washington focuses also on how Korea, on a limited basis, could better contribute to some of the regional security challenges with which the U.S. military must contend. This requirement for Korea to help bolster America's broader missions around the peninsula compels both to devise a more equitable division of labor that produces modest combined responsibilities, in, for example, rear-area support, including logistics, medical assistance, interdiction, and even force protection missions, such as air and naval escort, to U.S. operations in the region.

Force structure. As in alternative 1, the disappearance of the North as a central military threat changes the South Korean force structure. A draw-down focuses primarily on ground forces no longer needed to fight a major conventional land war on the peninsula. However, Seoul retains significant heavy armored and infantry units, deployed north of the thirty-eighth parallel, for contingencies related to civil unrest in the North, and, more indirectly, as a counter to China. At the same time, Korea would pursue an outward oriented force posture centered on strengthening key naval ports and airbases as a hedge against perceived threats from Japan, as well as from China.

The resources freed up from downsizing the army would be diverted to bolster Korea's air and naval power and to help demobilize, disarm, and retrain the North's defunct military. The new ROK force would have offensive components, but it would be limited largely to narrow self-defense missions. Given the resource constraints on a cash-strapped Korea in this scenario, Seoul would focus primarily on key pockets of excellence in air and naval power, and to a lesser extent on boosting missile defenses. The new Korean military would very gradually feature longer-range capabilities in air superiority and ground attack assets in the air and on the littoral waters of the peninsula to combat potential aggression. The need for highly skilled human resources for these niche capabilities would tempt Seoul to abandon the conscription system and introduce a smaller, smarter professional force.

Analogous to the arrangements of the U.S.-Japan alliance during the Cold War, Washington and Seoul maintain separate and unequal forces. In other words, each implicitly accepts operational and technological asymmetries within the alliance, at least for a period of time. While the U.S. military essentially loses its ground mission after unification, Korea's threat perceptions of China to its north still requires the stationing of an American ground-based presence, though significantly downsized. For instance, one highly deployable medium (*Stryker*-like) brigade stationed below the thirty-eighth parallel might replace the two full, active brigades deployed today. Its relative distance from the Chinese border avoids antagonizing Beijing, yet at the same time its presence is robust, agile, and visible enough to send a deterrent signal to China that could adequately reassure Korea. The United States also expands its air and naval presence to complement Korea's new orientation and to support its own set of regional and global missions. The 7th Air Force downgrades its ground-attack missions and focuses instead on air superiority assets and air expeditionary forces. It also could expand its facilities and command and control capabilities at Osan and Kunsan.

In a significant change, the U.S. military assigns a greater number of seagoing forces, including marines, to Pyeongtaek and Chinhae, perhaps on a rotational basis with naval forces attached to the U.S. command component in Japan. Pre-positioned assets expand and shift flexibly at key access points in tune with changing requirements. The forces deployed would facilitate and enhance joint and combined operations with Korean forces in the air and on the seas near the peninsula. The shift is also intended to fill the critical defense gaps that are likely to emerge during the transition phase as Korean forces adjust more slowly to carrying out their responsibilities effectively. In this scenario, it may be possible for Korea to replace U.S. air and naval power gradually, as it develops greater confidence and capabilities during the reconciliation and reunification process. In this sense, the naval and air power posture could be a transition phase, leading to the third alternative (regional/hemispheric posture) discussed below, as Korea slowly overcomes the challenges of reunification and feels increasingly secure.

Command structure. Modeled after the U.S.-Japan alliance, two separate American and Korean national commands emerge. The united Korea assumes primary command responsibilities on the peninsula alongside a substantially restructured USFK, while the CFC and the UNC are phased out. With substantial withdrawals of the U.S. Army from Korea, the headquarters and the combatant commander (likely an air force general officer) would be based in or near Osan airbase. The new command serves as a subcomponent to a newly organized U.S. regional combatant command for Northeast Asia based in Japan (similar to the U.S. Forces Northeast Asia proposed earlier). All U.S. strategic and operational decisions surrounding the Korean Peninsula flow from that command as a part of PACOM's area of responsibility over China, Japan, Korea, Taiwan, and the Russian Far East.

Under this alternative command structure, Korea's MND and armed forces are solely responsible for plans and operations concerning peninsular security and defense. However, this scenario inherits some legacies of the former (today's) U.S.-ROK alliance. In particular, plans associated with air and naval operations are closely coordinated through the new USFK for certain joint and combined missions, and a new bilateral security consultative mechanism would be established to facilitate collaboration.

Acquisition and procurement. This alternative posture envisions some levels of integration between U.S. and ROK military units in line with the force structure posited above. Since the defense of the peninsula still requires significant U.S. military involvement, Seoul's procurement of air and naval assets continues to center on modest interoperability with the U.S. military. However, given the financial constraints that the troubled unification process has imposed in this scenario, Korea's limited purchasing power forces its modernization agenda to drag far behind that of the United States. Seoul must rely primarily on its legacy systems for its defense while more slowly acquiring big-ticket items, such as next-generation fighters, extended-range surface ships and submarines, and enhanced AWACS capabilities. Korea focuses instead on systems integration via existing platforms to improve limited joint and combined operations with U.S. forces. In the meantime, new U.S. assets and capabilities developed under the proposed defense transformation plan are introduced on the peninsula (and around the region) to bolster Seoul's sense of security and to serve America's broader missions.

Alternative 3: Regional/Hemispheric Posture

This scenario contains a mix of assumptions embedded in the two postures described above. While uncertainties and elements of competition remain in Northeast Asia, the upward trend lines diminish the potential for instability in the region. The two Koreas unite under a negotiated plan that gradually and methodically integrates the North with the South. To be sure, the political and socio-economic challenges are immense even under such carefully deliberated circumstances. However, sufficient progress made in the unification process, underwritten in part by generous foreign assistance, increasingly suggests that the united Korea will likely enjoy a promising future. In this context, a more healthy form of Korean nationalism coalesces. The Korean public may become more willing to bear the cost of operations not directly associated with the country's immediate and narrowly defined interests. The combination of a greater sense of security and a confident national psyche enables Seoul to embrace more aggressively many of the regional security obligations that would appear to coincide with its emerging middle power status, such as regional peacekeeping or humanitarian relief missions.

Similar to the second alternative above, however, the international security environment remains precarious. At the regional level, China's future path as a regional power is far from clear. While Japanese-Korean ties are still punctuated by controversies associated with the past, ongoing regional (TCOG) and bilateral (joint exercises) mechanisms foster a more mature and stable relationship. Indeed, the degree to which Tokyo facilitated the reconciliation and reunification process (by being a constructive participant in the six-party process, for instance) is likely to dictate the long-term closeness between the two powers. In other words, a prominent and constructive Japanese role could, and in this scenario would, inaugurate unprecedented bilateral cooperation.

In this context, Korea remains engaged alongside the United States in a variety of regional and global contingencies. America's continued activism abroad begins to coincide with Korean extra-peninsular interests in this instance. In fact, over time, both Washington and Seoul view the ongoing and potential joint collaborations within broader "coalitions of the willing" as a common interest and a key component to sustaining the alliance. Seoul, in particular, no longer views the foundations for the alliance in narrow, Korea-centric terms focused almost exclusively on the defense of Korean territorial integrity. Domestically, as Korea further consolidates its democratic institutions and free market economic system, the protection and promotion of these values are accepted as a vital national interest.

The greater convergence of values and interests between the United States and Korea motivates both sides to restructure the security relationship more explicitly for broader regional and extra-regional contingencies not directly associated with Korea's self-defense. More importantly, the alliance's rationale increasingly centers on out-of-area missions in which Korea can seamlessly plug into U.S. deployment plans. In such a scenario, the mutual defense treaty as it stands today would no longer adequately reflect new strategic realities for the alliance. A major reassessment and revitalization of the security partnership would be required in this scenario. For instance, the legal mechanisms governing the alliance would have to incorporate new language and content, perhaps similar to NATO's Article 4, that would facilitate deploying joint and combined missions far beyond the peninsula in support of a wider range of contingencies (such as counter-proliferation missions and peace support operations) than classic collective defense against an armed attack on the ROK.[9] Clearly, such a reorientation would substantially deepen and widen the scope of the U.S.-Korea relationship.

Roles and missions. Given the consolidation of Korea as a reunited entity, Seoul assumes primary responsibility for its own defense and security. However, unlike in the previous scenario, a more confident Korea seeks to further complement and enhance U.S. military capabilities in the region and beyond, since it sees those missions as more directly connected to protecting its national interest. Rather than adopt an outward looking posture simply as a security hedge, Seoul reconfigures its military forces to maintain alliance cohesion and effectiveness for regional and hemispheric operations. In other words, Korea views itself as a critical force multiplier to U.S. forces and power projection, at least in situations where the two nations' interests coincide. Korea is also a more aggressive participant in regional security cooperation and actively supports the development of multilateral security institutions.

Further, informal trilateral defense collaboration among Washington, Seoul, and Tokyo becomes a prominent feature of the U.S. alliance architecture for Northeast Asia, where the United States serves as a bridge (as it does today) between Seoul and Tokyo. While the U.S. military is no longer involved directly with the defense of Korea, the United States incorporates Korea's defense posture into its own planning for extra-regional and hemispheric activities. In many ways, the burden-sharing arrangements between Washington and Seoul increasingly resemble the outcomes flowing from the U.S.-Japan alliance revitalization process in the 1990s, during which planners on both sides shifted away from the defense of Japan to contingencies beyond the home islands. Borrowing from the legacy of the pre-unification era, the level of bilateral cooperation and joint operational planning continues to deepen.

Force structure. As in the two previous scenarios, Korea downsizes its armed forces across the board. The heavy ground forces that have long characterized the ROK military are replaced by rapid deployment capabilities with elite units intended to fulfill regional and extra-regional tasks. In the meantime, air-naval expeditionary forces become the centerpiece of Korea's post-unification force structure. In contrast to the peninsular posture noted in scenario two, which focuses on deterring threats in the immediate neighborhood, the force projection capability is far more beyond-the-horizon in character (including Southeast Asia, for example). While the cost of modernization initially forces Korea to tailor its forces for rear-area support and escort, the envisioned "objective force" eventually is able to operate alongside U.S. forces across a broader range of military missions at longer distances and at higher levels of operational tempo. The U.S. military, for its part, expands its air and naval presence to complement and reinforce Korea's security posture. Again, a part of the rationale for the apparent redundancy is to fill in Korea's capabilities deficit during the transition on the peninsula.

The U.S. military presence in Korea largely resembles that of the naval/air posture described above, but the nature of its mission and its training focus is quite different. The USFK maintains less ground attack capability in the regional/hemispheric posture than in the second scenario (fewer fighters and attack helicopters), and a *Stryker* brigade might not be necessary (since Korea is more confident in its ability to deter aggression or intimidation by China or Russia). The only U.S. ground forces on the peninsula might be a contingent of marines that train specifically for combined missions with Korean forces. If the marines stationed in Korea are drawn from those already deployed in Okinawa, then this could also help reduce the USFJ footprint in Japan while maintaining a regional response capability. U.S. naval forces (essentially the 7th Fleet) would probably keep their current home-porting structure but would rotate in and out of Korean naval bases on a regular basis. U.S. and Korean forces would engage in regular joint exercises and training focused on interoperability in certain mission areas.

As further integration between the two forces proceeds, the alliance may adopt operational concepts similar to NATO's CJTF.[10] In the NATO context, the CJTF concept consists of politico-military structures and procedures that allow member and non-member states to contribute selectively to ad hoc multinational (combined) and multi-service (joint) task forces, designed for specific, short-duration operations that range from humanitarian assistance to peace enforcement/combat operations. Once the CJTF operation is deemed complete, the capabilities deployed would return to the respective parent military organizations.

Both the U.S. and the Korean command would develop doctrines and force structures for a flexible and readily deployable task force designed for operations other than the defense of Korea. Both would then be able to tailor their respective forces based on the operational requirements, the size and location of a crisis, and the unique capabilities that each can bring to bear on fairly short notice. In operational terms, the United States and Korea would boast the capacity to detach "organic assets" – parts that are essential to a larger military unit – from their respective military organizations and capabilities for a combined and joint operation.

In a hypothetical humanitarian crisis in Southeast Asia, an integrated U.S.-Korean CJTF headquarters under the command of PACOM would be able to rapidly organize an expeditionary naval unit to monitor the flow of refugees. Such a naval task force could include a mix of American and Korean combat and support ships that could operate together under a single integrated command and control architecture and that could share critical operational intelligence. Depending on the degree of Australian and Japanese involvement in such a joint and combined structure, it is conceivable that these countries could also deploy forces alongside U.S. and Korean forces within the CJTF construct.

Command structure. As the pre-unification command structures are phased out, two separate national commands emerge that enjoy far more equal statures than the commands that exist today. Similar to the naval/air power posture, a newly reorganized USFK subordinate to the regionally oriented Northeast Asia Command in Japan is createtd, though the focus of its planning is different. Despite Korea's sensitivities about working with a potentially new, sub-regional U.S. command based in Japan that oversees U.S. forces in Korea, the Korean national command eventually becomes fully integrated into the sub-regional command. Command integration enables the two sides to consummate the promise of the CJTF concept, in concert with Japan if desired or warranted. For instance, a new CJTF headquarters run by a permanent U.S.-ROK joint planning staff (or cell), based in the Osan/Pyontaek area, could be embedded within the Northeast Asia Command. Such an arrangement could help to retain (and build on) the very positive U.S.-ROK joint planning experiences established under the CFC, but do so within a more balanced framework less dominated by the United States.[11] In response to a contingency, the headquarters would select an overall commander who would then oversee a land- or sea-based headquarters element that could be rapidly fielded for command and control of the combined joint force tailored for the specific mission. That commander, moreover, might as often be Korean as American, a turn of events that would likely help to ease past perceptions among South Koreans of unnecessary inequities in U.S.-ROK command relationships.

Acquisition and procurement. Clearly, a far more collaborative acquisition process would be required for the alliance to fulfill the CJTF concept. Indeed, interoperability with U.S. forces becomes a major driving force behind Korean modernization plans under this scenario. Technological commonality would inform procurement on both sides, and platform acquisition and systems integration would be closely coordinated. However, even if the pace of U.S. defense transformation slows down for other, external reasons, Seoul would still not likely be able to reach technological parity in any given platform or system. In this case, the allies would have an opportunity to minimize redundancy (and costs) and invest in systems and capabilities that complement each other (and contribute to multilateral security activities). A joint study on military transformation and procurement would be useful, and it might also be possible to use a TCOG-like mechanism to expand the study by involving Japan.

Implications of the Three Alternatives

It is worth reemphasizing that the three alternatives are not the only possible outcomes for a united Korea within the five- to fifteen-year timeframe, and that other scenarios may very well crystallize. However, these projections do provide broader lessons and insights that are applicable to the future of the alliance. In many ways, the three scenarios reflect a timeline and sequence of events that could transpire after Korean unification. The first two alternative futures, which are driven by threat perceptions and national interests that will almost certainly become evident shortly after peace on the peninsula, are more likely to occur in the near to medium terms. The third scenario, on the other hand, envisions a new alliance premised, in part, on the convergence of values that would no doubt take more time to cultivate and develop.[12] In other words, scenarios based on threat levels and interests are far more determinant than those centered on amorphous ideational commonalities.

SUMMARY OF THE THREE ALTERNATIVES				
		Recessed	**Naval/Air**	**Regional/Hemispheric**
Roles and Missions	Korea	Primary Korean defense; eventually some limited off-peninsula missions conducted independently or in cooperation with coalitions of willing nations. To extent possible with downsized military: humanitarian relief, peacekeeping, sea lane protection, and other national interest protection missions.	Shared Korean defense with United States; modest logistical support for USFK off-peninsula missions that promote regional stability.	Primary Korean defense; eventually some long-range off-peninsula missions conducted jointly with U.S. forces and other nations. Often, but not limited to, logistical support. Potential for combined missions in humanitarian relief, peacekeeping, peace enforcement, sea lane protection, counter-terrorism, counter-proliferation.
	USFK	Cooperation with Korean forces on case-by-case basis when interests overlap or in concert with other countries. Pledge of assistance if Korea is attacked and vice-versa.	Cooperation with Korean forces on regular basis for Korea defense and to a lesser extent for certain off-peninsula missions. Pledge of assistance if Korea is attacked and vice-versa.	Cooperation with Korean forces on regular basis for above-mentioned missions in concert with other countries. Pledge of assistance if Korea is attacked and vice-versa.
Force Structure	Korea	Reduced ground forces (1/3 to 1/2) and increased mobility; small, gradual increase in air and naval forces.	Reduced ground forces (1/4) and increased mobility; modest increase in air and naval forces for Korea defense.	Reduced ground forces (1/3 to 1/2) and increased mobility; increase (eventually) long-range air and naval forces.
	USFK	Virtually none, except to facilitate joint planning and joint exercises.	2nd ID reduced and reconfigured (less heavy, more mobile). Fighter wing remains. Added contingent of marines. Rotational naval presence.	2nd ID withdraws. Added contingent of marines. Command support for CJTF missions. Rotational air and naval presence.
Command Structure		USFK, CFC, UNC dissolved. Korean command conducts joint planning and exercises with PACOM or its Northeast Asia subregional component.	UNC and CFC dissolved. Parallel Korean–USFK command established for combined operations. USFK serves as subcomponent to PACOM or its Northeast Asia subregional component.	UNC and CFC dissolved. Parallel Korean–USFK command established with CJTF capability. USFK serves as subcomponent to PACOM or its Northeast Asia subregional component.
Key Systems†	Korea	To extent reduced budget allows: C⁴ISR, KDX-III destroyer (*Aegis*) on a delayed basis, system upgrades for existing platforms. No priority on inter-operability with United States.	C⁴ISR, army tactical missile system, KDX-III destroyer (*Aegis*), mid-air refueling, missile defenses. High priority on interoperability with United States.	C⁴ISR, KDX-III destroyer (*Aegis*), LPX amphibious vessel (delayed), mid-air refueling, AWACS, missile defenses. High priority on interoperability with United States.
	USFK	No Korea-specific technologies. Continue Pacific-based carrier and enhance long-range strike capability via Japan, Guam, Hawaii, Alaska, and Diego Garcia.	*Stryker* brigade; *Apache* and *Black Hawk* helicopter upgrades; F-22 / joint strike fighter; continued intelligence gathering (U2); airlift, AWACS, and mid-air refueling deployable.	Airlift, AWACS, intelligence gathering assets, and mid-air refueling deployable until Korea develops indigenous capabilities. Otherwise supported by regional air and naval assets.

†   *Weapons and systems are listed only to illustrate operational emphasis.*

Indeed, if U.S.-Korea relations permit narrow interests to dictate the terms of the alliance, the partnership will either remain shallow or eventually render itself obsolete. Indeed, one key observation emerging from this analytical exercise is that if both sides desire a stable and enduring relationship, then each will have to engage the other to promote more intangible factors, such as common values, and to create and capitalize on opportunities to cooperate. As noted earlier, it is possible that an increasingly confident Korea in the naval/air power posture, in conjunction with American encouragement and inducements, might gradually assume responsibilities for the regional/hemispheric posture. Otherwise, Washington and Seoul may find themselves hijacked (once again) by geopolitical forces and divergent threat perceptions that (pre)determine certain elements of bilateral ties that are not necessarily conducive to long-term alliance cohesion.

That the conditions and trends of the security environment can drastically alter Korea's strategic outlook, and therefore the level of mutual interest in sustaining the alliance beyond the horizon, is abundantly obvious. Less apparent is that nationalism and shifting domestic consensus within Korea are wild cards beyond the control (and expectations) of the United States and of the political elite in Seoul. The December 2002 presidential elections, in which polarizing views of the alliance emerged, exemplified the unpredictability of internal political dynamics. Indeed, Korean public opinion could swing in directions that prove inimical to the alliance and to U.S. interests in the region regardless of the prevailing external security environment outlined above.

In contrast to the recessed posture, it is also conceivable that a benign security environment might not ease Korea's perceptions and judgments of external threats (however implausible) that in turn result in strategic responses similar to those outlined in the second alternative. Heightened nationalism could convince Seoul to view Japan and China with greater suspicion even if existing conditions do not warrant such hostility. It is likely that Korea would then opt to seek a reassurance role from the United States. To be sure, negative threat perceptions in Seoul would ensure that Washington remains anchored to the fate of the peninsula. However, a threat-based alliance would likely impose its own set of opportunity costs. For instance, an insecure united Korea would be less willing or able to divert its energies toward fulfilling broader U.S. global and regional responsibilities.

Alternatively, contrary to the naval/air power posture as described, an abundance of threats in the region might not reduce nationalistic sentiments sufficiently to protect the rationale of a security partnership with the United States. In other words, domestic politics could still generate enough support to push out U.S. military presence, regardless of the objective risks to the peninsula. It is even possible, under this projection, that Korea would seek accommodation with China as an alternative security option. Such an outcome is perhaps the least desirable because of the ripple effect that a Sino-Korean entente would have across the region. An isolated Japan in this context could either strengthen its alliance with the United States or choose to bolster its defense capabilities and chart a more independent security course. Either scenario could easily trigger the competitive dynamics that have historically animated the region – and not for the better.

From an institutional and legal perspective, the need to revise the substance of the U.S.-ROK defense treaty rises in direct proportion to the degree of expansion and diversification of the alliance beyond the peninsula. In the recessed posture, the more limited nature of the alliance would obviate the need to change the treaty (if it indeed is retained), while the regional/hemispheric posture would require substantial modifications that broaden the scope of mutual obligations. The latter option would surely entail lengthy discussions and soul searching about the exact purpose of the alliance and a prolonged process of negotiations and compromises. There is thus a need to look beyond ongoing efforts to modify and streamline the alliance, and that is why a follow-up to the FOTA will be required.

A persistent theme that emerges from the three scenarios is that force structures and command structures will invariably require dramatic changes in the post-unification era. In terms of force structure, unless an overt continental threat emerges from China, Seoul will almost certainly draw down its ground forces and most likely adopt a more outward looking security strategy. The absence of a land threat would also have significant implications for the U.S. Army's posture that prevails today on the peninsula. Indeed, there will almost certainly be pressure from Korea and the United States to withdraw substantial numbers of American ground forces, though the number, types, and missions of remaining U.S. forces will be different in each case.

In terms of command structure, revisions and changes to organizations and institutions are perhaps the most difficult to achieve, given the political sensitivities associated with authority and power. For instance, proposals for subsuming a new USFK under a streamlined regional command based in Japan are likely to meet stiff resistance from Korean policy makers, who understandably fear losing an independent operational command (especially to Tokyo). Moreover, inter-service rivalries within the U.S. military could arise, since the U.S. Army will resent a major draw-down that could diminish its role in Asia. In this sense, the U.S. proposal to transfer its army headquarters in charge of Asia Pacific (I Corps) from the United States to a location in Japan could soften that sense of loss.[13] From an alliance perspective, depending on Korea's strategic orientation that may range from an insular to a participatory outlook, Seoul's military command could be either plugged seamlessly into U.S. operational planning or superficially aligned with the U.S. military posture in Asia. Organizational innovations will therefore need to be carefully thought through and deliberated as soon as possible.

Yet another common thread is that under all conceivable scenarios U.S. defense transformation in the region will not be slowed by the varying acquisition processes undertaken by Korea. The technology gap that has been so persistent in transatlantic relations will be an inescapable reality in U.S.-Korea relations as well. In an ideal world, strategy, doctrine, and operations should be the guiding elements behind technological innovation and procurement. However, history has shown that technical developments can often force changes on the doctrine and planning that harness them, and technological asymmetries that are bound to widen will invariably strain the alliance. Given the uncertainties of the technological aspects of the alliance, Washington and Seoul need to tackle the strategic dimensions of the partnership to lessen the shocks that could emerge from a major capabilities rift.

A net assessment of the three scenarios suggests that the regionally oriented outcome benefits Washington and Seoul the most and maximizes the goals envisioned in the ideal situation described in chapter 4. Moreover, a diversified posture is more conducive to trilateral security cooperation among the United States, Korea, and Japan that could promote burden sharing, and it would facilitate the ability of the U.S. military to fulfill its extra-regional obligations and commitments. But the objectives of such an alliance are also the most difficult to realize. Indeed, despite the obvious benefits of this diversified and ambitious alternative, it is not immediately evident that the U.S.-ROK alliance is moving, or is capable of leaning, in that direction in the absence of direct policy intervention at the highest levels.

In order for both sides to look beyond narrow interests and to facilitate a convergence in broader values, which are the critical ingredients for the alliance to diversify its potential capabilities, a more proactive public diplomatic effort to solicit Korean views of the future will be required. In sum, all of the projections and associated analysis above suggest that joint U.S.-ROK preparations should be made now in order to pave the way for the major changes and upheavals that will almost certainly accompany the strategic transformation on the Korean Peninsula.

Notes for Chapter Eight

1   In a speech marking the fifty-eighth anniversary of Korea's liberation from Japanese rule at the end of World War II, President Roh said that he would "prepare a basis for our military to posses an independent defense capability within the next decade." *JoongAng Daily,* August 16, 2003.

2   The ROK government intends to submit these MOUs to the National Assembly for approval, handling them almost as if they were international treaties. In the United States, Congress will only be involved to the extent that appropriations are required to fulfill U.S. obligations, and these funds will probably be a part of larger appropriations bills for the Defense Department or military construction.

3   "U.S. Said to Seek Regional Role for Forces in Korea," *JoongAng Daily,* October 10, 2003, http://joongangdaily.joins.com/200310/10/20031 01000004305439900090209021.html.

4   Yoo Yong-won, "U.S. Troops Not Leaving JSA So Fast," *Chosun Ilbo*,
    September 3, 2003, http://english.chosun.com/cgi-bin/printNews?i
    d=200309030034 (December 19, 2003).

5   Ser Myo-Ja, "Security Meeting Comes Up Short," *JoongAng Daily*,
    November 17, 2003, http://joongangdaily.joins.com/200311/17/200
    31117230901110990009030903.html.

6   OSD refutes this line of reasoning by pointing out that the USFK
    move south provides no sanctuary from longer-range North Korean
    missiles and that they are in some ways an easier target for the KPA
    because U.S. forces can be attacked with less expected Korean civil-
    ian collateral damage.

7   The ROK National Security Council document instead says that
    North Korea "still remains a direct threat to our security." Choi
    Jie-ho, "'Main Enemy' is Dropped as Description of North Korea,"
    JoongAng Daily, March 4, 2004.

8   Article 6 of the Treaty of Mutual Cooperation and Security between
    the United States of America and Japan begins, "For the purpose
    of contributing to the security of Japan and the maintenance of in-
    ternational peace and security in the Far East, the United States of
    America is granted the use by its land, air and naval forces of facili-
    ties and areas in Japan." This reference to "international peace and
    security in the Far East" is a broader mandate than that mentioned
    in the Mutual Defense Treaty between the ROK and the United
    States, which is concerned only with an "armed attack in the Pacific
    area on either of the Parties in territories now under their respective
    administrative control..."

9   Article 4 of the Washington Treaty allows for consultation among
    the NATO Allies on a wider range of security risks than direct
    armed attacks on Allied territory (which are covered under Articles
    5 and 6), and, when deemed appropriate, for Allied coordination in
    responding to such risks. It was to Article 4, therefore, that NATO
    member states increasingly turned as the Atlantic Alliance took
    steps in the 1990s to address a growing list of post-Cold War chal-
    lenges – including ethnic conflict, terrorism, and WMD proliferation
    – that directly influenced NATO security, but had little to do per se
    with NATO's core collective defense mission as enshrined in Arti-
    cles 5 and 6. See, for example, Part I, Paragraph 12, in *The Alliance's
    Strategic Concept Agreed by Heads of State and Government Participating
    in the Meeting of the North Atlantic Council*, Rome, November 8, 1991,
    http://www.nato.int/docu/basictxt/b911108a.htm.

10 The 1994 Brussels summit endorsed the development of the CJTF
    concept intended to facilitate NATO's ability to cope with non-
    collective defense contingencies (and, when required, to operate
    alongside other non-member states). After NATO determined that
    the CJTF required a test phase before further execution in 1996,
    subsequent trials and assessments from 1997 to 1998 proved that

the concept was viable and strong enough for future implementation. Since the late 1990s, many training exercises and post-September 11 operations, such as the CJTF Horn of Africa operation in Djibouti, have solidified the operational standing of the concept.

11   In a recent interview in *The Oriental Economist,* Michael McDevitt underscored the operational value of retaining a closely integrated U.S.-ROK binational planning staff and some form of combined command structure in any successor organization to CFC. See Michael McDevitt, "U.S. Commitment to Asia is Strong," *The Oriental Economist* 72, no. 3 (March 2004): 12-13.

12   For a comprehensive discussion of values-based alliance renovation, see Victor D. Cha, "Values after Victory: The Future of U.S.-Japan-Korea Relations," *Comparative Connections, E-Journal on East Asian Bilateral Relations,* Pacific Forum CSIS, special annual issue, July 2002. http://www.csis.org/pacfor/annual/2002annual.html.

13   "U.S. Eyes Japan for Army Headquarters," *International Herald Tribune/Asahi Shimbun,* March 3, 2004.

CHAPTER NINE

Conclusions & Recommendations

///

As this study demonstrates, the U.S.-ROK alliance has arrived at an important crossroads, perhaps the most pivotal time in its history, and it coincides with fundamental changes in South Korean society, American strategic planning and military transformation, and the region's geopolitical and economic environment. The two nations' diverging threat perceptions and security priorities are undermining some of the basic foundations of the bilateral alliance, and, if it is not nurtured, the alliance will almost certainly weaken and potentially wither. Despite the sense by many in both countries that a U.S. military presence in Korea has potential value even after unification, the prospects for the alliance (and, by extension, that presence) look uncertain in the event of a united Korea.

At the same time, however, the maturation of South Korea's economy and democracy is contributing to new bilateral linkages and offers an opportunity for Washington and Seoul to find broader common ground, diversify the alliance, and build a new platform for security and other forms of cooperation. Eventually, this new platform could become the basis for a reinvigorated and more stable security relationship, long after the original premise and its accompanying command and force structures cease to apply. There is a desire to move in this general direction in both capitals, but with several other domestic and international challenges demanding attention, it is difficult for policy makers to spend the time and political capital necessary to move forward more aggressively.

Although the United States and the ROK have improved the frequency and quality of official dialogues regarding these issues in the past two years, the discussions are still not adequate in their current form to develop a comprehensive, mutual understanding of each other's future goals and objectives for the alliance (including the public perspective). This is in part because neither government, particularly the ROK, has decided for certain what it wants from the other in the long term. The political turmoil in South Korea and a long election year in the United States exacerbate the problem. South Korea says that it wants to improve U.S.-Korean relations and, at the same time, to pursue an independent national defense posture, but it is not adequately seizing the opportunity that the FOTA offers to pursue alliance diversification in support of its stated goals. With the clock running out on the FOTA, there is not enough time in this forum to develop a detailed plan to achieve future alliance objectives that enjoys wide Korean public support and that meshes well with other U.S. strategic adjustments in the region.

If the United States and South Korea are serious about strengthening and maintaining their alliance for the future (and this study outlines several reasons why they should pursue this course), then they must consider a substantive process to follow the FOTA and build on its momentum. This process needs to identify and articulate American goals more broadly and clearly, while at the same time it solicits and incorporates South Korean viewpoints and priorities more comprehensively. Although the details and circumstances are different, this effort (as suggested throughout this study) might not be unlike the revision of the U.S.-Japan Defense Guidelines in the mid 1990s or NATO's New Strategic Concept in 1991 (fifth revision) and 1999 (sixth revision). In the U.S.-ROK case, the purpose is less to enhance the alliance (as in the U.S.-Japan experience) than it is to diversify its function in preparation for an eventual de-emphasis of its original, peninsula-focused rationale.[1] The style could mirror the U.S.-Japan example (that is, bilateral talks with a chief executive mandate), but the substance might hew more closely to the NATO revisions (given the potential for joint peacekeeping and similar stability-minded missions abroad).

It is clear from this study that there are numerous barriers and complicating factors with which to contend before a U.S.-ROK consultation process can be successful. Largely because of these complicating factors, however, the task is urgent and should not be avoided or delayed much longer. If former President Carter's mission to Pyongyang in 1993 had failed and the Clinton administration carried out its plans to strike the Yongbyon nuclear facility, the U.S.-ROK alliance would have suffered a serious blow, but it is likely that the alliance would have survived, given the political climate in Seoul and the regional strategic environment at the time. With all that has changed in the last ten years, however, it is unclear how the bilateral relationship would fare if Washington decided that it had to take a similar action today to protect its national security. There is no doubt that such a move would inflict greater damage on the alliance now than in the past, and perhaps even cause irreparable harm to the relationship. This fragility will persist without a concerted effort by both governments.

The United States and South Korea must begin by acknowledging their increasingly divergent threat perceptions and security priorities, and then take steps to bridge those gaps as much as possible. As a part of this process, the United States needs to better define and articulate its goals for the alliance and make a greater effort to convince the ROK and its citizens of America's continued, strong commitment to South Korea's security, as well as explain the potential benefits to Seoul of alliance diversification. In order to achieve this, the United States should encourage Seoul to define and articulate its own goals more clearly, especially now that South Korean foreign policy appears to be in a period of transition. U.S. officials will have to listen carefully to Seoul's positions and demonstrate that they understand South Korea's perspective, trying to accommodate its priorities as best they can, while still pursuing America's security agenda. The rest of this chapter outlines a series of steps that Washington can take to begin this process in earnest, and it proposes recommendations for a diversified alliance posture that promotes U.S. and ROK interests in a practical manner.

Establishing a Broader, Deeper Dialogue for the Short and Long Term

The initial step toward realizing alliance diversification and re-invigorating the U.S.-ROK security relationship is to establish a bilateral dialogue specifically designed for this purpose. Although the FOTA talks have been productive, they were not able to stimulate a thorough enough debate, either in government circles or among the public, about how the future of the alliance could be shaped, let alone provide a forum for exploring, detailing, and deciding upon alternative visions. This new dialogue could quite easily pick up from where the FOTA leaves off (call it FOTA 2), but it will ultimately be a different process, one that is more ambitious and open-ended, and one that more directly enjoys presidential imprimaturs in both capitals.

FOTA 2 might not even require the launching of a totally new, formal set of talks; instead an existing bilateral coordination mechanism could be specifically (and publicly) charged with moving more aggressively on the original agenda planned for the FOTA's second year. OSD is already considering ways that the allies could monitor the implementation of FOTA agreements such as mission transfers and the other MOUs. One idea is for the Policy Review Subcommittee (PRS) of the SCM, which now meets only once or twice a year, to meet more frequently to oversee the FOTA accords. The PRS involves many of the same government and military officials who have been involved in the FOTA.

The downside of the PRS approach, however, is that it could become consumed with smoothing out wrinkles and refereeing disagreements regarding FOTA implementation. This would not only distract from the alliance diversification task, but it would also fail to sufficiently separate the logistical issues of USFK re-alignment from broader, long-range alliance issues, which was a weakness of the original FOTA in the first place. In this sense, allowing the PRS to deal solely with FOTA implementation and setting up a separate (though perhaps linked) set of negotiations might be the best answer. Whatever format is adopted, FOTA 2 should be specifically focused on alliance diversification and be capable of incorporating a diverse range of inputs from government and public sources.

Even though FOTA 2 could still be led by OSD in the United States and the ROK's MND, both presidents should invest more political capital in the process, and the White House and the Blue House will have to play a larger role in energizing and driving the dialogue. There is almost as much work to be done to create a consensus on the alliance's future within each government as there is between the two countries, so a delicate balance between the domestic and bilateral discussions will need to be managed in the early stages of the talks.

The early goal should be an agreement on a broad set of alliance diversification principles, which can then be turned into something similar to the U.S.-Japan Joint Declaration on Security that was signed by President Clinton and Prime Minister Hashimoto in 1996.[2] That document set the stage for a review and revision of the Japan-U.S. Defense Guidelines, which ultimately allowed for such unforeseen developments as the provision of Japanese logistical support for operation Enduring Freedom in Afghanistan and the application of the allies' acquisition and cross-servicing agreement to U.S. and Japanese troops serving in Iraq. The first round of FOTA talks was launched at the ministerial level, but a more comprehensive set of discussions that would truly remake the alliance would need to be inaugurated in some form by the two presidents.

It might be possible, indeed even advisable, to break down FOTA 2 into two different discussion tracks, one focused on long-term issues related to alliance diversification and the future of

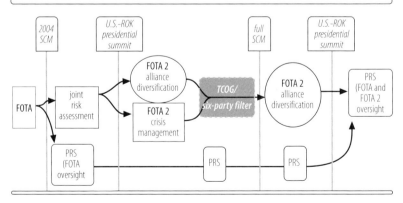

POTENTIAL FLOW of BILATERAL CONSULTATIONS
RELATED to U.S.-ROK ALLIANCE DIVERSIFICATION

the security relationship (including the enduring interests and identity of the alliance), and the other dedicated to short-term, crisis management contingencies that could arise in the next few years, while the two governments are working on the longer-range details. A joint risk assessment study (building on past efforts) might be a useful start to feed into both of these tracks, by identifying which risks require immediate attention and helping to harmonize the objectives of a diversified alliance.

The first track should be a methodical and relatively transparent process. As noted above, the early stages involve a period of internal and bilateral consensus building regarding both countries' regional outlooks, their threat perceptions and strategic priorities, and their long-term expectations for (and tolerance for financial and political investment in) the alliance. It would begin by dealing with and agreeing upon broad concepts, and then progress to greater levels of specificity regarding future roles and missions, complementary force and command structures, capabilities and technologies, advisable treaty changes and other legal adjustments or enhancements, and the alliance's place within a regional context.

This is not to suggest that, simply given enough time, such an ambitious and far-reaching dialogue will somehow naturally yield an agreement on alliance diversification. The U.S.-Japan and NATO experiences are, to some extent, success stories that might not be replicable in the US-ROK case. Chapters 5 and 6 identified numerous obstacles to agreement in both countries, and new impediments will almost certainly come to the fore. Simply initiating this dialogue does not ensure success. By engaging sincerely in this effort, however, the United States has a better chance of shaping the regional security environment to its liking than if it does not try. For the United States to achieve its goals, a certain amount of persuasion will be required, since diversification is essentially about forging a grand bargain that will involve a series of tradeoffs – costs and benefits – for both countries. If Washington does not achieve all of its objectives, the effort will still have been worthwhile, since the allies will be better able to cope with the transition to a new, constructive security relationship in the future, even if it does not include a permanent USFK presence.

As the discussions mature, the public in each country (particularly in South Korea) should be involved as much as possible. This can be accomplished indirectly, perhaps by including (or at least regularly briefing) elected officials in the process, and it can be pursued directly, through public appearances by government officials in person, in town hall meetings, on broadcast media, and via print interviews. Bilateral and multilateral policy conferences involving academics, think-tank policy analysts, and the media are another means of public engagement. It is also a way to extend the discussions beyond just the United States and South Korea, in order to reassure neighboring countries of the allies' intentions. In particular, Seoul and Washington might want to utilize a version of the TCOG (involving Japan) as a means of extending the coordination of roles and missions and military investments, though this might come later on in the process. The views of China will also have to be taken into consideration, possibly through separate bilateral discussions with South Korea and the United States. The next section in this chapter outlines in more detail a set of recommendations, from the U.S. perspective, for the first-track dialogue and alliance diversification in general.

The second track, however, would probably be more technical in nature and could include identifying near-term (and possibly sensitive) crisis scenarios involving North Korea that have the potential to place severe strain on the alliance if not managed effectively and in close cooperation. Such scenarios might include attempts by Pyongyang to export WMD components or other illicit cargo (particularly if it is caught in the act), a North Korean nuclear weapons test, or some form of DPRK military incursion, either unprovoked or in response to a ratcheting up of economic sanctions pressure on the North (by the UN or a coalition of willing nations) due to delay or failure in the six-party talks. The discussions would focus not only on the concrete, coordinated response to an incident, but also on minimizing the potential diplomatic fallout when a particularly sensitive event threatens to drive a wedge between the allies.

Bilateral discussions on the second track would be handled more discreetly and could involve table-top exercises, and gaming out various contingencies and possible coordinated policy and military responses. In certain cases, other members of the six-party process (Japan, China, and Russia) might also be included in (or simply briefed on) the exercises. There is no doubt that the fear of leaks or otherwise tipping the North Koreans off to likely U.S. policy responses would be a limiting factor on the amount and type of detail discussed on the second track, but it is also clear that the United States and South Korea cannot wait until an incident occurs and then expect to quickly react in harmony with one another. In this sense, while the first track is geared toward alliance diversification, the second track is focused on alliance preservation.

The second track might also deal with the USFK's role during the process of Korean unification, since the alliance would likely play a unique and important stabilizing role during this uncertain time. This is especially true in the event that the early stages of reconciliation are accompanied by a rapid decline in the North's ability to maintain governmental control. Managing a potentially large flow of North Korean refugees toward China or South Korea is one concern, as is accounting for and monitoring the dismantlement of the DPRK's nuclear weapons program or other WMD stockpiles. Even if North-South reconciliation follows a carefully orchestrated timetable of CBMs and deepening economic cooperation, the oversight of CBM implementation (such as pull-backs of conventional forces and weapons systems) could involve the USFK. The details of command structure adjustments will also need to be considered during this transition period.

The First Steps toward a
Post-Unification Force Structure

While it is impossible to predict exactly how a FOTA 2 dialogue might evolve, how the ROK will react, or what kind of outcome could emerge, it is possible to sketch out an initial game plan for U.S. officials to follow based on prudent assumptions about the regional strategic landscape and America's security priorities. In this context, the third alternative (regional/hemispheric posture) described in chapter 8 can serve as a useful starting point for discussion, since it is not overly optimistic or pessimistic, and because it clearly has the potential to serve both countries' national interests in the long run. Moreover, as noted in chapter 8, this alternative is not determined solely by the course of events and it requires more active deliberation and nurturing by the allies for it to evolve properly, so it lends itself to a proactive approach.

The first step, therefore, is to initiate an interagency discussion in the U.S. government considering all three strategic posture alternatives outlined in chapter 8, but focusing primarily on the regional/hemispheric posture. Overlapping this internal debate, the United States should engage ROK officials and listen to their thoughts regarding the long-term future of the alliance, incorporating their feedback into the discussions in Washington. A joint study assessing the peninsular and regional risks to both countries could be a part of this process. The goal is to test the waters in the first few meetings for various diversification concepts, ideally settling on a rough framework that administration officials in both countries can build upon to prepare the alliance for a united Korea. The fundamentals of alliance diversification, which focuses on mutuality and compatibility, will likely include the following:

- In the intervening period prior to Korean reconciliation and unification, diversification is supplemental to (and does not detract from) defense of the ROK against DPRK aggression.
- For the United States, a diversified alliance provides versatility to U.S. forces for carrying out counter-terrorist and stabilization missions off-peninsula that are supported by a more able and complementary ally.
- For the ROK, a diversified alliance facilitates a non-threatening (to neighbors) and cost-effective power projection capability to ensure its basic national security goals, including self-defense and the protection of its economic and energy security interests, in addition to enhanced independence in a more stable region.
- Diversification lays the groundwork for a post-unification, U.S.-Korea security relationship, should one be desired by the two countries at that time.
- Diversification involves bridging multiple gaps between the separate tracks of the alliance relationship

(for example, military, diplomatic, economic, and, of increasing importance, civil society).

· Diversification is part of a regional effort that aims to dampen military competition and enhance security cooperation in the Asia Pacific as a whole.

The second step is to move beyond a discussion about broad concepts and begin detailed negotiations on a road map for diversifying the alliance that both presidents can endorse publicly in a high-profile setting, such as a bilateral presidential summit. The 1996 Japan-U.S. Joint Declaration on Security was a sweeping document, expressing the president's and the prime minister's concurring beliefs regarding a number of issues, including the bilateral alliance, their security treaty, and the importance of bilateral, regional, and global cooperation under the auspices of their security relationship. Within the declaration were both broad statements (about continuing close consultation on defense policies and military postures, for instance) and specific policies (such as formally launching the review of the Defense Guidelines and singling out the F-2 support fighter program as a model for cooperative research and development). The declaration provided a strategic direction and a political foundation for the subsequent Defense Guidelines revision process, and it put presidential/prime ministerial credibility on the negotiating table. Equally important was the declaration's emphasis on common values that underpin the alliance: "the maintenance of freedom, the pursuit of democracy, and respect for human rights."

As alluded to earlier, there are several reasons why a similar attempt at a U.S.-ROK declaration on security might evolve differently than in the U.S.-Japan case. The trickiest aspect is the possibility that Washington and Seoul could still be in the midst of a mild security crisis (a tense standoff with the North) while they discuss the outline of a new relationship for a situation that cannot be known at this time. In contrast, the U.S.-Japan talks took place in a relatively benign security environment. It is worth remembering, however, that during their negotiations, the United States and Japan thought that they were most likely planning for a North Korean contingency, yet the early tests for the new guidelines came in such unexpected locations as the Indian Ocean and Iraq.

The GWOT was not on U.S. and Japanese minds during the guidelines revision, but their recent cooperation in this contingency (including the PSI) would probably not have been possible were it not for those discussions in the late 1990s. In other words, the U.S.-Japan experience demonstrates that there is not always a direct correlation between the expectations and planning assumptions underlying exercises in alliance adaptation and the payoffs resulting from such a renewal process. In the U.S.-ROK case, a dialogue about new forms of security cooperation in the region will always be supplemental to the primary focus on the DPRK, but negotiators should keep in mind that the supplemental or diversified alliance activities may someday become primary functions when the DPRK threat recedes, and they may become such in unanticipated ways in support of missions not yet imagined.

Another key difference in the South Korean case is that it does not have the same constitutional restrictions as Japan on offensive firepower or collective defense actions. On the one hand, this allows the ROK to participate in a wider range of joint operations with the U.S. military, but on the other hand it means that Seoul has more flexibility to develop its own force projection capability and spurn U.S. collaboration. In this sense, the U.S.-Japan Defense Guidelines revision was a relatively simple process, since the range of options for joint military activity was narrower than would be the case for the United States and South Korea. This has implications for everything from the nature and intensity of public debate to the potential need for treaty or other legal adjustments.

In short, the more strategic choices that the ROK enjoys in the future, the broader the range of issues that can be addressed, and the more that can potentially go wrong in the dialogue. This key difference between Japan and South Korea leads to a surprisingly similar result, which is that the United States is wise to begin with a modest agenda of adjustments at first, and then seek input from its ally as to what modifications are feasible in the short term. For example, pursuit of the CJTF concept and conducting joint peace enforcement or combat operations off-peninsula are not advisable at this time, but a focus on humanitarian operations, civil emergencies, and consequence management is appropriate. Over time, the agenda of alliance adjustments can be expanded (for example, to involve peace support and counter-proliferation activities), as each country evaluates progress, domestic reaction, and the regional security environment.

Once the political endorsement for alliance diversification has been agreed to by the two capitals, the next step is for both sides to flesh out the details regarding logistics and procedures (i.e., the operational endorsement). It is likely that Washington and Seoul will be in the midst of implementing the FOTA results when they reach this stage of FOTA 2, so an early focus should be on identifying any obvious synergies (or inconsistencies) between FOTA investments and the potential adjustments under FOTA 2. If the optimal end result is a regional posture outlined in alternative 3 (chapter 8), then the allies can expect that facilities in the Osan/Pyongtaek area would become an even more important asset for the alliance over the long term. Mid-air refueling capacity, enhanced strategic airlift capability, and the close proximity of U.S. and ROK troops (marines or special operations forces) ready for rapid deployment would be consistent with an alliance prepared to respond to various regional contingencies.

Over time, the 2nd Infantry Division, as currently configured, could essentially be replaced by ROK forces (depending on progress toward North-South reconciliation) and by more mobile U.S. forces, while the U.S. naval presence in South Korea could be slowly enhanced. The latter would probably not involve permanently stationing U.S. ships at ROK bases, but instead would include sharing assets with Japan, more frequent port-of-call visits, increased joint training activities, and a more sophisticated U.S. infrastructure in South Korea for logistical support. The CJTF opportunities can be explored in more detail at a later date, after alliance diversification has been initiated.

Other issues that will need to be looked at during this phase are any treaty or legal adjustments that would be necessary to accommodate the changing roles and missions. The U.S.-ROK Mutual Defense Treaty is a relatively brief document that does not go much beyond a commitment to aid each other if either of the parties is attacked (Article 3). It might be necessary to build upon Article 2, for example, which outlines a consultative process in case "either of the Parties [thinks it] is threatened by external armed attack," and suggests that they consult on how to "maintain and develop appropriate means" to "deter armed attack...by self-help and mutual aid." It might be possible to expand upon the spirit of consultation and response flexibility in Article 2 in determining how to respond to a wider variety of threats to regional stability, such as protection of vital sea lanes, assisting failing states, or countering illicit trading activities. In this sense, an agreed interpretation – or, if necessary, revision – of Article 2 may be warranted to bring it closer to the consultative process allowed for the NATO Allies under Article 4 of the North Atlantic Treaty, which, as noted earlier in chapter 8, has paved the way for NATO policy coordination and joint military action on security challenges beyond Europe and having little to do with a direct armed attack on Allied territory. Still another example that might serve as a guide would be Article 6 of the U.S.-Japan Security Treaty, which specifically identifies "the maintenance of international peace and security in the Far East" as a reason for allowing U.S. forces to reside in Japan.

In the context of the overall U.S. alliance structure in Northeast Asia, there will inevitably be a certain degree of overlap between the capabilities of the USFJ and the USFK, which is to some extent by design. Even if similar assets reside in both Japan and South Korea, they are likely to be deployed in different ways and will also require joint training tailored to the specific roles of indigenous forces. Some of this can be achieved by sharing certain assets between the USFJ and the USFK and by conducting training exercises in both countries, perhaps at times coordinating trilaterally. But if U.S. and ROK forces are truly going to operate jointly in off-peninsula missions, then there will be no substitute for a permanent U.S. presence in Korea, particularly at a command and control level, to facilitate bilateral cooperation and communication in-country and in coordination with U.S. military commanders at PACOM. This is especially true if the potential exists for the USFK and ROK forces to operate together in a combat environment, which would be a distinctly different form of cooperation than that between the USFJ and Japan's SDF.

Building a Regional Coalition to Fight Terrorism and Promote Stability

As described in chapter 4, one of America's main objectives should be to build a regional coalition in East Asia to be prepared to fight terrorism and promote regional stability. This coalition could become the means by which U.S.-ROK alliance diversification operates, and it would center around America's treaty and major non-NATO allies in Asia: Japan, the ROK, Australia, Thailand, and the Philippines (and involve other security partners like Singapore). The coalition should also involve other regional powers, namely Russia and China, as much as possible. The so-called "founding members" of this coalition (the treaty and major non-NATO allies) would probably agree to a comprehensive relationship that includes a significant military function, but other (lesser) partners might be able to pick and choose those support activities that best suit their national interests and local political conditions.

China is particularly important in this effort, both in terms of what it can contribute to the region and because of the destabilizing effect an isolated China (or a China that perceives itself as such) could have in Asia. The focus on countering terrorism should be reassuring to the PRC, since it would be clear that the coalition is not aimed at containing China. In fact, the coalition would seek the involvement of the PRC, and Russia, whenever possible, since both of these countries have a stake in combating terrorist networks and limiting their access to WMD.

Against the backdrop of recent bombings and related acts of terror within Russia proper by Chechen extremists, Moscow's interest in broader cooperation on anti-terror/counter-WMD activities may be quite high. As for China, the prospects for attracting broader support from Beijing on this front also seem to have grown in recent years (and months, really) as Chinese authorities have moved away from their somewhat blasé, "we can understand it," attitude toward North Korean proliferation activities, and begun to worry openly about the possible transfer of WMD capabilities (be it via a deliberate act or as a result of domestic chaos) from the DPRK to dissident factions in the PRC (notably among the Islamic Uighurs of Xinjiang province).

Ideally, U.S.-ROK alliance diversification should be a part of a broader effort to enhance regional security cooperation overall, and this goal needs to be kept in mind during the bilateral negotiations. The allies do not necessarily have to consult with Chinese officials during the talks, but some method of reassuring Beijing will pay dividends over the long term. As for the ROK, it can decide how aggressively it wants to participate in this coalition, but every effort should be made to facilitate its involvement (and chapters 4 and 6 outline several reasons why participation might be attractive to Seoul). Discussions on the future of regional security cooperation (and Korea's role in the region) are closely linked to the FOTA 2 talks, and they can be mutually reinforcing. Alliance diversification is aimed at integrating Korea into a system of regional cooperation, and regional cooperation will be significantly enhanced by Korea's active participation.

That said, there will undoubtedly be some difficulties in linking the FOTA 2 talks with discussions on regional security cooperation, and, if anything, it should be recognized as well that bilateral negotiations between the United States and the ROK – as well as between the United States and its other major non-NATO allies in the Asia-Pacific region – will be the driver behind future regional collaboration, not the other way around. Knitting together a regional security architecture out of the six-party talks, the ARF, or from scratch will be a time-consuming process, and success could be ambiguous and tenuous. Numerous potential stumbling blocks were outlined in chapter 4. FOTA 2, therefore, should not be dependent on progress in the more broadly cast effort to create a stronger structure for security cooperation in Asia overall.

Because the vision for regional cooperation proposed in this study is based on the prior existence of healthy, future-oriented bilateral agreements, the emphasis first and foremost should be on strengthening America's primary bilateral security relationships in the region and on identifying ways that they can complement each other in a loose, multilateral framework. Expanding the range of topics discussed in the TCOG and strengthening that trilateral connection is one way of facilitating this transition. There is already a solid analytical foundation for a coordinated bilateral/multilateral approach, as demonstrated in the literature review in chapter 3 of this study. Such an approach can also serve as a useful hedge against the possible slow development of regional cooperation or its failure to emerge any time soon as a credible and effective component of a new security architecture in the Asia-Pacific region.

Overall, the presence of U.S. forces in Korea could indicate to neighboring nations a low likelihood for military conflict on the peninsula by limiting any prospect for an unnecessary ROK arms buildup, while at the same time making it more difficult for any regional heavyweight to intimidate a temporarily fragile country obsessed with the task of unification. In theory, at least, Russia, China, and Japan could thereby reduce the amount that they would need to spend on border or coastal defense (compared to what they would likely spend in an environment of open competition). A long-term U.S. military presence on the Korean Peninsula, therefore, can be viewed as a means to lower regional military expenditures, which will allow for greater investments in productive infrastructure and, by extension, brighten the prospects for peace and prosperity.

Strengthening the Non-Military Aspects of the Bilateral Relationship

The final major recommendation of this study is for the United States to adopt policies aimed at strengthening the non-military aspects of the bilateral relationship, much in the same way that it does with Japan and other European allies. While it is true that a military alliance can be founded (and even endure, to some extent) solely on mutual strategic interest, such a relationship tends to be vulnerable to obsolescence when strategic interests begin to diverge. By the same token, a military alliance that is embedded within a strong and multi-faceted bilateral partnership can still lose its relevance under similar circumstances, even if the other aspects of the relationship continue to flourish. The threshold for alliance deterioration, however, is much higher in the latter scenario, which is to say that a wider gap in common interests can be accommodated in a broad-based alliance and still retain its military component. The U.S.-ROK alliance is certainly not a one-dimensional, military-only relationship (as this study demonstrates), but neither is it as deeply rooted as the U.S.-European or U.S.-Japanese relationships, and there are steps that U.S. policy makers can take to address this deficiency.

Although there is no simple way to strengthen bilateral ties at the grassroots level, educational and professional exchange programs are effective over the long term, such as those supported by the Japan-United States Friendship Commission, the German Marshall Fund of the United States, and other organizations. A similar, U.S.-based foundation to promote U.S.-Korean ties does not exist, but it could be a productive investment in an important alliance relationship, and Congress should consider endowing such a foundation. Endowing a United States-Korea foundation (at anywhere from $10 million to $100 million) would allow for the funding of a broad range of programs including Korean studies at U.S. universities, pre-college educational exchanges, policy studies and Track II policy dialogues, cultural exchanges, journalism and other professional fellowship programs, and possibly even documentary film projects. This foundation could collaborate to some degree with the Korea Foundation (which is affiliated with MOFAT), as well as initiate its own projects.

It is easy to underestimate the impact that these kinds of programs can have on a bilateral relationship. Each project, individually, only touches a small number of people, but taken together they can be influential over the long term. This is especially true when combined with efforts by organizations in the counterpart country (such as the Japanese government's Japan Exchange and Teachers Program, other projects supported by the Japan Foundation, as well as private companies in both countries). Strengthening mutual understanding and personal friendships among average citizens and the intelligentsia in the two nations is a long-term strategy for building public support of a diversified alliance.

In 2000, for example, there were nearly fifty-one thousand American high school students enrolled in Japanese language courses, compared to about twenty-four thousand in 1990.[3] This is due in large part to the provision of financial resources from various private and public organizations, and it helps make Japanese the fifth most popular foreign language at that level (after Spanish, French, German, and Italian). In contrast, only two hundred U.S. high school students were studying Korean in 2000. This gap can be explained in part by the larger size of Japan's economy and the popularity of its products and pop culture, but it is also a function of more available resources for teachers: teacher training, textbooks, and audio-visual aids.

Another valuable Japan-centered program supported by U.S. government funds is the Mike Mansfield Fellowship Program. This program enables U.S. federal government employees to learn Japanese and experience long-term placements in Japanese government offices, and it could be a model for a new, Korea-specific program. Government-to-government ties can be further supported by increasing the quality and quantity of legislative exchanges between the two countries, including strengthening the U.S. congressional caucus on Korea . This caucus meets occasionally in Washington, but in general it is less vibrant than other caucuses focused on America's relationships with its security partners.

Expanding involvement in Korea by the U.S. National Endowment for Democracy (NED) is yet another opportunity to strengthen the relationship, as is fostering interaction between U.S. and Korean NGOs in humanitarian and relief activities. In 1998, President Kim Dae-jung and President Clinton established the Democracy Forum to further democracy and market economies in East Asia. The NED and the Sejong Institute in South Korea were designated as the organizing institutions to carry out this forum's joint program of mutual exchange, education, and networking. The Democracy Forum could be developed into a more formal organization with enhanced programming funded by a U.S.-Korea foundation. An additional example is the Conference on North Korean Human Rights and Refugees, now in its fifth year. This three-day international conference was held in Poland in 2004, and it was organized by the Citizens' Alliance for North Korean Human Rights (winner of the NED's 2003 Democracy Award) and the Helsinki Foundation for Human Rights. The NED and the *Chosun Ilbo*, a large ROK news organization, were sponsors.

These kinds of efforts only supplement official military and governmental exchanges, and they do not include the vast amount of private sector interaction that is arguably the most important channel, but they underscore a commitment to common values of democracy and human liberty that has the potential to be the strongest bond between our two nations. All of these efforts, tied together, can be part of a proactive American strategy to redesign and reinvigorate the U.S.-ROK alliance for a mutually beneficial future.

Realizing Alliance Diversification

U.S.-ROK alliance diversification is a practical and prudent step for mitigating the potential negative impacts that dramatic change on the peninsula could have on the U.S-Korean bilateral relationship and on the regional security environment as a whole. Nevertheless, the road map for success on this front is neither obvious nor easily drawn by the two countries. Diversification ultimately involves overcoming numerous political, logistical, cultural, and legal hurdles. The beginning of this process, however, probably has more to do with creating a positive atmosphere for open and constructive dialogue than it does with tackling technical details.

Discussions with U.S. alliance managers in Washington reveal that many perceive an underlying difference in tone when they hold meetings with their South Korean counterparts, compared to talks with Japanese officials. U.S.-ROK negotiations are described as having a slightly harder edge to them or a tinge of zero-sum mentality that suggests one side's gain is another side's loss. Similarly, ROK officials sometimes complain that they find themselves responding to U.S. demands instead of working together to craft a mutually agreed upon agenda at the outset.

The point of this observation is not to lay blame on one side or the other, but instead to recognize that the way in which these bilateral talks are conducted will need to accommodate South Korea's political and economic maturation. To accomplish this, the two countries will have to make adjustments in how they interact with each other and look to capitalize on the growing convergence of national values and broad national interests. Seoul must be less defensive and more open to new ideas for revising the division of labor regarding the maintenance of security on the peninsula and in the region, commensurate with the ROK's rising status. Enhanced status and an increased level of respect in the region will require Korea to take on more responsibility, to be more accountable for its own fate, and to develop a broader, less Korea-centric world view.

For its part, Washington should work harder to solicit and incorporate South Korean opinions early in the agenda-building process for any subsequent negotiations on alliance issues, recognizing that the ROK has become less dependent on the United States over the years and that its leaders are more accountable to the voting public than ever before. Understanding and factoring in Korean perspectives and requirements will be central to any successful effort to reform and diversify the U.S.-ROK alliance relationship. Such an approach, in fact, is perhaps the only way to assure the level of mutual commitment that will be necessary for a FOTA 2-like alliance review.

Historically, the Korean Peninsula has played a subsidiary role in the broader regional context ever since its first encounter with the United States. From the great power competition over Korea at the turn of the twentieth century to the division of the peninsula during the Cold War, Korea was generally considered by the United States as just one part of a much bigger geopolitical tapestry. These larger concerns and events essentially underplayed, if they did not subsume, Korea's importance as an individual player. It is high time to treat the Korean Peninsula on its own terms. This period of fluid transition presents a unique opportunity to turn the historical tide in a way that both recognizes and elevates the strategic significance of Korea, and to do so in a manner that secures vital U.S. and ROK interests while minimizing the negative forces that have for so long troubled this critical region.

Notes for Chapter Nine

1   In the U.S.-Japan case, the defense of Japan remains the central pillar of the alliance, and the coordination of security operations surrounding Japan (upon which the revisions focused) was already a part of the U.S.-Japan Security Treaty. In this sense, the revisions were an enhancement of a pre-existing alliance function. In the U.S.-ROK case, "diversification" implies that an entirely new alliance function would be added to the Mutual Defense Treaty.

2   The U.S.-Japan Joint Declaration on Security: Alliance for the 21st
     Century was signed by President Clinton and Prime Minister Hashi-
     moto on April 17, 1996. It followed more than a year of bilateral
     discussions on the evolving political and security environment of
     the Asia-Pacific region and of various aspects of the Japan-U.S. se-
     curity relationship. The declaration was several pages long and
     reaffirmed the allies' concurrent views on the regional outlook, the
     bilateral security treaty, and regional and global cooperation. The
     document essentially launched a joint review of the 1978 Guidelines
     for Japan-U.S. Defense Cooperation and emphasized that the allies
     share "a commitment to the profound common values that guide
     our national policies: the maintenance of freedom, the pursuit of de-
     mocracy, and respect for human rights."
3   Jamie B. Draper and June H. Hicks, "Foreign Language Enrollments
     in Public Secondary Schools, Fall 2000," American Council on the
     Teaching of Foreign Languages, May 2002.

Abbreviations & Acronyms

APEC	Asia-Pacific Economic Cooperation
ARF	ASEAN Regional Forum
ASEAN	association of Southeast Asian Nations
AWACS	airborne warning and control system
BRAC	base re-alignment and closure (United States)
C^{4}ISR	command, control, communications, computers, intelligence, surveillance, and reconnaissance
CBM	confidence building measure
CFC	combined Forces Command (United States-Republic of Korea)
CJTF	Combined Joint Task Force
DMZ	demilitarized zone
DoD	Department of Defense (United States)
DPRI	Defense Policy Review Initiative (United States-Japan)
DPRK	Democratic People's Republic of Korea
FIP	Force Improvement Plan (Republic of Korea)
FOTA	Future of the Alliance Policy Initiative (United States - Republic of Korea)
GDP	gross domestic product
GNP	Grand National Party (Republic of Korea)
GWOT	global war on terrorism
HEU	highly enriched uranium
ICC	International Criminal Court
IFPA	Institute for Foreign Policy Analysis
JIACG/CT	Joint Interagency Coordination Group for Counterterrorism (United States)
JSA	joint security area
KEDO	Korean Peninsula Energy Development Organization
KPA	Korean People's Army (Democratic People's Republic of Korea)
LNG	liquefied natural gas
LPP	land partnership plan (United States - Republic of Korea)
MDP	Millennium Democratic Party (Republic of Korea)
MLSA	mutual logistics support agreement

MND	Ministry of National Defense (Republic of Korea)
MNNA	major non-NATO ally
MOA	memorandum of agreement
MOFAT	Ministry of Foreign Affairs and Trade (Republic of Korea)
MOU	memorandum of understanding
NATO	North Atlantic Treaty Organization
NED	National Endowment of Democracy (United States)
NORAD	North American Air Defense Command (United States)
NPT	Nuclear Non-proliferation Treaty
NSC	National Security Council (United States)
OSD	Office of the Secretary of Defense (United States)
PACOM	Pacific Command (United States)
PRC	People's Republic of China
PSI	Proliferation Security Initiative
RMA	revolution in military affairs
ROK	Republic of Korea
SCM	Security Consultative Meeting (United States-Republic of Korea)
SDF	Self-Defense Forces (Japan)
TCOG	Trilateral Coordination and Oversight Group
	(United States-Republic of Korea-Japan)
TMD	theater missile defense
UNC	United Nations Command
USFJ	U.S. Forces Japan
USFK	U.S. Forces Korea
WMD	weapons of mass destruction
WTO	World Trade Organization

About *the* Authors & *the* Institute *for* Foreign Policy Analysis

Dr. Charles M. Perry is vice president and director of studies at the Institute for Foreign Policy Analysis. He has written extensively on a variety of national and international security issues, especially with respect to defense trends and security policy in the Asia-Pacific region, NATO affairs and European security, arms trade and technology transfer problems, WMD proliferation concerns, missile defense options, and regional conflict issues. Principal areas of current research and analysis center on U.S.-allied cooperation on crisis/consequence management, strategic developments and alliance adjustments in Northeast Asia, and challenges to regional stability along NATO's flanks, especially in the Nordic-Baltic and Balkan regions. Recent publications include *The U.S.-Japan Alliance: Preparing for Korean Reconciliation and Beyond* (Brassey's, 2003) (co-author); *Defense Reform and Modernization in Southeast Europe* (IFPA, 2002); and *Strategic Dynamics in the Nordic-Baltic Region: Implications for U.S. Policy* (Brassey's, 2000) (co-author). Dr. Perry received his B.A. from Middlebury College, and holds an M.A. in international affairs, an M.A. in law and diplomacy, and a Ph.D. in international politics from The Fletcher School of Law and Diplomacy, Tufts University.

Jacquelyn K. Davis is executive vice president of the Institute for Foreign Policy Analysis. Dr. Davis has written and lectured extensively on a wide range of topics related to U.S. alliance relations (both in NATO-Europe and the Asian-Pacific region), defense transformation and military technology trends, counter-proliferation and post-Cold War deterrence issues, and regional security dynamics, especially as they affect U.S. policies regarding forward presence. Recent publications of note include *Central Asia in U.S. Strategy and Operational Planning: Where Do We Go From Here?* (IFPA, 2003); *Reluctant Allies and Competitive Partners: U.S.-French Relations at the Breaking Point?* (Brassey's, 2003); *Euro–Atlantic Institutions: Ready for the 21st Century?* (Brassey's, 2000); and *Strategic Paradigms 2025: U.S. Security Planning for a New Era* (Brassey's, 1999) (co-author). Dr. Davis serves as a member of the Chief of Naval Operations Executive Panel, the U.S. Special Operations Command's Futures Group, and the U.S. European Command's Senior Advisory Group. She holds an M.A. and a Ph.D. in international relations from the University of Pennsylvania.

James L. Schoff is a senior staff member at the Institute for Foreign Policy Analysis. He joined IFPA after serving as the program officer in charge of policy studies at the United States-Japan Foundation for nearly four years. Mr. Schoff specializes in East Asian economic and security issues, international crisis management, and American foreign policy. Before working at the foundation, he spent five years (three based in Tokyo) developing new business and managing building projects in Asia for Bovis Construction, an international construction and project management firm. Prior to his work at Bovis, he assisted with foreign policy studies at the Brookings Institution. His recent publications include *Crisis Management in Japan and the United States: Creating Opportunities for Cooperation amid Dramatic Change* (Brassey's, 2004); *The 108th Congress: Asia Pacific Policy Outlook* (National Bureau of Asian Research, 2003); and *WMD Challenges on the Korean Peninsula and New Approaches* (IFPA Conference Report, 2003). Mr. Schoff graduated from Duke University and earned an M.A. in international relations at The Johns Hopkins University School for Advanced International Studies (SAIS).

Toshi Yoshihara is a research fellow at the Institute for Foreign Policy Analysis. His special areas of focus include U.S. alliances in Northeast Asia, Japan's defense policy, China's military modernization, and Taiwan/PRC cross-strait relations. He recently co-authored, with Dr. Perry, an IFPA study entitled *The U.S.-Japan Alliance: Preparing for Korean Reconciliation and Beyond* (Brassey's, 2003). Mr. Yoshihara completed and successfully defended his doctoral dissertation on Chinese strategic culture and military innovation in March 2004, and will formally receive his Ph.D. from The Fletcher School in June 2004. He also holds an M.A. in international affairs from The Johns Hopkins University School of Advanced International Studies (SAIS).

The Institute for Foreign Policy Analysis (IFPA) is an independent, non-partisan and not-for-profit (501(c)(3)) research organization that conducts research, publishes studies, convenes seminars and conferences, promotes education, and trains policy analysts in the fields of foreign policy and national security affairs. The institute maintains a staff of specialists at its offices in Cambridge, Massachusetts, and Washington, D.C. IFPA is associated with The Fletcher School of Law and Diplomacy, Tufts University. Since its founding in 1976, IFPA has provided a forum for the examination of political, economic, security, and defense-industrial issues confronting the United States in a rapidly changing world.

Mutual Defense Treaty
between the
Republic of Korea *& the* United States *of* America

Signed at Washington: October 1, 1953
Entered into Force: November 17, 1954

The Parties to this Treaty,
Reaffirming their desire to live in peace with all governments, and desiring to strengthen the fabric of peace in the Pacific area,
Desiring to declare publicly and formally their common determination to defend themselves against external armed attack so that no potential aggressor could be under the illusion that either of them stands alone in the Pacific area,

Desiring further to strengthen their efforts for collective defense for the preservation of peace and security pending the development of a more comprehensive and effective system of regional security in the Pacific area,

Have agreed as follows:

Article 1
The Parties undertake to settle any international disputes in which they may be involved by peaceful means in such a manner that international peace and security and justice are not endangered and to refrain in their international relations from the threat or use of force in any manner inconsistent with the purposes of the United Nations, or obligations assumed by any Party towards the United Nations.

Article 2
The Parties will consult together whenever, in the opinion of either of them, the political independence or security of either of the Parties is threatened by external armed attack. Separately and jointly, by self-help and mutual aid, the Parties will maintain and develop appropriate means to deter armed attack and will take suitable measures in consultation and agreement to implement this Treaty and to further its purposes.

Article 3
Each Party recognizes that an armed attack in the Pacific area on either of the Parties in territories now under their respective administrative control, or hereafter recognized by one of the Parties as lawfully brought under the administrative control of the other, would be dangerous to its own peace and safety and declares that it would act to meet the common danger in accordance with its constitutional processes.

Article 4
The Republic of Korea grants, and the United States of America accepts, the right to dispose United States land, air and sea forces in and about the territory of the Republic of Korea as determined by mutual agreement.

Article 5
This Treaty shall be ratified by the United States of America and the Republic of Korea in accordance with their respective constitutional processes and will come into force when instru-

ments of ratification thereof have been exchanged by them at Washington.

Article 6
This Treaty shall remain in force indefinitely. Either Party may terminate it one year after notice has been given to the other Party.

IN WITNESS WHEREOF the undersigned plenipotentiaries have signed this Treaty.

Republic of Korea:	United States of America:
(signed) Y.T. Pyun	(signed) John Foster Dulles

Done in duplicate at Washington, in the Korean and English languages, this first day of October, 1953.

Understanding of the United States of America
It is the understanding of the United States that neither Party is obligated, under Article 3 of the above Treaty, to come to the aid of the other except in case of an external armed attack against such party; nor shall anything in the present Treaty be construed as requiring the United States to give assistance to Korea except in the event of an armed attack against territory which has been recognized by the United States or lawfully brought under the administrative control of the Republic of Korea.